IMAGES
of America

Skiing in New Mexico

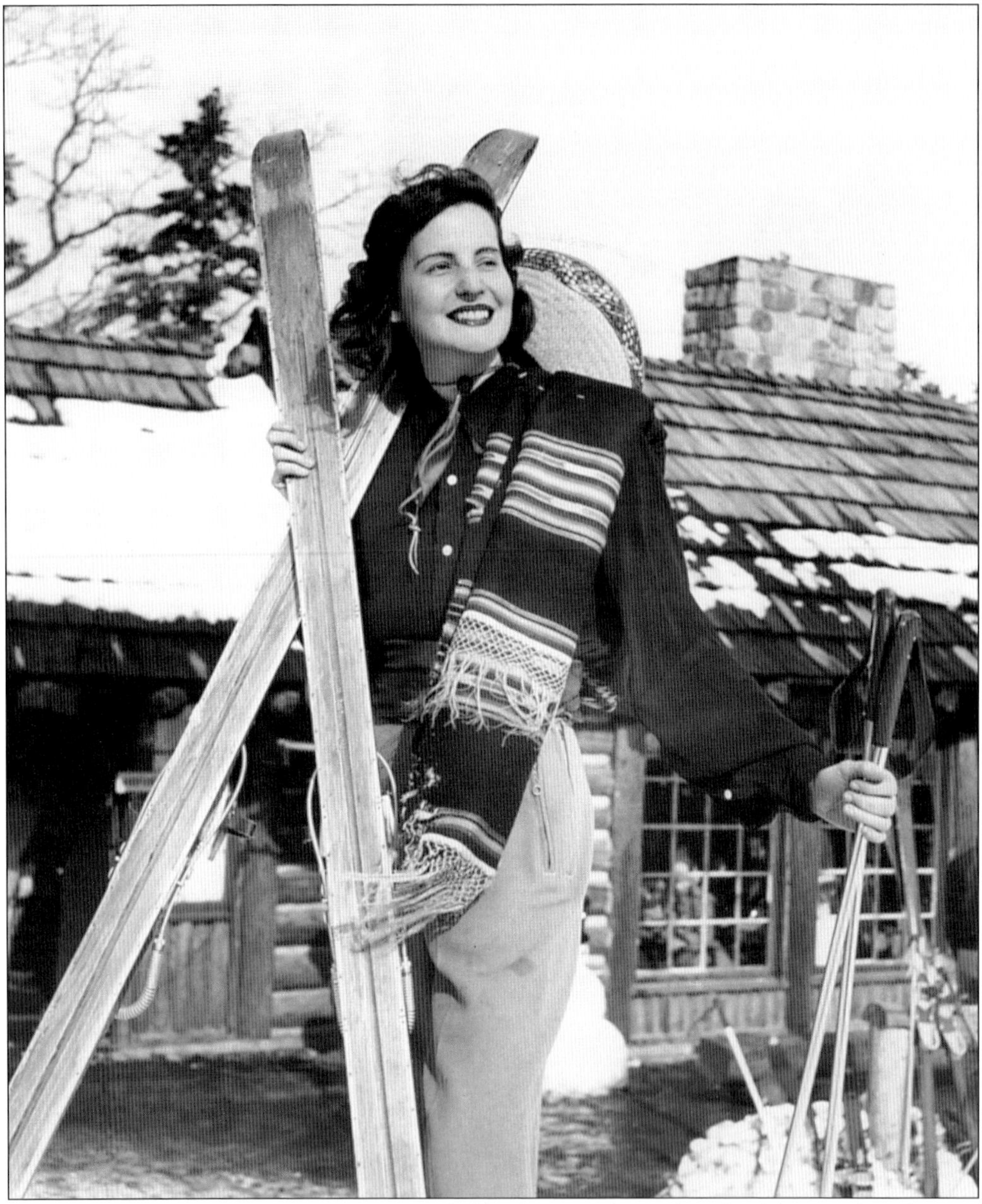

A vivacious ski señorita with a Mexican-style blanket tossed over her shoulder stands in front of the original La Madera Lodge in this image produced for a state tourism brochure in the 1950s that plays up the state's Hispanic roots. La Madera ("The Woods") was launched in 1937 by New Mexico's own Robert Nordhaus and other Duke City families. (Courtesy Sandia Peak Ski Area.)

On the Cover: Three women try out New Mexico's *other* ski medium, the rare gypsum sand dunes of White Sands National Monument, in the 1950s. Truth be told, skiing on sand is difficult, and now that White Sands is a national park, skiing is no longer allowed there. But snow discs are okay, and many families enjoy this activity year-round here in the Tularosa Basin of south-central New Mexico. (Photograph by Barnes/Caplin for the state highway department, courtesy State Archives of New Mexico, Item No. 007596.)

IMAGES
of America

SKIING IN NEW MEXICO

Daniel Gibson and Jay Blackwood

ARCADIA
PUBLISHING

ISBN 978-1-4671-0702-0

Published by Arcadia Publishing
Charleston, South Carolina

Printed in the United States of America

Library of Congress Control Number: 2021934523

For all general information, please contact Arcadia Publishing:
Telephone 843-853-2070
Fax 843-853-0044
E-mail sales@arcadiapublishing.com
For customer service and orders:
Toll-Free 1-888-313-2665

Visit us on the Internet at www.arcadiapublishing.com

I would like to dedicate this book to my parents,
John and Shirley Blackwood, for instilling the skiing bug
in my brother, sister, and myself at an early age.
—Jay Blackwood

This is dedicated to Kitty Leaken, who has accompanied me on many skiing outings, and to my grown children, Travis and Isabel Gibson, who carry on the love of skiing and New Mexico's high country.
—Daniel Gibson

Contents

ACKNOWLEDGMENTS

This book would not have been possible without the tireless work and determination of the founders of New Mexico's ski areas and the many willing volunteers who aided their efforts. It has been our privilege to know many of these ski pioneers and to have heard many of their stories firsthand over the years.

Many living people contributed to this book, beginning with personnel at the state's ski areas: media mavens Greg Ralph and Krysty Ronchetti at Angel Fire Resort, along with vice president Christy Germscheid; Tom Long, general manager at Pajarito Mountain, and public relations director Christine Hudson, who also runs Sipapu's media outreach; marketing director Reed Widmer at Red River; Jessica Fox, who directs media for both Ski Santa Fe and Sandia Peak; Tania McCormack and Erin Dolin, who oversee media for Taos Ski Valley; and owner and manager Ellen Miller-Goins of Enchanted Forest Cross Country Ski & Snowshoe Area.

Many others who had various roles within the state's ski community also provided help, particularly Mickey Blake of Taos Ski Valley's Blake family; the Pitcher family, including Davey, Roseanne, and their office assistant Carol McGiffin; and Bruce Bolander of Sipapu heritage. The cooperation and assistance of the New Mexico Ski Museum and its Ski Hall of Fame are also greatly appreciated.

Several individuals also contributed photographs and information, such as Rick Holben, whose father helped develop La Madera; Mike Lord; Paul "Snappy" Smith of Red River; Valerie Wood of the Los Alamos Ski Club; Dena Hunt, archivist for the State Archives of New Mexico; and Kitty Leaken.

Our editor at Arcadia Publishing, Caroline Vickerson, also deserves a big *abrazo* of thanks. And thanks go to Arcadia's patient acquisitions editor Lindsey Givens for roping us into taking this on.

Some images used here were obtained from the US Forest Service (USFS), Taos Ski Valley (TSV), Ski Santa Fe (SkiSF), Sandia Peak Ski Area (SP), Red River Ski Area (RRSA), the New Mexico Ski Museum (NMSM), the Blake family collection (BFC), the Pitcher family collection (PFC), and the Los Alamos Ski Club (LASC).

INTRODUCTION

New Mexico's skiing history is among the oldest in the American West, with prospectors in the late 1800s and early 1900s trying out their "long boards" on the region's abundant and famously light powder snow, often over ground that would later become beloved ski areas.

No photographs of these early skiing miners could be found, but there are rare written references to them, and images of the era from Colorado, California, and other Western states show people on skis for both practical purposes and for fun. New Mexico does have the distinction of being home to perhaps the oldest-known image of a Native American on skis, a Taos Pueblo man around 1900, included in this book.

The first developed ski areas in the state came in the 1930s, with the creation of the Albuquerque Ski Club and La Madera near Duke City in the Sandia Mountains, and at Hyde Park (today's Hyde Memorial State Park) above Santa Fe. Students at the Los Alamos Ranch School in today's town of Los Alamos were also hiking and skiing in the Jemez Mountains in the 1930s, and in the 1940s, scientists at Los Alamos National Laboratory—busy developing the world's first atomic weapons—took to skiing in their few off hours.

Major developments blossomed across the state in the 1950s and 1960s, with the launch of Taos Ski Valley by the remarkable Blake family, Sipapu by the Bolander clan, and Sierra Blanca under the guidance of the ambitious Kingsbury "Pitch" Pitcher. The Santa Fe Ski Basin took form in this period, first under the Blakes and then the Pitchers. Red River, "Ski Town of the Southwest," took form, as did Pajarito Mountain above Los Alamos and Angel Fire. Some changed names, like La Madera morphing into Sandia Peak with the construction of its world-class aerial tram. Development continued in the 1970s and 1980s at all these resorts, as at Ski Santa Fe with the able Abruzzo family at the helm.

Many ski areas were also born and died in these early years, among them Agua Piedra, which is well represented in this book. Powder Puff, which arose and then faded just down the valley from today's Red River Ski Area, was most notable, with two chairlifts and some longish runs. Valverde was a tiny operation near Eagle's Nest in the lovely Moreno Valley, while Sugarite was just east of Raton in Sugarite State Park. Near Ruidoso was Cedar Creek, and in the Sandias was Tree Springs. A ski area was almost built in the Gila region of southwestern New Mexico, and an aborted effort was made near Chama in the Brazos Mountains. Most significant was the creation and closure of Ski Rio near the Colorado border. But even today, one of the early micro-areas lives on, in good snow years: Ski Cloudcroft. Located east of the town of Cloudcroft in south-central New Mexico, it is among the southernmost ski destinations in the nation.

Cross-country skiing has long been popular here, with routes in every high-altitude mountain range—from popular areas above Albuquerque, Santa Fe, and Taos, and in the Jemez range near Los Alamos, to obscure outings on Mount Taylor near Grants, the Sacramentos near Ruidoso, and the Brazos Range. Back in the 1970s, and even as far back as the 1930s, as pictures in this book reveal, other skiers were beginning to explore far outside the boundaries of ski areas. Today, backcountry skiing is the fastest-growing portion of the state's skiing and snowboarding community. What was old is new again.

Today, skiing remains an integral aspect of winter life in the state. A sizeable percentage of its population ski or snowboard, and tens of thousands of out-of-state, and even international, travelers come to sample the skiing, as well as the state's renowned arts, culture, food, and history.

Many people are surprised there is any skiing in the state, but the southernmost range of the Rocky Mountains, the Sangre de Cristos, bisects northern New Mexico, with several peaks topping out at more than 13,000 feet in elevation. Taos Ski Valley's Kachina Peak chair climbs to 12,450 feet, and Ski Santa Fe's parking lot sits at 10,350 feet. The high elevation traps storms and then holds the snow in a deep freeze, which piles up deeper and deeper all winter. From summits, one can often see a hundred miles or more in all directions, in some cases over pale-brown, red, and yellow desert lowlands below. It is a transfixing environment, a place of harsh beauty.

The founders of the state's ski community were a fascinating cross section of America and the world. Most were American, but Ernie Blake was Swiss German, and he brought over many Europeans to help him create Taos Ski Valley, which had French hoteliers and Austrian ski instructors. Many who hailed from other parts of the country came during World War II, when New Mexico was home to many US military bases, while others were native. This includes attorney Robert Nordhaus, founder of Sandia Peak ski area and tram company. Born and raised in Las Vegas, New Mexico, he attended Yale. Another New Mexican—by association, not birth—was Robert O. Anderson, founder of Atlantic Richfield Oil Co. He financed the 1961 opening of today's Ski Apache in south-central New Mexico near Ruidoso on the flank of 11,981-foot Sierra Blanca Peak. Other areas were managed and kept functioning by veterans of the US 10th Mountain Division of World War II and the affable and wild skier Pete Totemoff, an Aleut Indian from Alaska.

Luckily, the early days of skiing in New Mexico were well documented. Thousands of photographs of people and places exist, and there are incredible scenic images, action shots, and portraits. They reveal a tight-knit cadre of like-minded people, men and women of immense vision, courage, strength, and audacity to believe they could create a viable ski center in an area so remote from the rest of the country, set in the most foreign state in the nation, amidst the high deserts of New Mexico.

One

Early Days
19th and Early 20th Centuries

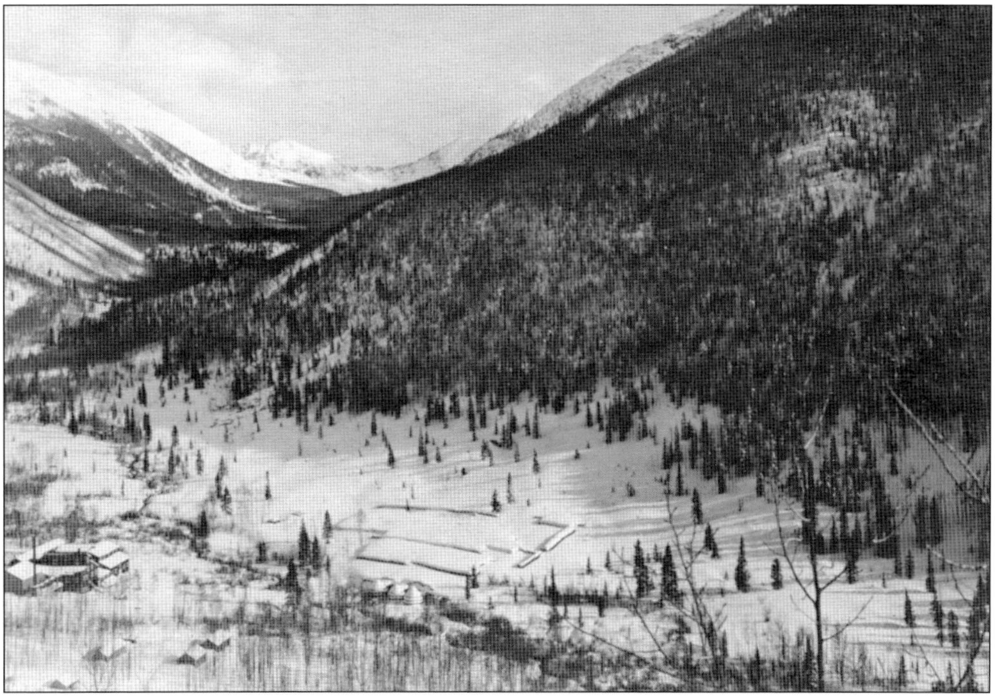

The base site of Taos Ski Valley was previously the mining community of Twining, as seen in this c. 1910 image. The view is looking up the Lake Fork Valley toward the state's highest point, Wheeler Peak. The squares in the center are cords of stacked firewood used to feed the conical coke ovens, seen just below them and roughly on the site of today's Blake hotel. (Courtesy TSV.)

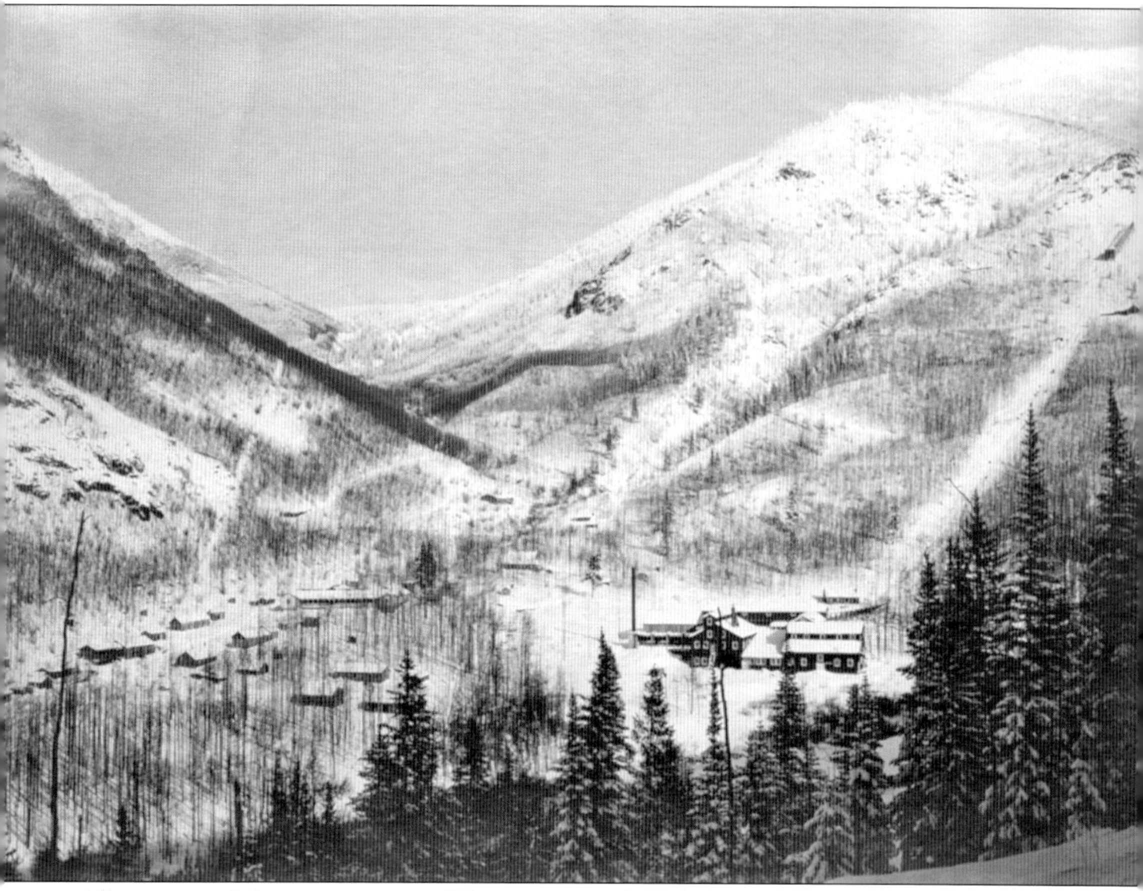

This image of the mining town of Twining was taken about 1910 from what is now Taos Ski Valley's famed Al's Run. The immense mill, as well as the mine tailings slope above it, dominates the picture, but to its left are the Twining Hotel and various miner cabins and mercantile stores. The mill burned in 1932, but its foundations are still visible. Twining was the second mining community in the Hondo Valley. The first arose a few miles down-valley in the late 1800s, where Al Helphenstine and his wife, Amizette, ran a post office and hotel. (Courtesy TSV.)

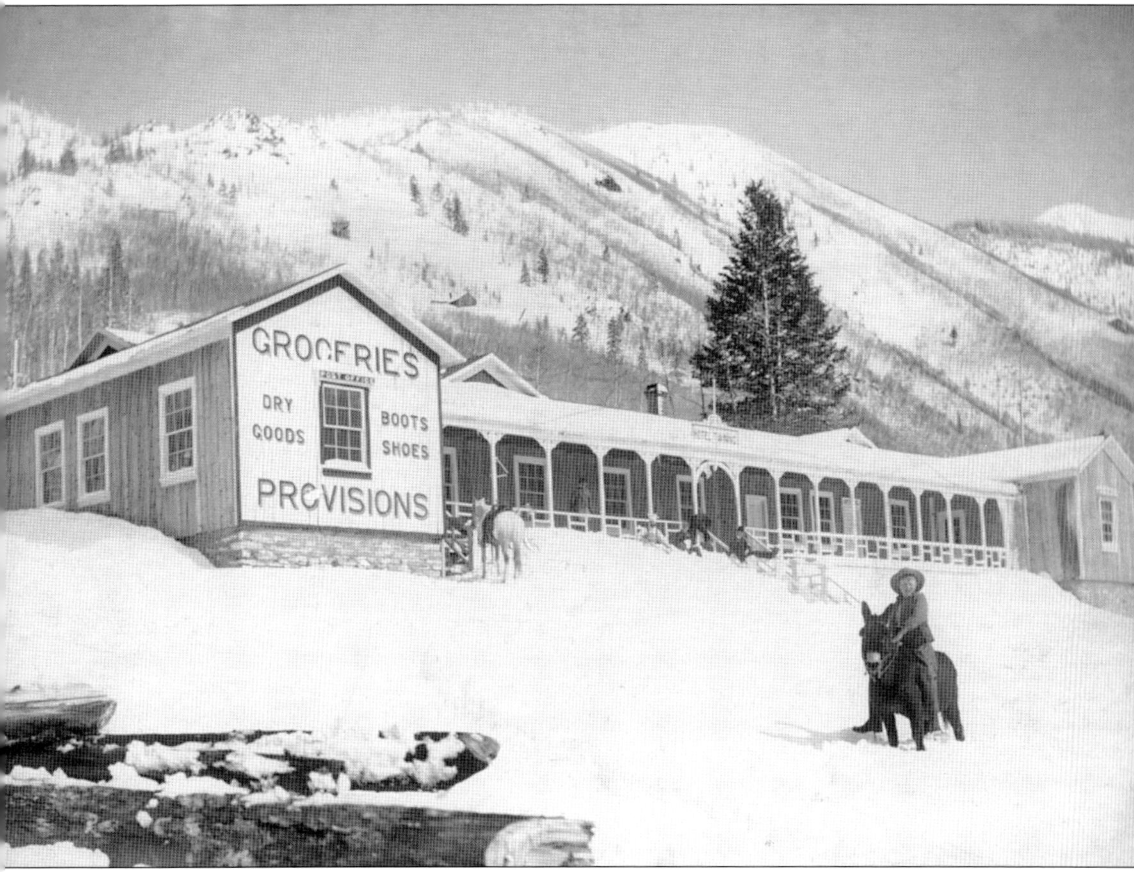

The Twining Hotel is pictured here. In the early 1900s, Twining had a Pelton waterwheel that generated electricity, and the hotel's cook, Tenderfoot Katie, dished out fine meals. Her name graces the resort's main dining establishment today. A founder of the town of Taos's famed art community, Bert Phillips, worked his own claim on nearby Gold Hill, and as noted in Rick Richard's fine book *Ski Pioneers: Ernie Blake, His Friends and the Making of Taos Ski Valley*, "he fitted out a pair of skis from barrel staves on which he would ski down from the mine." (Courtesy TSV.)

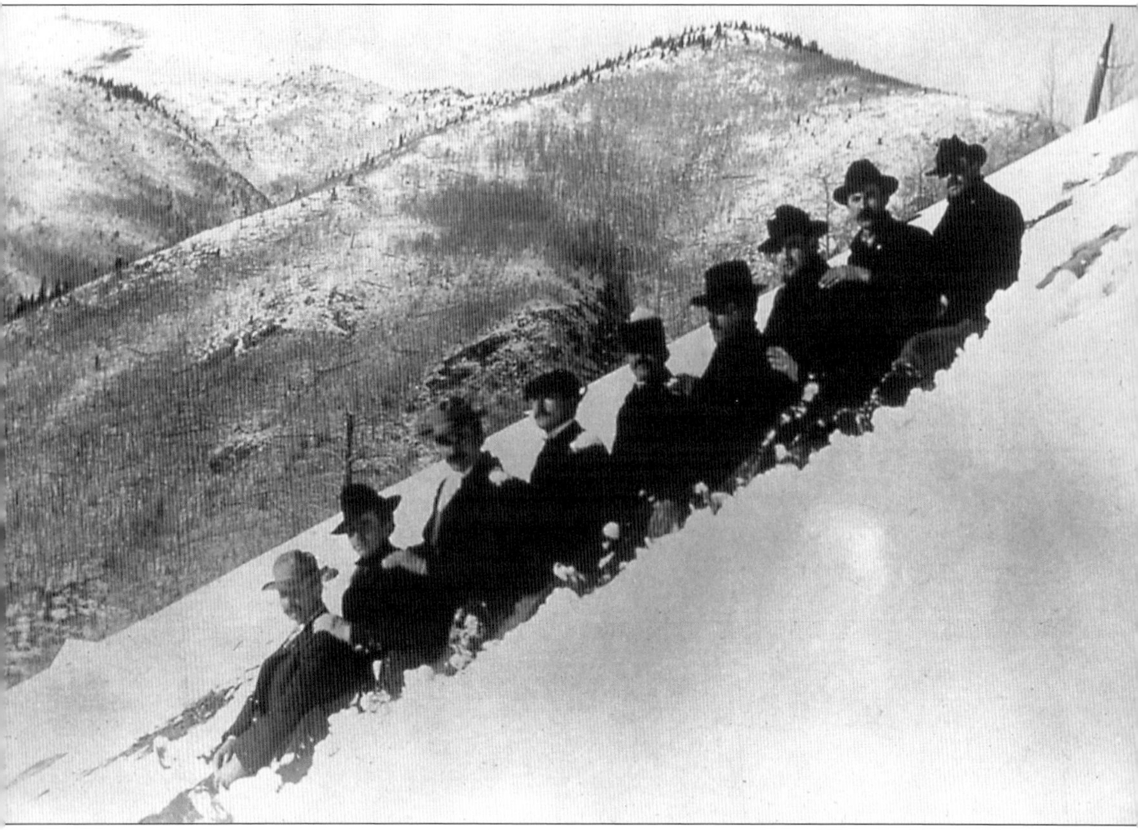

Nine men, directors of the Fraser Mine at Twining, line up on their mine tailings slope around 1900. Some sources suggest they are mimicking riding a toboggan, but it is not clear. It is known that early miners in Colorado, California, and elsewhere did pursue snow sports, including sledding and skiing, but no such New Mexico images have been found. William Fraser, mine co-owner, is thought to be in the rear at far right. He and the mine's primary investor, Albert C. Twining of New Jersey, planned on using low temperature–burning aspen to heat the smelter. With the initial firing in 1903, molten copper ore solidified on the furnace sides, destroying the smelter. Bankruptcy ensued, Twining was imprisoned, and the town site was largely abandoned by 1910. Its metal and milled wood were sold as scrap, and by the 1930s, Twining had essentially vanished, but Mickey Blake reports that he found remnants of the woodpiles when his father acquired the site in 1955 to launch Taos Ski Valley. (Courtesy TSV.)

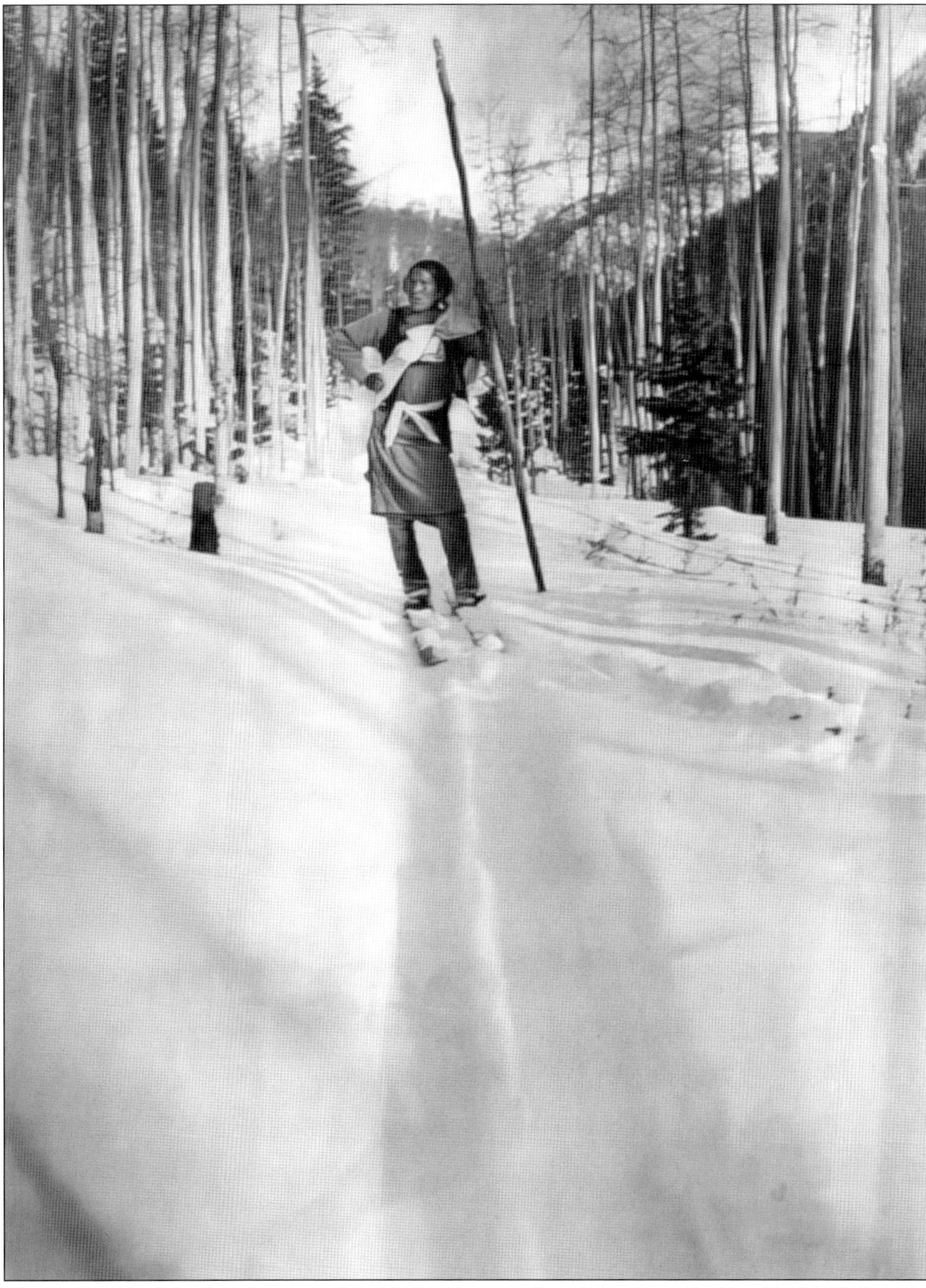

The exact details of this photograph are lost to history, but this image of a Taos Pueblo Indian on skis is believed to have been taken in the Hondo Valley a few miles down-valley from Amizette around 1900. He is thought to have been a mail carrier who delivered letters in a pouch on his back to the mining community of Twining. His long single pole was the early favored means of controlling speed and turning. The effort, both uphill and down, generated lots of body heat; note his trim figure and relatively light clothing. (Courtesy TSV.)

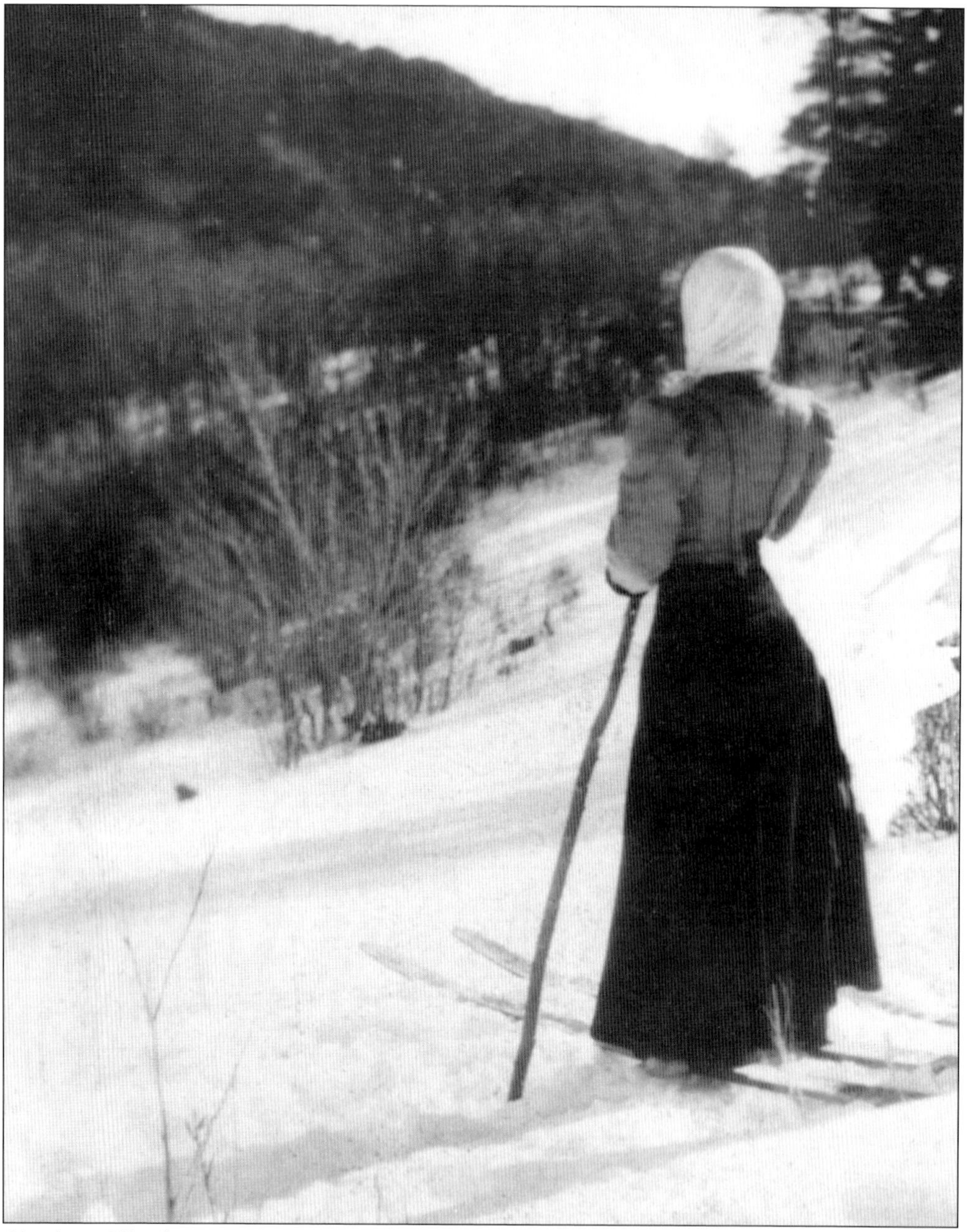

Charlotte Ellis, born in 1875, was a member of the Ellis family who homesteaded on 160 acres in the Sandia Mountains east of Albuquerque in 1905, in the well-watered Las Huertas Canyon. She is seen here on skis on the property in 1896, making this the oldest-known photograph of anyone in New Mexico on skis. Skis were used by many early pioneers as transportation across snowy landscapes rather than as a form of recreation. Ellis was surely hindered by her full-length dress, but one senses that she was enjoying her outing and not at work. Her single wooden pole would have been used as a brake and for balance. (Photograph by Bob Cooper, courtesy NMSM.)

Two

The Base Layer
1930s and 1940s

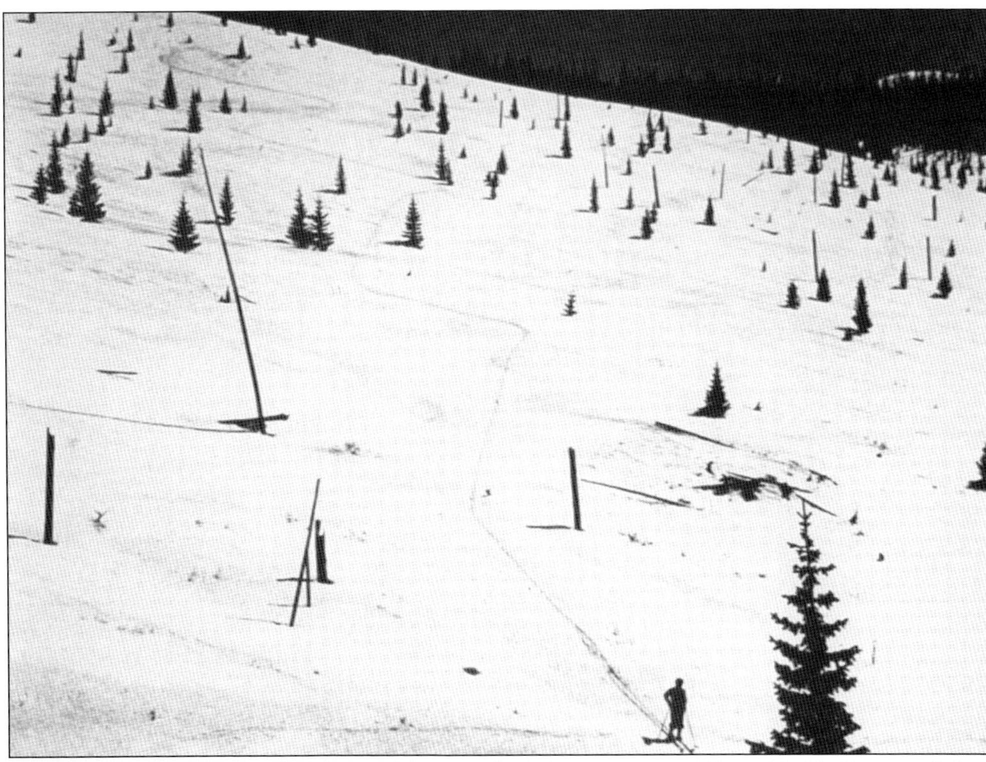

Pictured here is an area called Sacate Blanco, which became part of Santa Fe Ski Basin and then today's Ski Santa Fe. The photograph was shot on March 11, 1937, by Graeme McGowan, who had been hired by a group of Santa Fe businessmen to see if developing a ski area nearby was feasible. (Courtesy NMSM.)

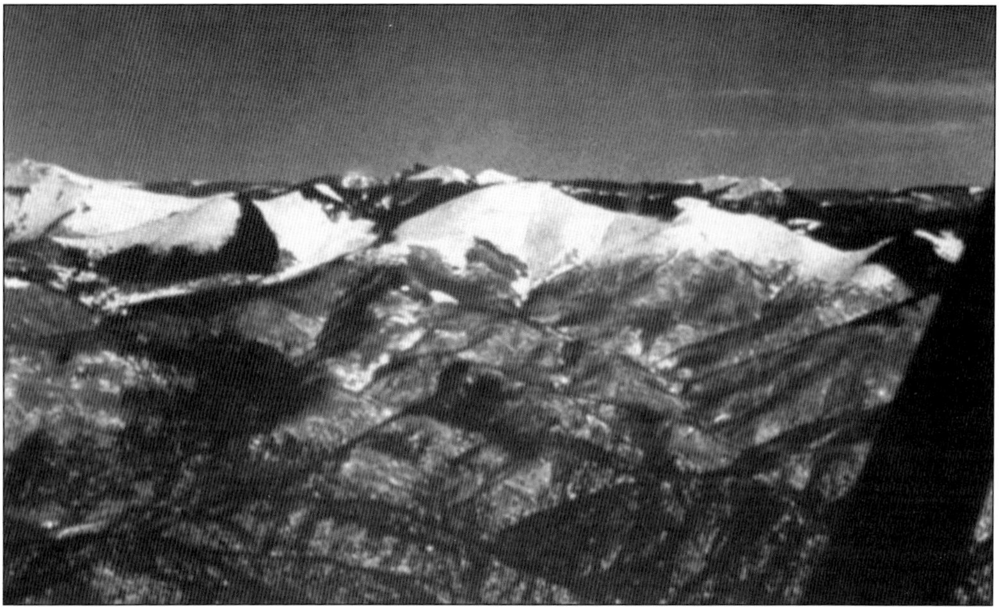

In March 1937, Graeme McGowan took this aerial photograph of a portion of the Sangre de Cristo ("Blood of Christ") Mountains near Santa Fe, the southernmost range of the Rockies. The image reveals vast swaths of treeless slopes, which had burned in a massive fire in the early 1900s. Today, Ski Santa Fe is just to the left of the white central mass, Tesuque Peak. McGowan's determination that it would support a successful ski area proved correct. He spent many years working for the US Forest Service on similar projects in Colorado, New Mexico, and Arizona. (Courtesy NMSM.)

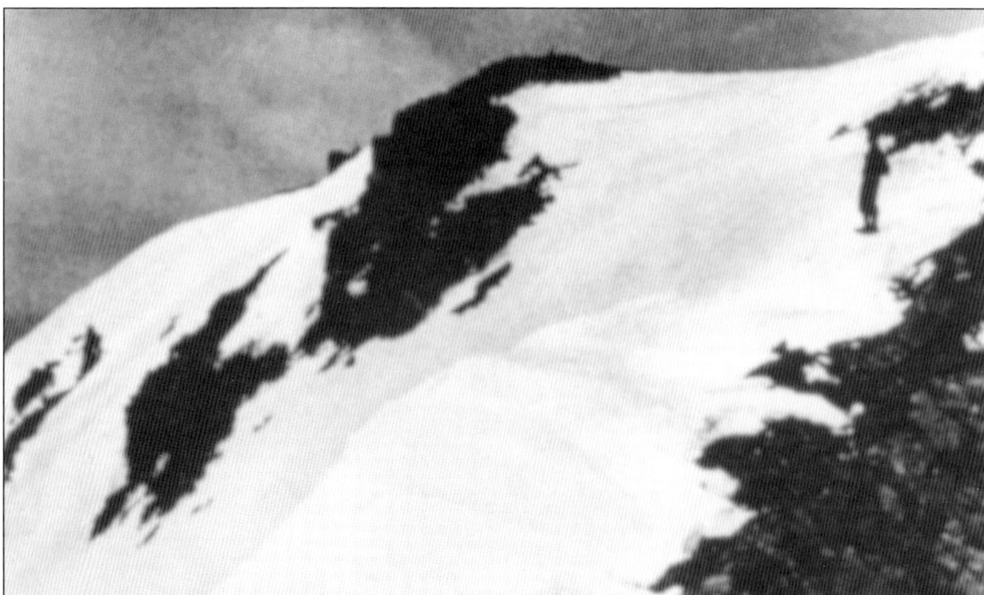

In another McGowan image, a lone skier on foot nears the summit of 12,408-foot Lake Peak, just outside the current Ski Santa Fe boundary, in March 1937. The adventure would have been a multiday outing with many miles of ascent from the end of the road at Hyde Park. McGowan took snow measurements, conducted interviews, and read various studies to produce a detailed report that enthusiastically endorsed the concept of creating a ski area in the vicinity. (Courtesy NMSM.)

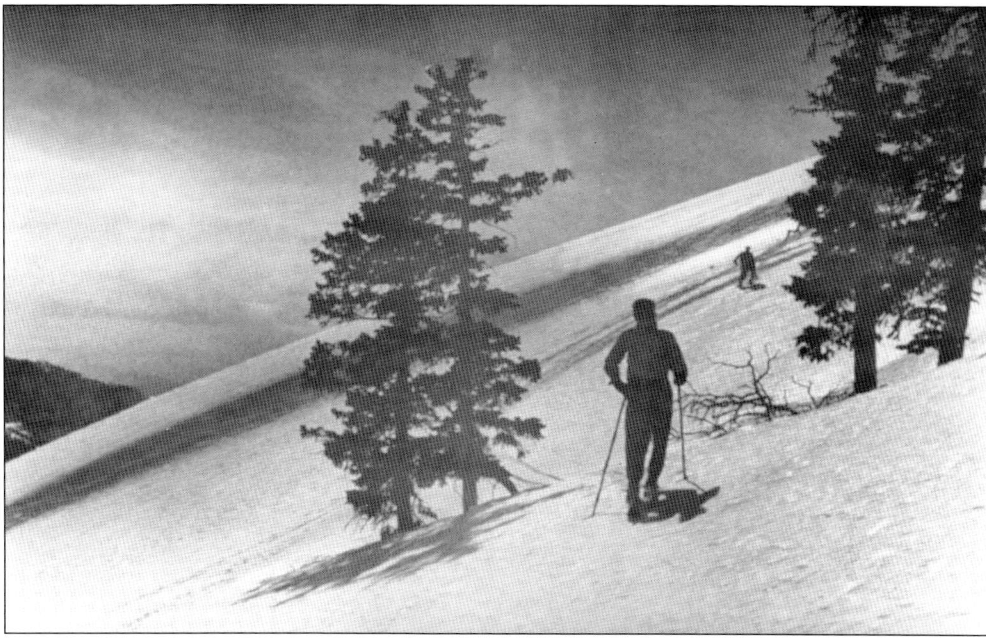

In the 1930s, two skiers are on foot on the sun-scalded slopes of Santa Fe Baldy. This foray required an even longer approach than Lake Peak, and at 12,631 feet, an even tougher climb. This was probably taken in late spring when the snowpack had consolidated. Even with today's gear, this route is not commonly tackled by Santa Fe's backcountry skiing enthusiasts. (Courtesy USFS.)

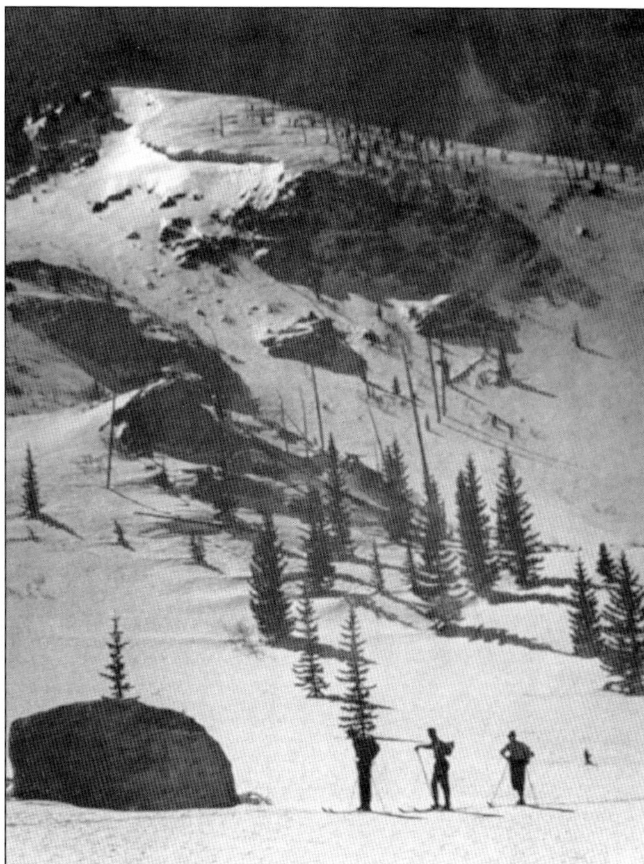

Three skiers pause to catch their breath on Nambe Pass between Lake Peak and Santa Fe Baldy in the 1930s. They most likely made the daylong excursion along the still-existent Winsor Trail, but from a much more distant starting point than today's ski touring aficionados. (Courtesy USFS.)

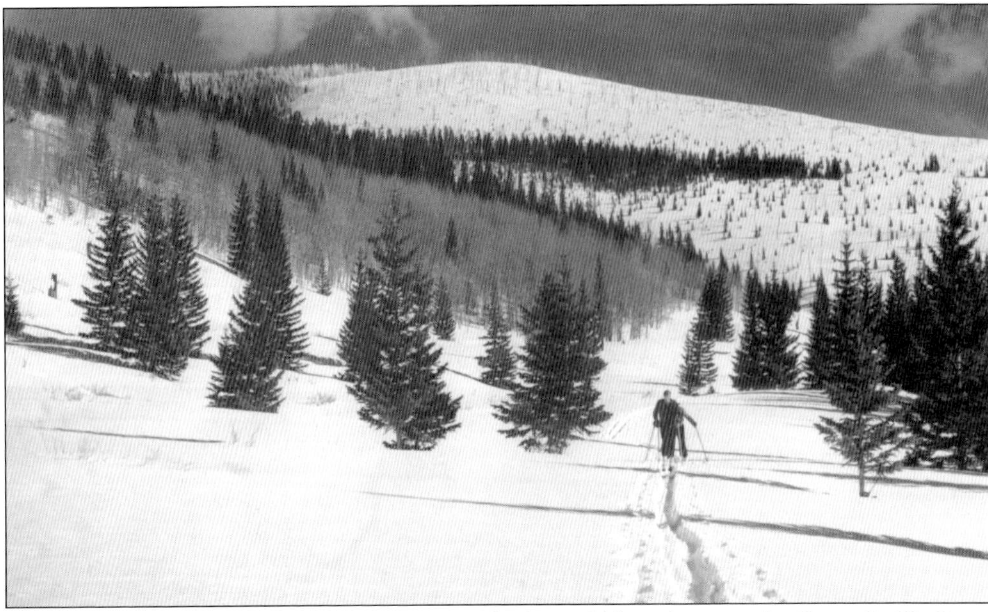

In 1940, two skiers head out of Aspen Basin, which would later become the Santa Fe Ski Basin and finally Ski Santa Fe. This view is from what now is the lower mountain's beginner section, looking upward to Tesuque Peak (12,047 feet), which had been swept by a major fire in the early 1900s. Today, pine trees have crowded out many of the aspen trees on the left, and the open slopes have largely filled in as well. This tree-free terrain is memorialized in current upper mountain trail names South Burn and North Burn. (Courtesy USFS.)

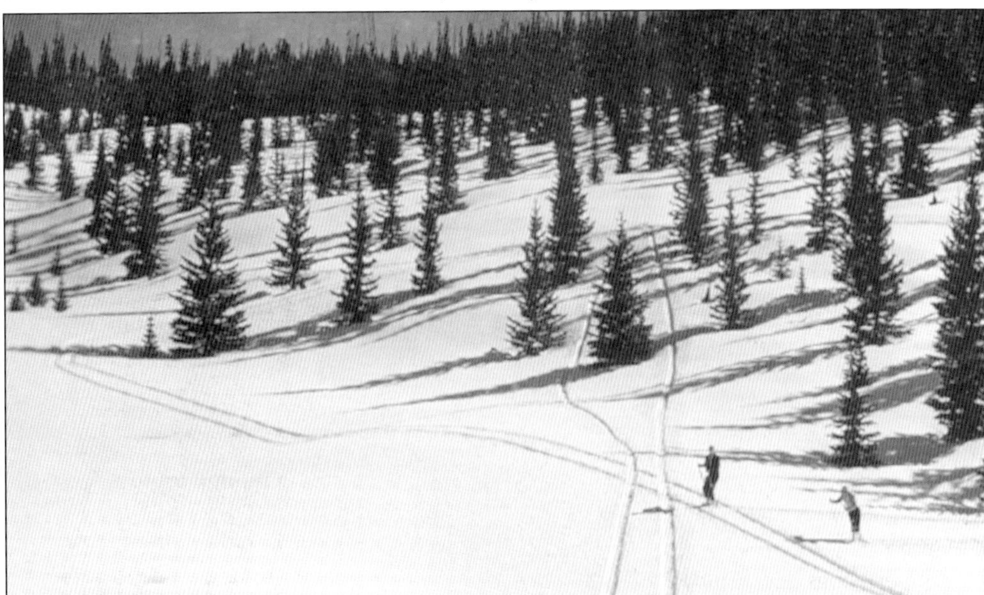

In another image taken in 1940 in Aspen Basin, the Gran Quemado ("Big Burn") is crisscrossed by a handful of ski trails. To get to the basin and higher peaks noted previously, skiers had to drive past the developed ski hill at Hyde Park to the end of the road at Tesuque Creek and ascend the Winsor Trail for miles. The payoff was deeper snow and isolation. A tiny cabin was built here to allow for extended outings. The rush was on! (Courtesy USFS.)

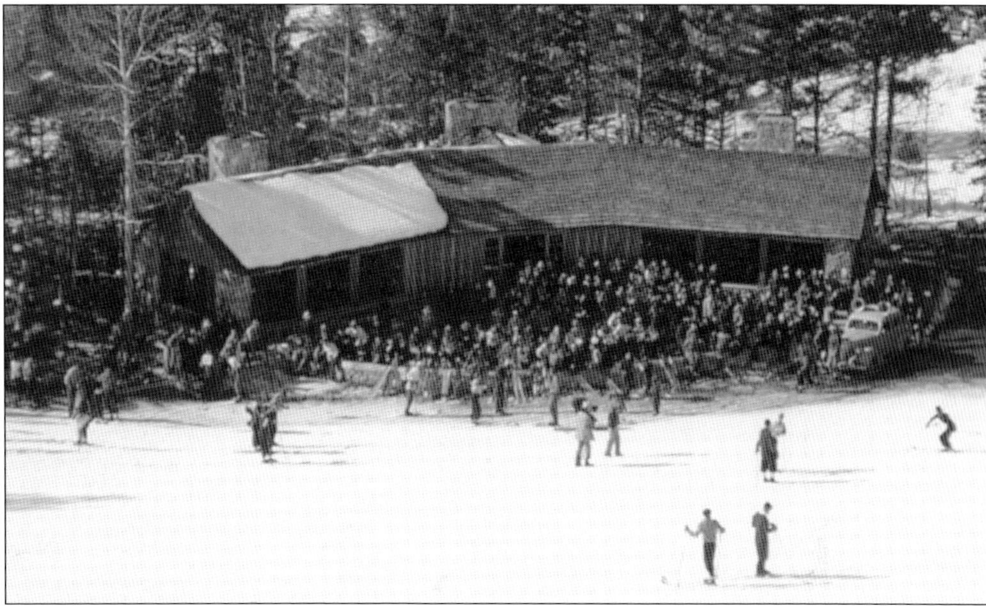

Meanwhile, the developed ski scene at Hyde Park was thriving. Just eight miles from Santa Fe Plaza, Hyde Park boasted a two-story stone-and-timber lodge built in 1938–1939 by the Civilian Conservation Corps (CCC), with fireplaces, a dining room, rental shop, and a flagstone patio. Skiers were dragged uphill by several rope tows and descended wide slopes cleared by the US Forest Service, which was then enthusiastically supporting the development of ski areas in national forests. Hyde Park first opened in the winter of 1937, complete with a concession tent, bus service, and instruction program. (Courtesy USFS.)

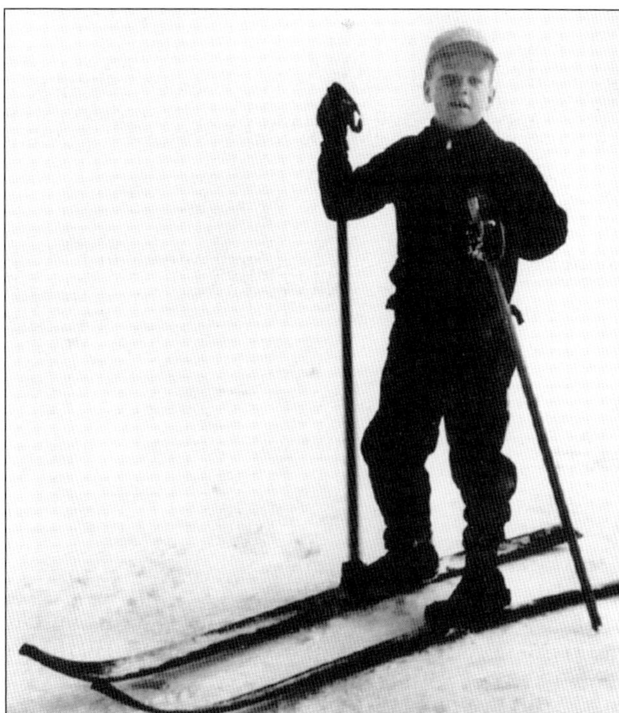

This young skier in 1937 could have used some better poles, but no matter! His long wooden skis did the trick. Hyde Park began as a dream of Santa Fe Rotary Club members, then spread to the chamber of commerce. In January 1937, the Santa Fe Winter Sports Club was formed with members including Robert Nordhaus of Albuquerque, Ferdinand Koch, John Watson, Mrs. Bates Wilson, Moris Burge, Mary Moore, Hunter Clarkson, T.B. Catron, Daniel Kelly, and others. The group joined the National Ski Association, and with the blessings of consultant Graeme McGowan, the US Forest Service began clearing a hill here in the summer of 1936 and resumed their efforts in 1937. (Photograph by Mrs. Karl Richards, courtesy NMSM.)

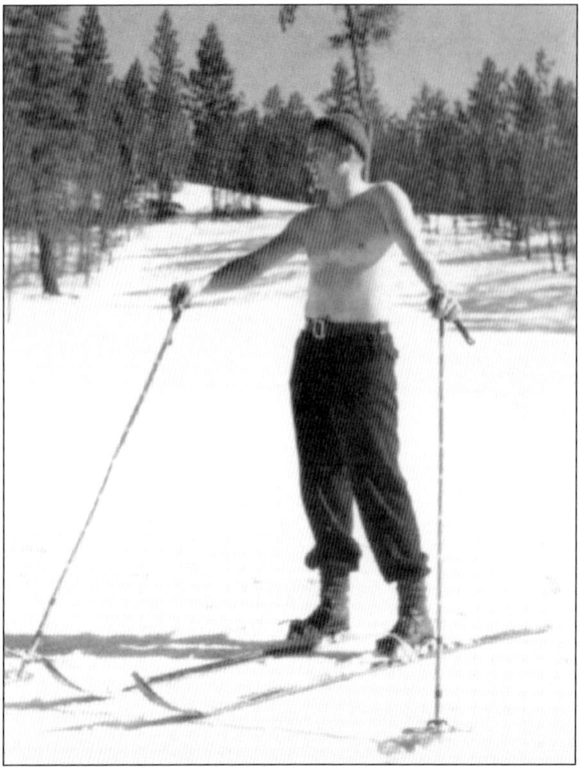

This fine specimen of manhood bares it all on the Hyde Park slopes on a sunny late-winter or early-spring day. Note his strap-over-boot bindings. By the winter of 1940–1941, the ski hill had a 700-foot tow installed that boosted skiers 175 vertical feet. Lift tickets cost 50¢ a day for adults and half that for kids and ski club members. The state highway department had improved the road, and public transportation was even available to Hyde Park. (Photograph by Mrs. Karl Richards, courtesy NMSM.)

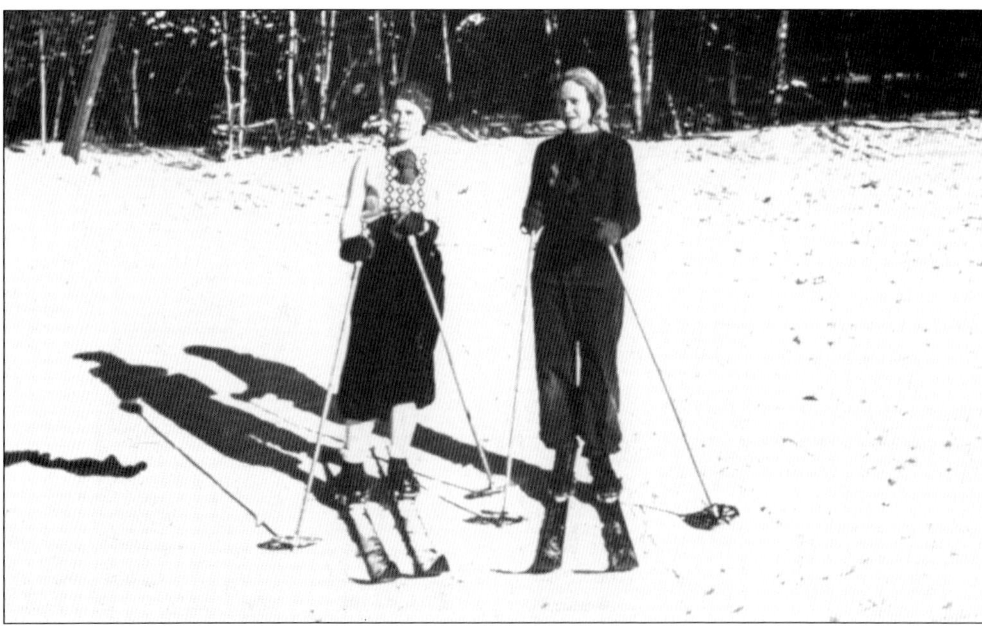

Ski area development consultant McGowan labeled this 1937 photograph he shot at Hyde Park, "Two of Santa Fe's better skiers." In his report to the Santa Fe Winter Sports Club, he also noted, "The mountainous area adjacent to Santa Fe offers skiing possibilities equal to the finest in the world and much better than elsewhere in the Southwest. Santa Fe, itself, is below the snow-belt and is graced with a very pleasant winter climate." (Courtesy NMSM.)

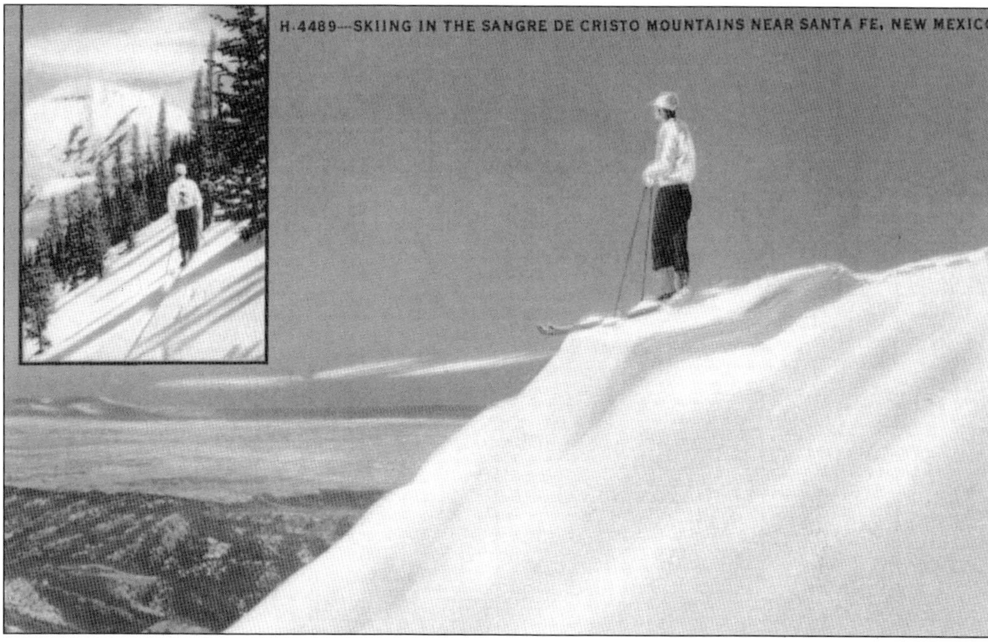

This postcard produced by the Fred Harvey Company in the early 1940s stated, "Most winter sport enthusiasts are surprised to learn that there is good skiing in sunny New Mexico. The high peaks of the Sangre de Cristo Mountains afford good practice runs of varying degrees; while open slopes, far-reaching views, marvelous sunshine and dry air all help make this region ideal for winter sports. Good skiing is available at the end of a few minutes' drive from Fred Harvey's La Fonda Hotel in Santa Fe. Skiing is fast becoming popular at other points in New Mexico and Arizona." (Courtesy NMSM.)

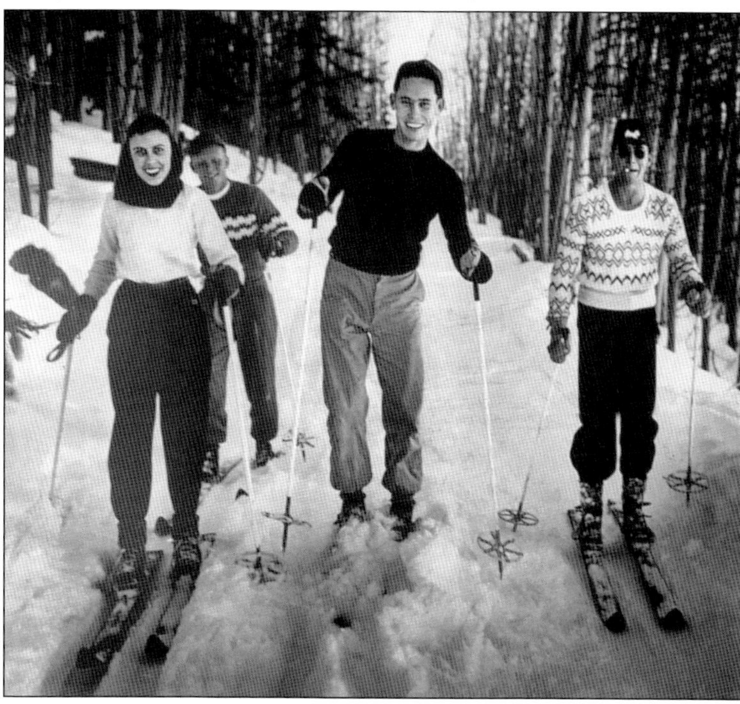

These cheerful young adults are skiing uphill on the Winsor Trail, which provided access to Aspen Basin and the high peaks near Santa Fe. For many years, this was the only way to reach the deeper snow and more expansive terrain above Hyde Park and Tesuque Creek. A road eventually replaced the trail, allowing for the post–World War II development of the Santa Fe Ski Basin. (Courtesy NMSM.)

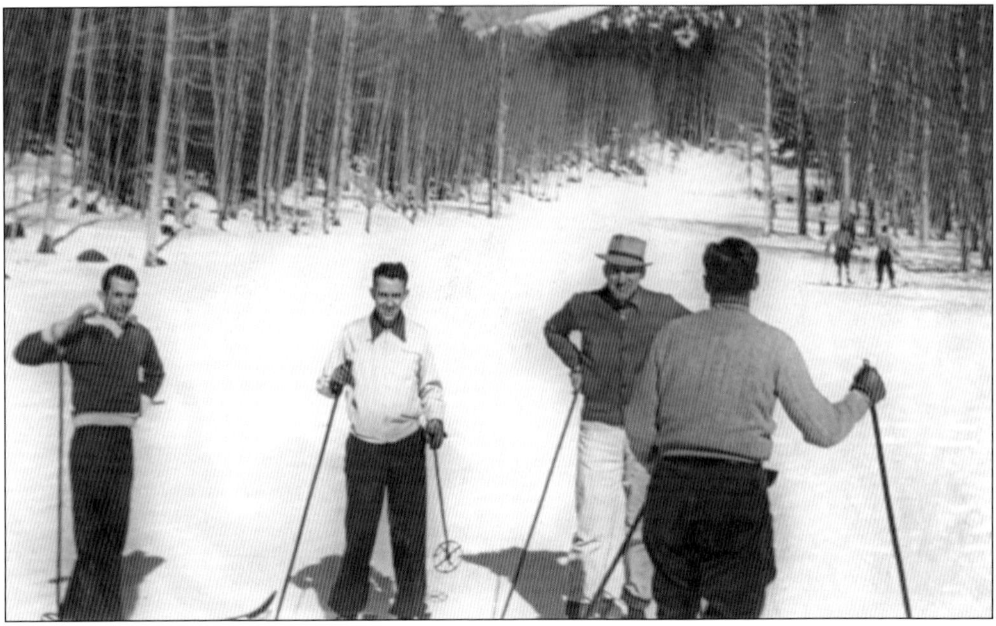

Four men yuck it up at a short-lived ski area at Tesuque Creek above Santa Fe in the winter of 1938–1939, where a single lift provided some diversion. At a higher elevation than Hyde Park, it had more dependable snow, and intrepid skiers could forge their own way upward into a zone called the Horse's Head—a patch of trees spared in an earlier fire that from town resembled its namesake. Robert Nordhaus oversaw the installation of several lifts here in 1940. (Courtesy NMSM.)

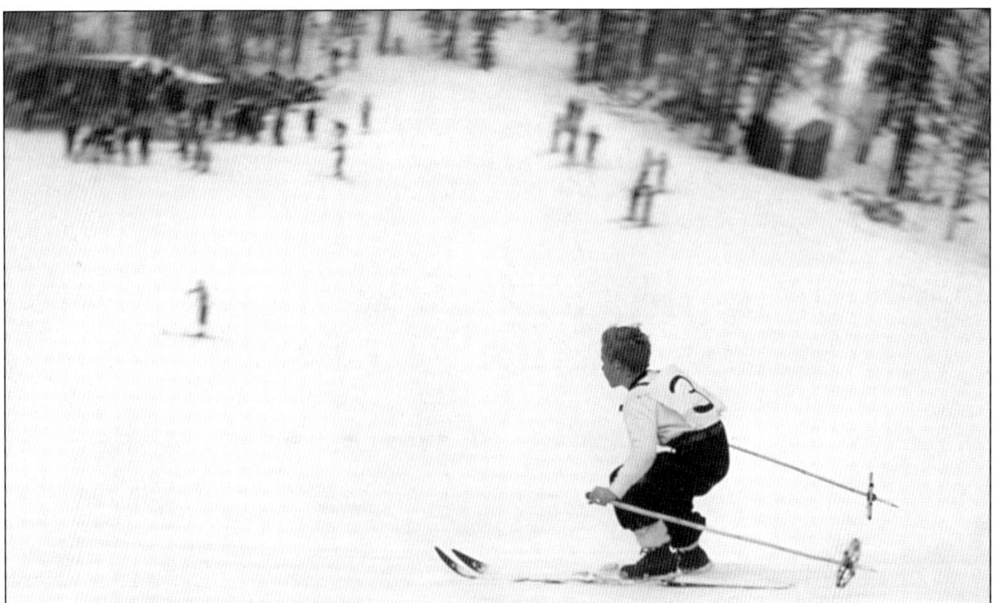

Young racer Jerry Groswold, son of ski manufacturer Thor Groswold, lets it rip at La Madera in its earliest days, as evidenced by the temporary warming tents and food concession at the base. La Madera was known for its ambitious races. In January 1938, racers from the Los Alamos Ranch School and clubs from the University of New Mexico, Albuquerque, and Santa Fe turned out for races here, including a mile-long downhill with a drop of 1,000 feet. (Photograph by Robert Nordhaus, courtesy NMSM.)

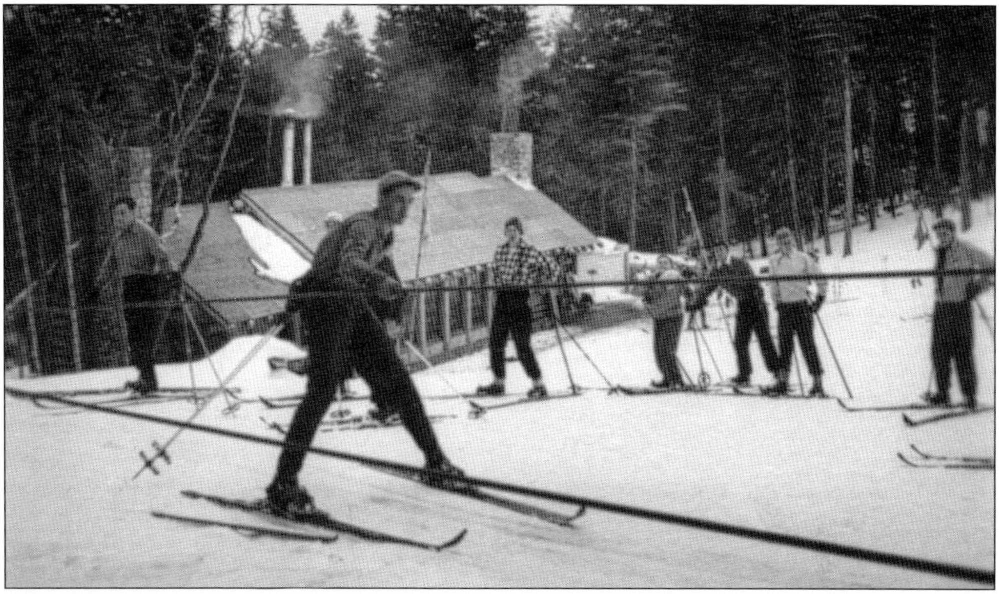

A member of the Armstrong family grabs one of the rope tows at La Madera Winter Sports Area for a ride to the modest slopes above. The first rope tow was installed here in 1937 by members of the Albuquerque Ski Club, including president Robert Nordhaus and Dan McPherson, Wiley Banes, Charlie Davis, and Dave Matthews, who cut a single run some 20 feet wide that snaked to Sandia Crest more than 2,000 feet higher. The warming lodge in the background was built in the summer of 1938 by the CCC. (Courtesy SP.)

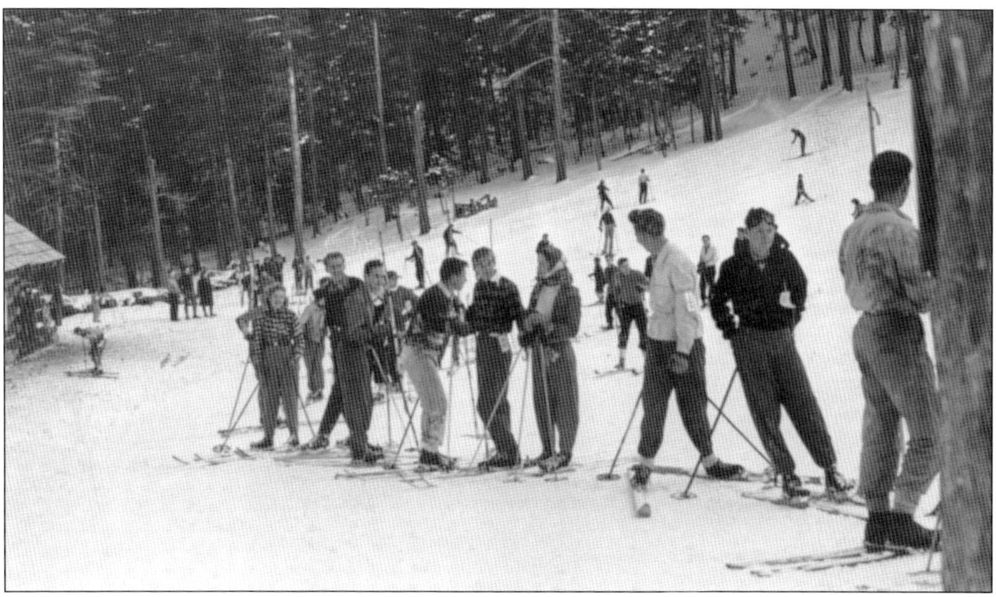

Skiers line up for the 1,500-foot rope tow at La Madera in 1941. Its first lift opened in December 1937 during a snow carnival, which also included a slalom race and exhibition skiing. The *American Ski Journal* for the 1938–1939 season reported that the lift "was a great success, despite a miscalculation by the Club's 'engineers,' which resulted in a climbing speed of 20 to 25 miles per hour instead of the intended 8." The ski area hosted the state's first downhill ski race in 1940, and that year, some 4,000 people bought lift tickets. (Courtesy SP.)

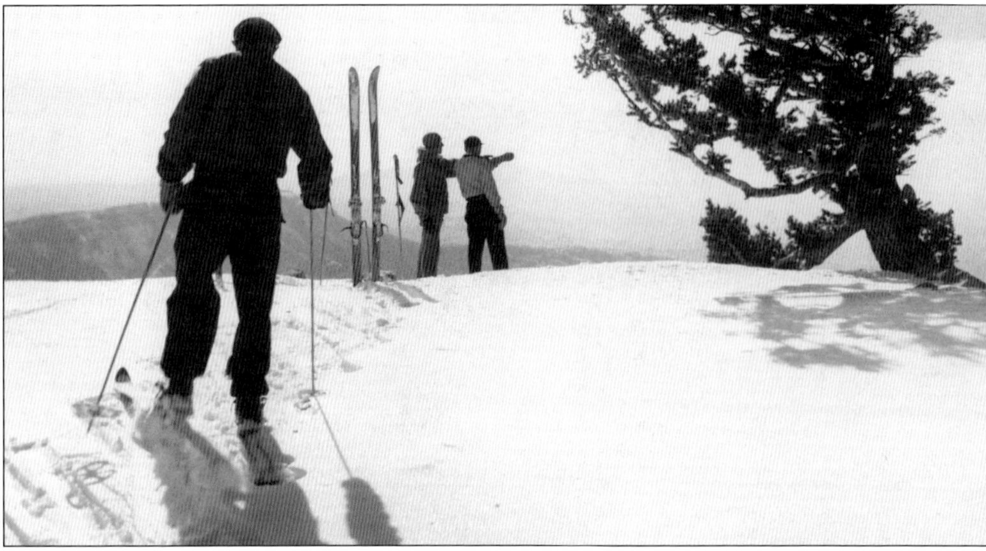

Around 1940, a skier takes the final few steps to the rim of the Sandia Mountains, which tops out at 10,678 feet. The men ahead of him are pointing to the west, perhaps toward Mount Taylor, some 80 miles away. Albuquerque sits at the foot of this limestone-topped range that tumbles precipitously into town. The Crest, as it is called, was connected by miles-long trails to La Madera Winter Sports Area, which sat at a lower elevation on the range's moderate eastern slope. (Courtesy SP.)

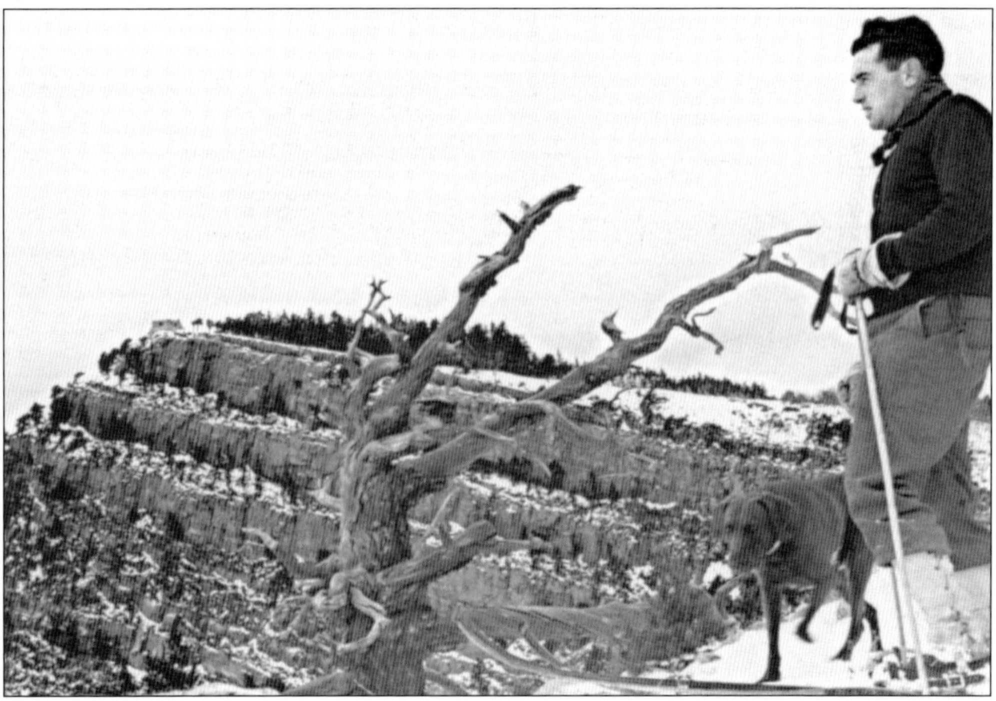

Neil "Nick" Foley stands on Sandia Crest overlooking its rugged west face in 1938 after climbing up from the La Madera T-bar. Foley was La Madera's first ski patrol volunteer and went on to serve in the 10th Mountain Division in World War II before returning home. When ski consultant Graeme McGowan first viewed this side of the mountain, he declared it unsuitable for skiing, and it largely is, though a few have dared it. (Courtesy SP.)

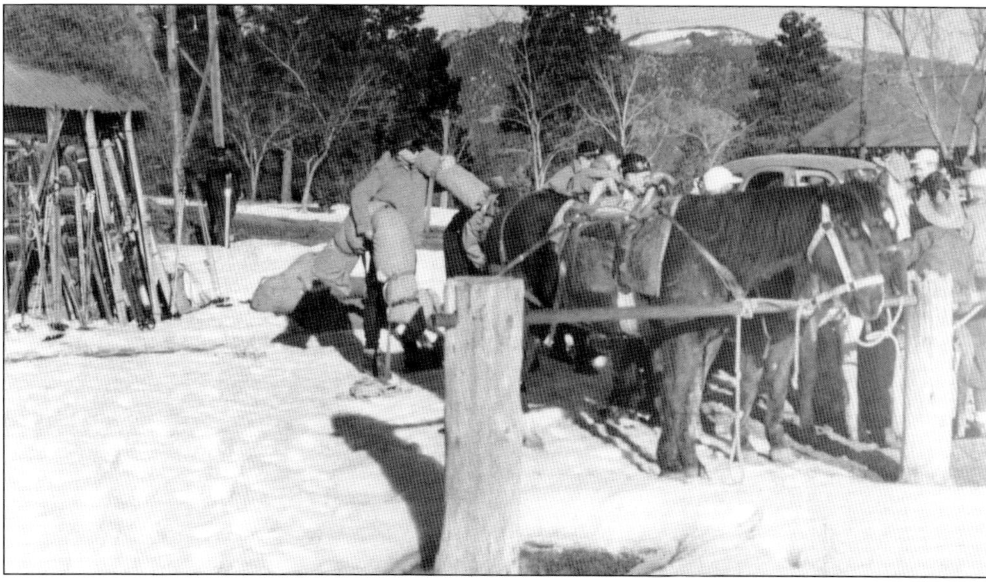

Students at the Los Alamos Ranch School were among the earliest New Mexico skiers. The boarding facility in the remote Jemez Mountains west of Santa Fe encouraged robust outdoor activities as well as rigorous academics. Founded in 1917 by Ashley Pond and directed by A.J. Connell, it never exceeded 46 students per semester. Here, the young men are loading horses on school grounds to begin the first leg of their climb to a distant cabin—Camp May, established in 1924—and excellent skiing terrain. Participation was mandatory. (Photograph by T. Harmon Parkhurst, courtesy LASC.)

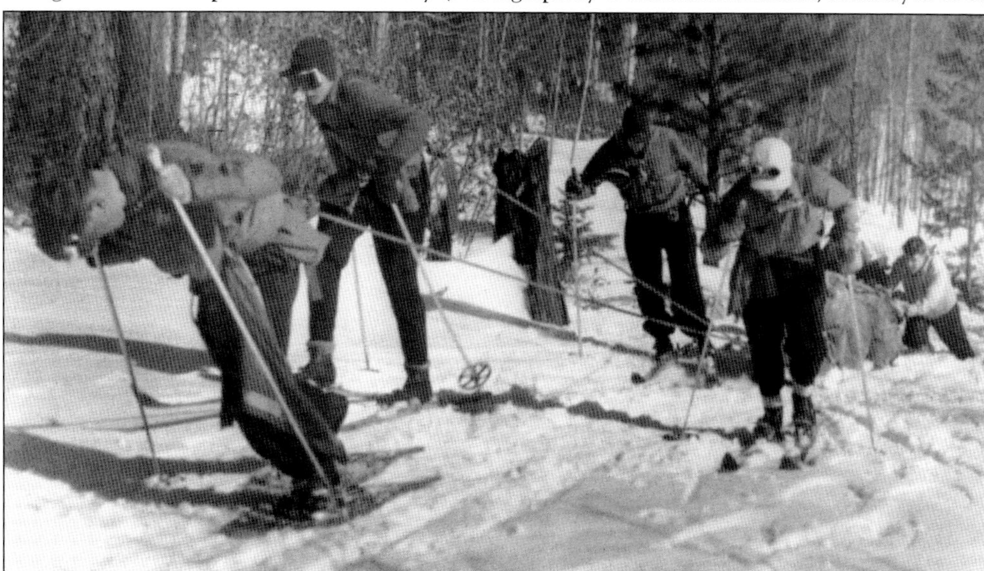

The students needed every ounce of fortitude and strength to pull their gear-laden sledges up the final leg to Camp May. It was an annual endeavor and introduced many young men to the sport, which they then spread to their homes across the nation. Graduates included Sears & Roebuck president Arthur Wood, anthropologist Edward Hall, Chicago White Sox owner Bill Veeck, American Motors Corp. president Roy Chapin, Santa Fe Opera founder John Crosby, and author William S. Burroughs. Author Gore Vidal wrote home that he was most unhappy here. (Photograph by T. Harmon Parkhurst, courtesy LASC.)

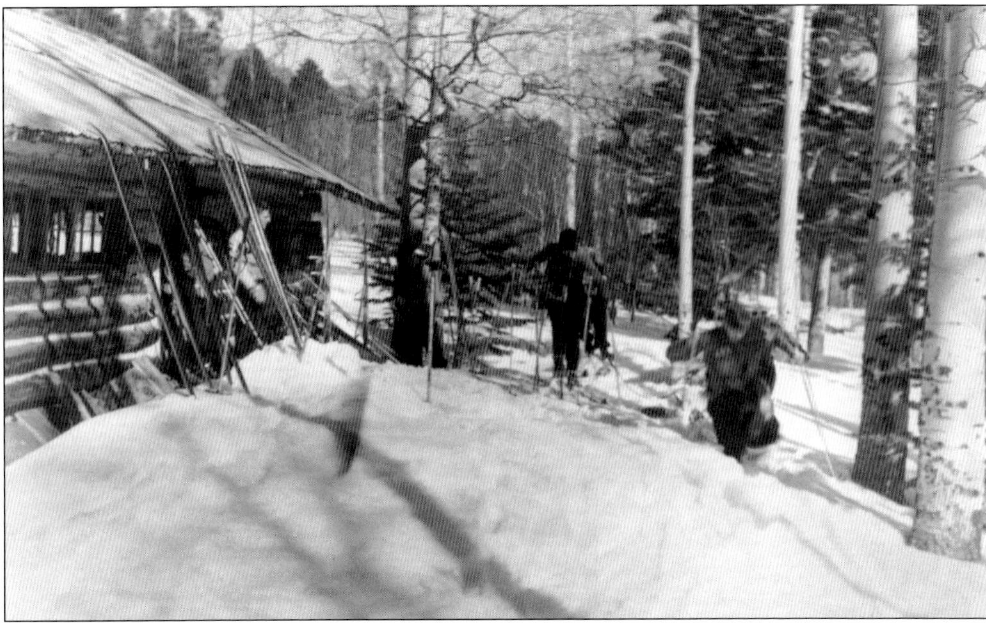

The promised land at last! Here, the weary students could warm up, sleep, and dine, and once restored, they took to the nearby slopes. The school was closed abruptly in January 1943 when the US government decided the campus would make the perfect location for a top-secret program to develop the world's first atomic weapon. The Manhattan Project (Project Y) was about to take root, and Los Alamos National Laboratory was born. (Courtesy LASC.)

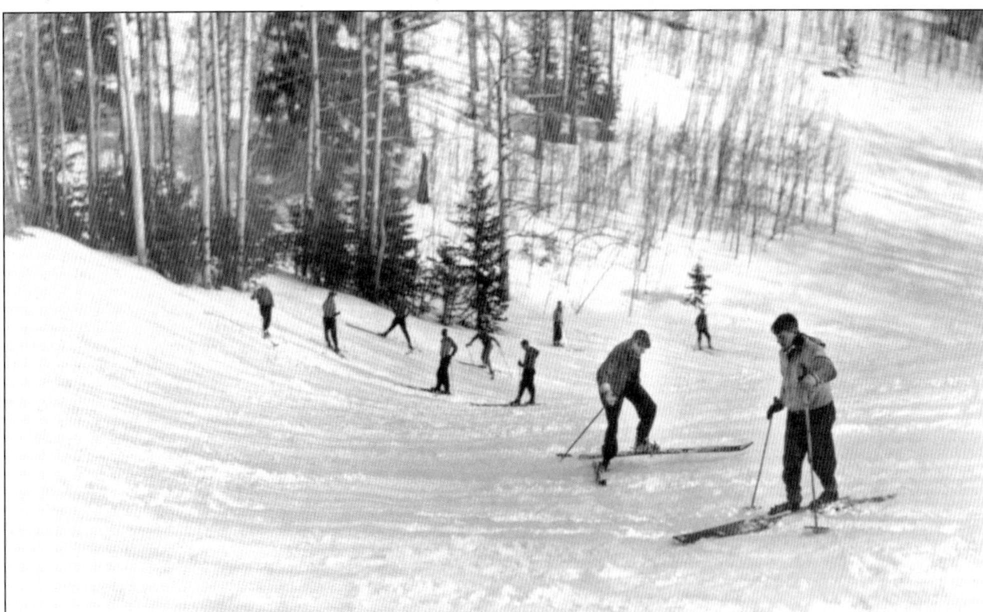

Finally, out on the slopes, the students found the going even here difficult, with no lifts to carry them to the summit overlooking the immense Valles Caldera to the south. They often made the trek to the rim. Here, they are working their way up a slope nicknamed Mother. It is incorporated today inside Pajarito Mountain, still going by its original moniker. (Photograph by T. Harmon Parkhurst, courtesy LASC.)

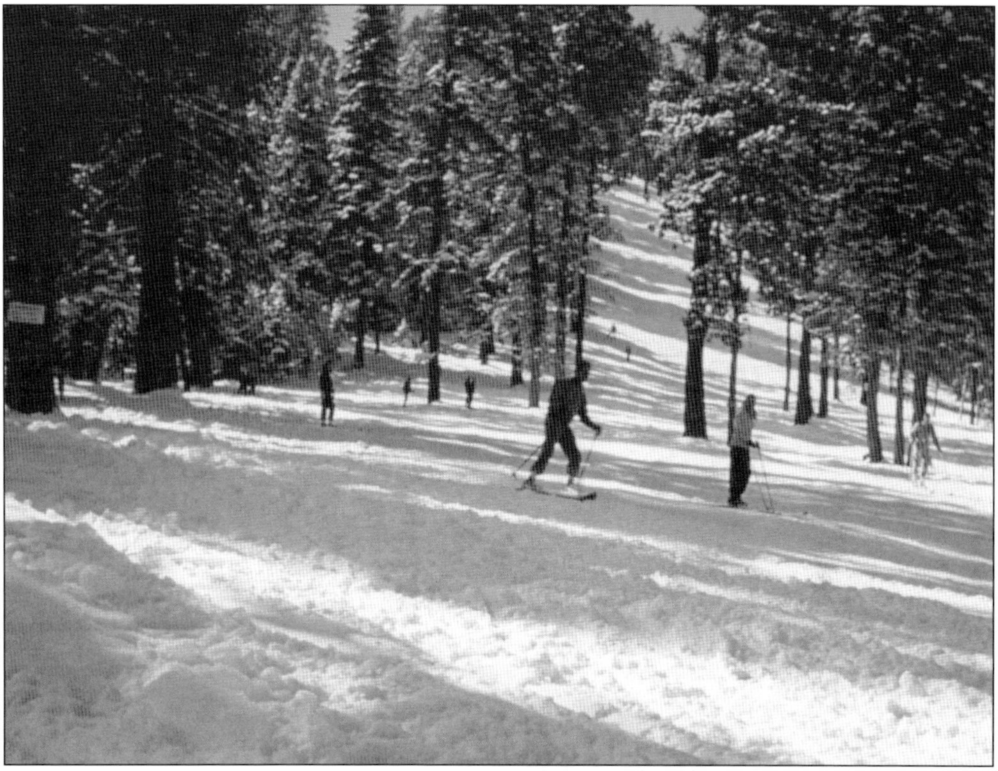

With the start of World War II and the launching of the atomic bomb project at Los Alamos, some 5,000 men and women suddenly found themselves ensconced at this remote location. To boost morale and allow staff to get some exercise and fresh air, laboratory administrators okayed funds in 1944 to put up some tows and clear some slopes for skiing close to the lab. With the strong support of the Sawyer's Hill Tow Association—formed in 1944 and still going as the Los Alamos Ski Club—Sawyer's Hill was up and running. (Courtesy LASC.)

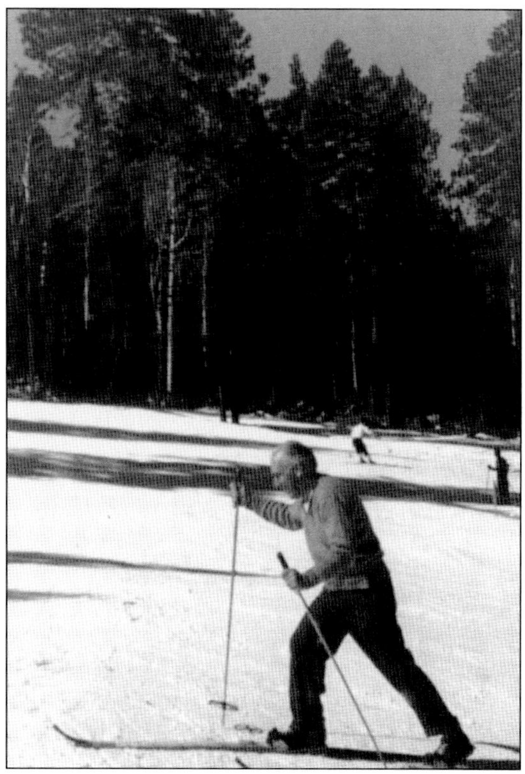

Many of Project Y's top scientists were Europeans who had fled the Nazi regime, and they brought with them a passion for skiing. Seen here at Sawyer's Hill is Niels Bohr, a Danish physicist who received the Nobel Prize in physics in 1922. Note his free-heel bindings. By 1947, Sawyer's Hill sported a 360-foot vertical drop and rope tows of 1,200 feet and 800 feet in length. (Courtesy LASC.)

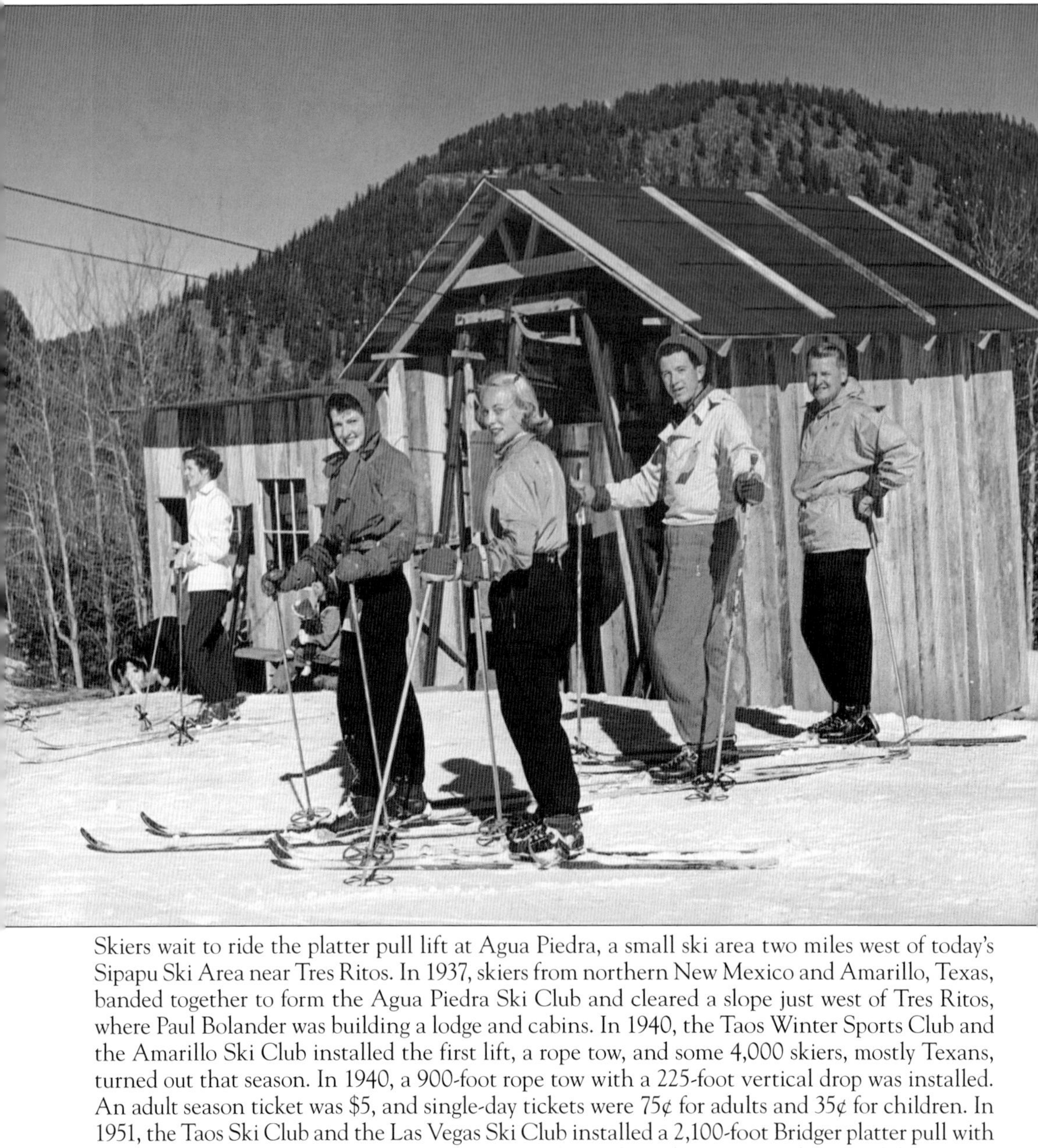

Skiers wait to ride the platter pull lift at Agua Piedra, a small ski area two miles west of today's Sipapu Ski Area near Tres Ritos. In 1937, skiers from northern New Mexico and Amarillo, Texas, banded together to form the Agua Piedra Ski Club and cleared a slope just west of Tres Ritos, where Paul Bolander was building a lodge and cabins. In 1940, the Taos Winter Sports Club and the Amarillo Ski Club installed the first lift, a rope tow, and some 4,000 skiers, mostly Texans, turned out that season. In 1940, a 900-foot rope tow with a 225-foot vertical drop was installed. An adult season ticket was $5, and single-day tickets were 75¢ for adults and 35¢ for children. In 1951, the Taos Ski Club and the Las Vegas Ski Club installed a 2,100-foot Bridger platter pull with a vertical drop of 600 feet, and the Bolander family was brought in to run the area. (Photograph by Verne Sackett, courtesy State Archives of New Mexico, Item No. 002468.)

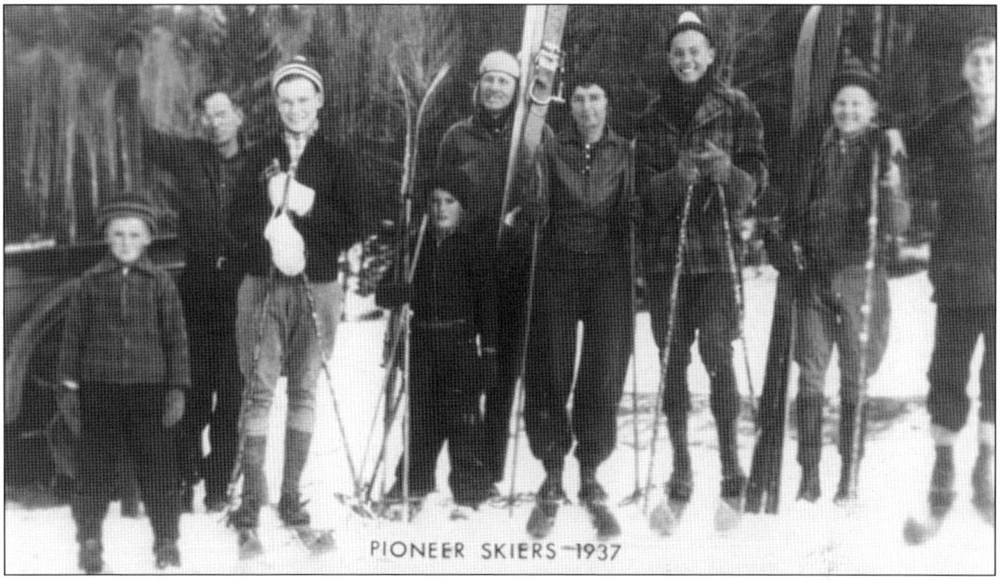

Skiers from Amarillo flocked to Agua Piedra—often referred to as Tres Ritos—helping lift the fledgling New Mexico ski community from its nest. Seen here in 1937 are, from left to right, Don Bolander, Archie Bolander, unidentified, Lloyd Bolander, John Maynerd, Ruth Bolander, two unidentified, and Curtis Maynerd. After World War II, the area sported two rope tows that provided access to a mile-long racecourse in Cordova Canyon where wild downhills were run over the years. Its deep snows were legendary, often stranding skiers, who had to sleep at the Bolanders' places in Tres Ritos on pool and roulette tables. (Courtesy Bolander family.)

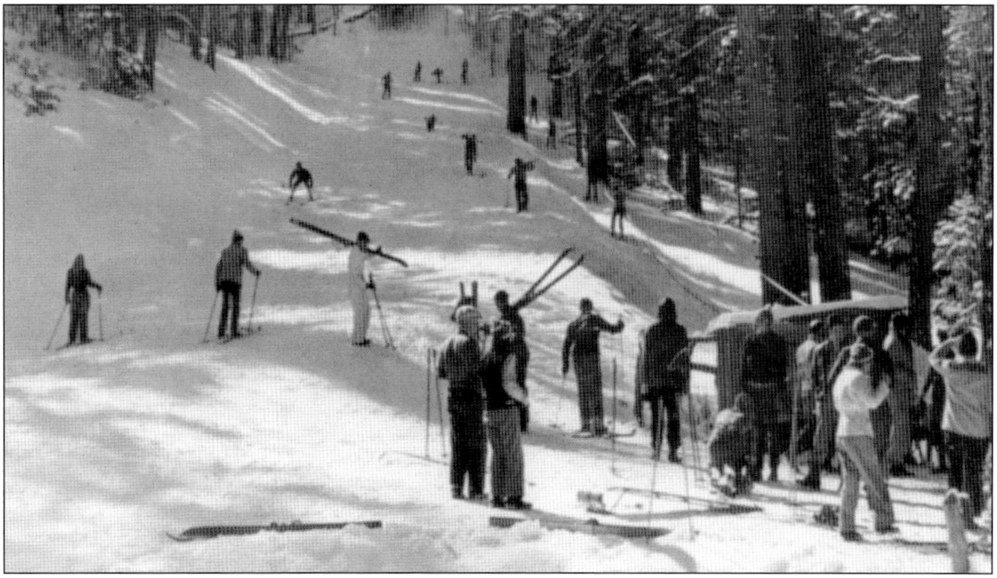

Cedar Creek opened in 1938 near Ruidoso in south-central New Mexico as an open slope with a few log shelters built by the CCC. In 1939, W.A. Hart, Carmon Phillips, Ray Izard, and Charles Milligan formed the White Mountain Sports Association in Ruidoso and sold shares for $100 to 45 stockholders. They persuaded the CCC to build a road and clear a trail on US Forest Service land along Upper Cedar Creek. A rudimentary rope tow was installed and operated for several winters. It continued after World War II into the 1950s, but low elevation doomed it. (Courtesy NMSM.)

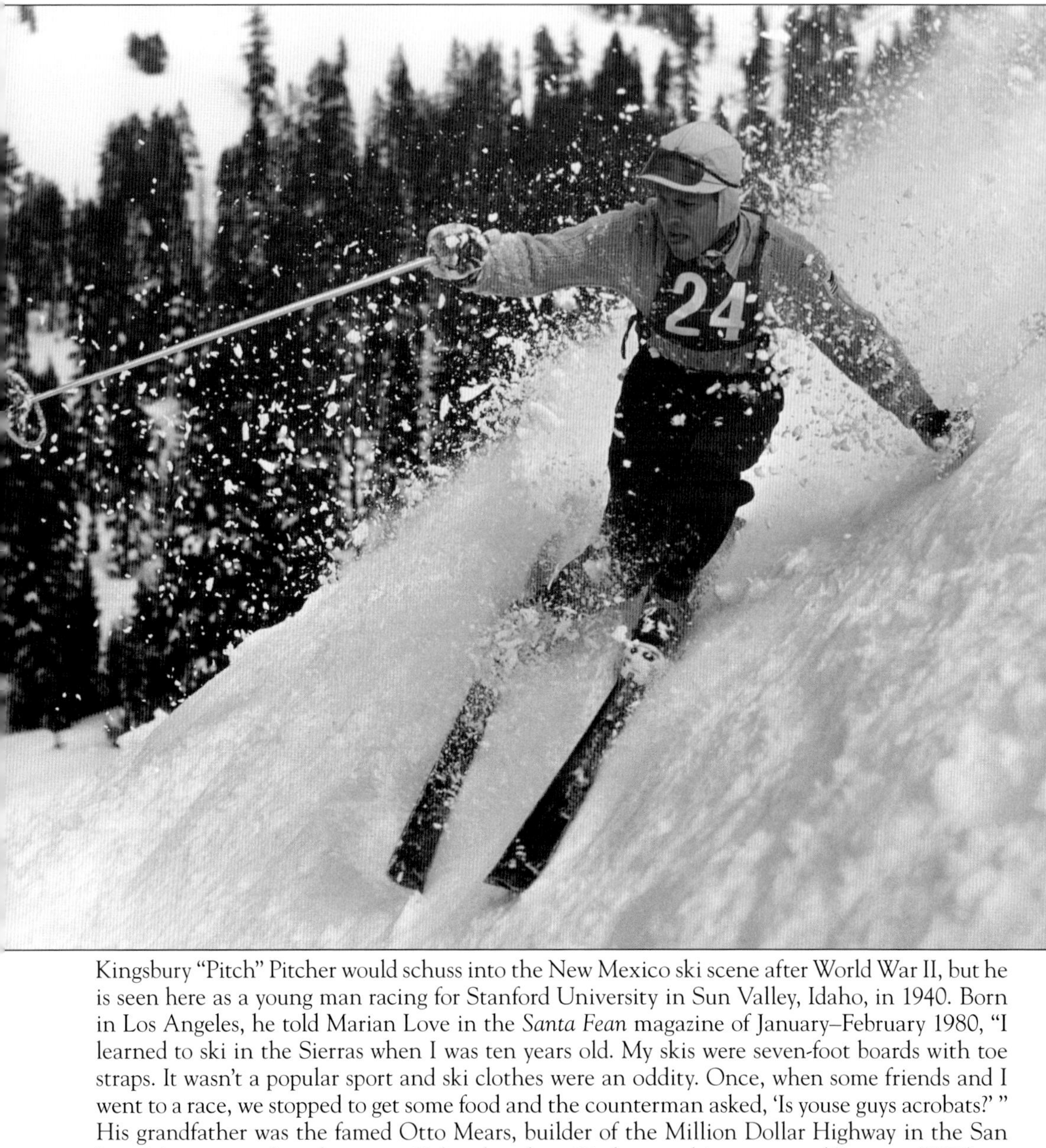

Kingsbury "Pitch" Pitcher would schuss into the New Mexico ski scene after World War II, but he is seen here as a young man racing for Stanford University in Sun Valley, Idaho, in 1940. Born in Los Angeles, he told Marian Love in the *Santa Fean* magazine of January–February 1980, "I learned to ski in the Sierras when I was ten years old. My skis were seven-foot boards with toe straps. It wasn't a popular sport and ski clothes were an oddity. Once, when some friends and I went to a race, we stopped to get some food and the counterman asked, 'Is youse guys acrobats?' " His grandfather was the famed Otto Mears, builder of the Million Dollar Highway in the San Juan Mountains of southwestern Colorado, where Pitch spent his summers. (Courtesy PFC.)

Three

BOOM YEARS
POSTWAR AND 1950S

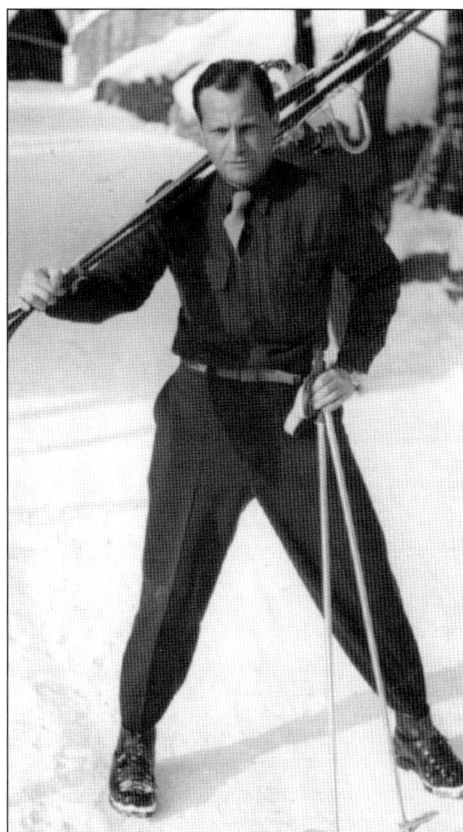

Ernie Blake worked for US Army intelligence in World War II, as he spoke German, French, English, and Italian. Born Ernst Bloch, of Swiss-German heritage, he grew up skiing in the Alps. A member of Gen. George Patton's staff, he is seen here in 1945 on leave in Switzerland going skiing. He would become the single most important figure in the nascent ski community amidst the mountain ranges of New Mexico. (Courtesy BFC.)

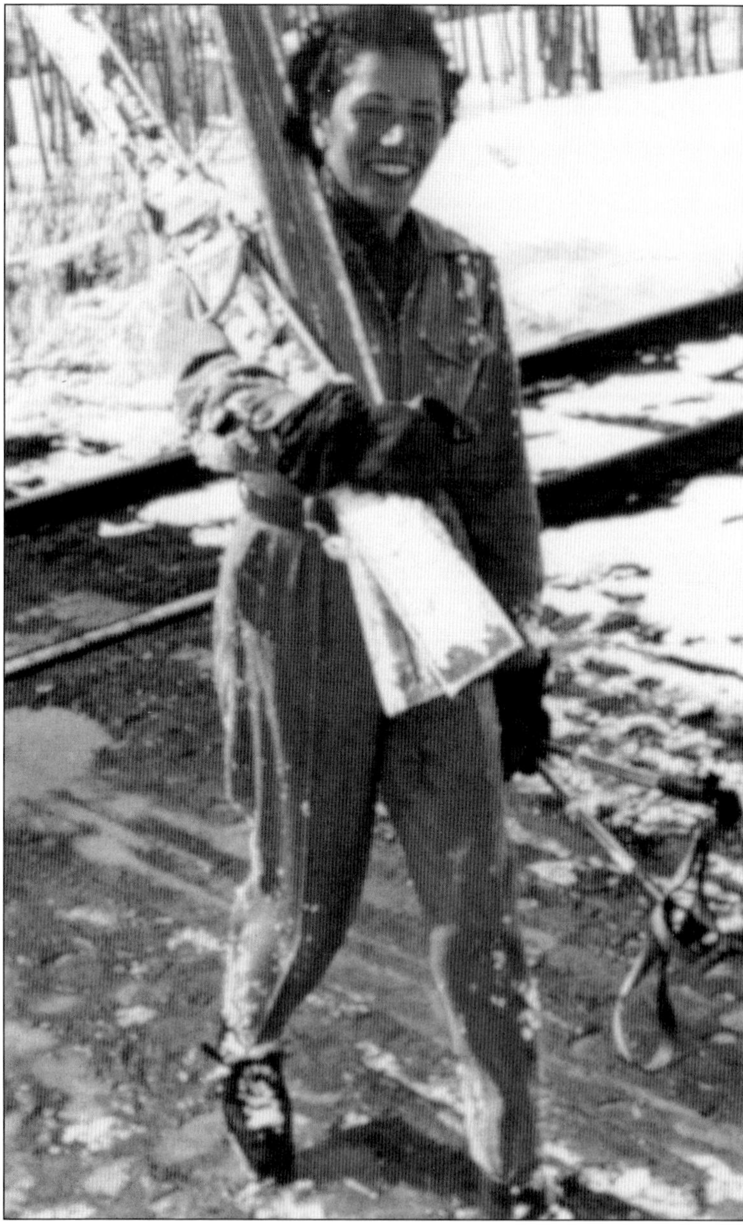

Rhoda Blake ambles along on her honeymoon in Sun Valley, Idaho, in February or March 1942, shortly after her marriage to Ernie Blake. Born Doris Rosenberg in London on April 8, 1918, Rhoda was orphaned during World War I, and Herbert and Irma Limburg of New York City adopted her when she was three. Raised on Park Avenue, largely in the Drake Hotel, she attended Dalton School and Bryn Mawr College. "Mom always wanted to escape from her mother," explains her eldest son, Mickey Blake. "She hated the whole society thing." As an aspiring artist, she convinced her parents to let her come live in Santa Fe for a year to study art in 1939. She met Ernie at the Octagon Restaurant while skiing at Stowe, Vermont, in December 1940, but the bond really began to form that summer and during a ski trip to Alta, Utah, in June 1941. He did not make a great first impression, reading the *New York Times* while riding the slow Mount Mansfield lift and stuffing it into his jacket for the ski down. She said later he "looked like a dumpy penguin." (Courtesy BFC.)

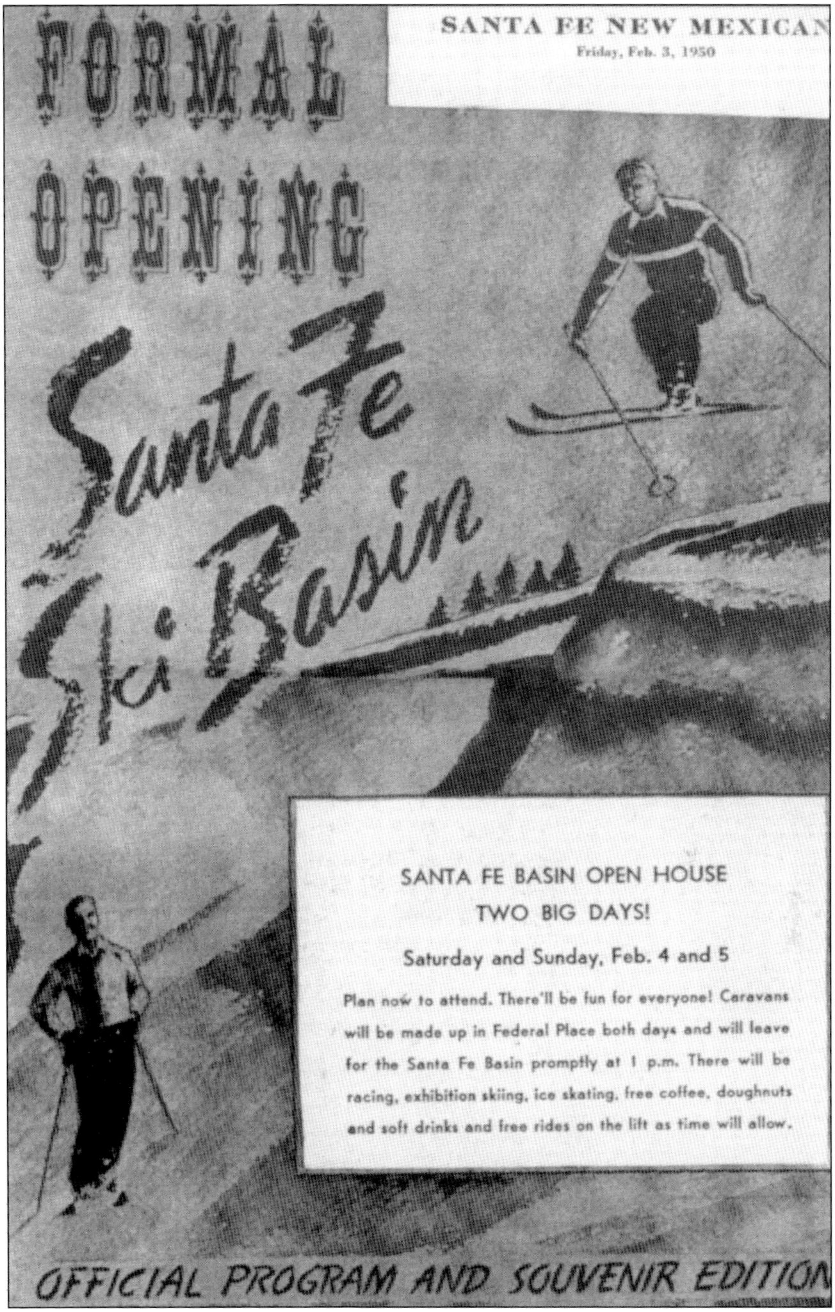

This official program published in the *Santa Fe New Mexican* on February 3, 1950, announced the opening of Santa Fe Ski Basin on February 4–5, 1950. It promised "There'll be fun for everyone!" Caravans left Federal Place both days at 1:00 p.m. Events included racing, exhibition skiing, and ice skating, with free coffee, doughnuts, and soft drinks, as well as free rides on the lifts. Running the show was Ernie Blake, who had first visited Santa Fe in 1941 with Rhoda, settling here in 1949. Looking for work, Ernie visited the chamber of commerce office, and when they found out he was a skier, they directed him to the Santa Fe Winter Sports Club, which was overseeing the ski area development. He was hired as the first manager. (Courtesy SkiSF.)

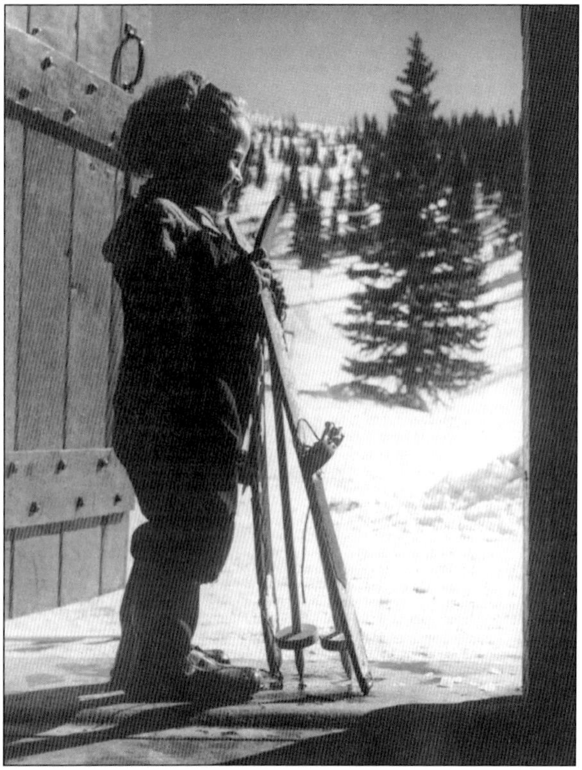

In January 1952, Wendy Blake, Ernie and Rhoda's middle child, stands in a doorway with her pint-sized skis at Aspen Basin. The family sometimes spent the night in a small metal trailer at the ski area when work or weather demanded. Ski competitions were popular in the early 1950s, with the annual May Day Race held on a milelong course down the creek bed of the Big Tesuque Creek, while Washington's Birthday Race was held off Lake Peak down to the Aspen Basin parking lot. Hup Wallis directed the races and was assisted by A.G. "Buzz" Buster Bainbridge and Graeme McGowan. (Courtesy BFC.)

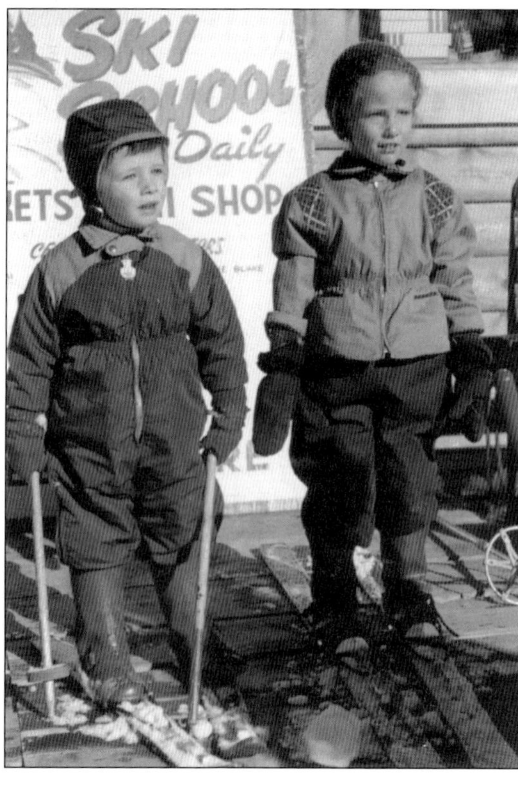

Wendy and younger brother Peter Blake hang out in front of the ski school office at Aspen Basin around 1954. The Blakes had a nice adobe home in Santa Fe and made many friends in the budding town, which was filled with artists and iconoclasts. Ernie Blake stayed on board until March 1954, when he resigned to begin the process of launching Taos Ski Valley. (Courtesy BFC.)

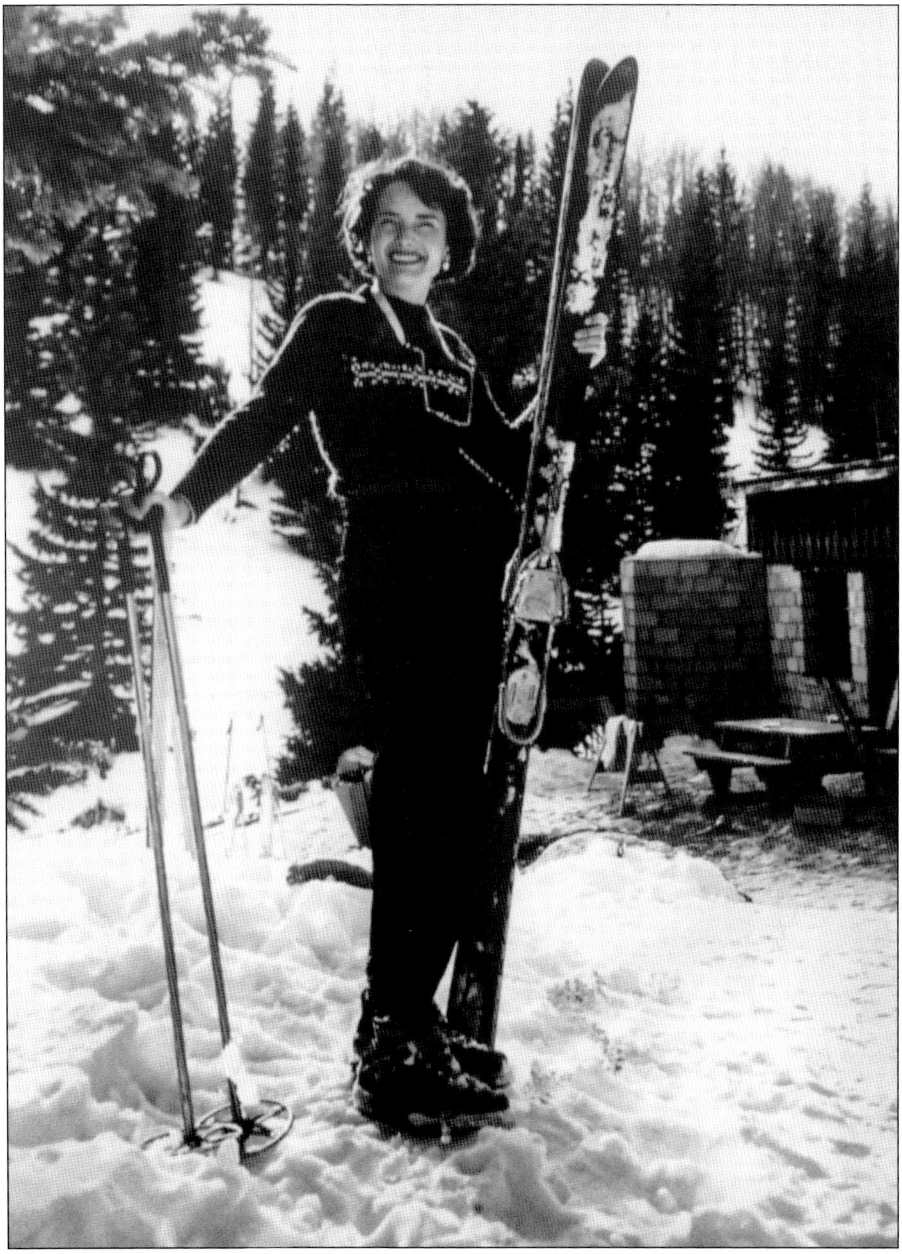

A skier strikes a pose at the newly renamed Santa Fe Basin in 1950, when a work-in-progress lodge was unveiled, seen here in the background, along with a 2,600-foot double chair—the state's first—ski school, ski shop, and skating rink. The chairs, with great effort from two lift operators, could be detached from a moving cable for easy loading and unloading and hung from cables salvaged from the former Eureka Mine of Silverton, Colorado, with seats from B-24 bombers. If not securely reattached to the moving cable by the operators, the chairs were known to roll backwards! Daily tickets ran $3, with a single ride to Lookout Point at 11,200 feet costing 75¢. The basin's 1950–1951 brochure stated, "Enthusiastic skiers are traveling west for deep powder snow, vast open slopes and brilliant sunshine. American skiing at its best is found in the Rocky Mountains, and the West's newest development is the Santa Fe Basin." (Courtesy SkiSF.)

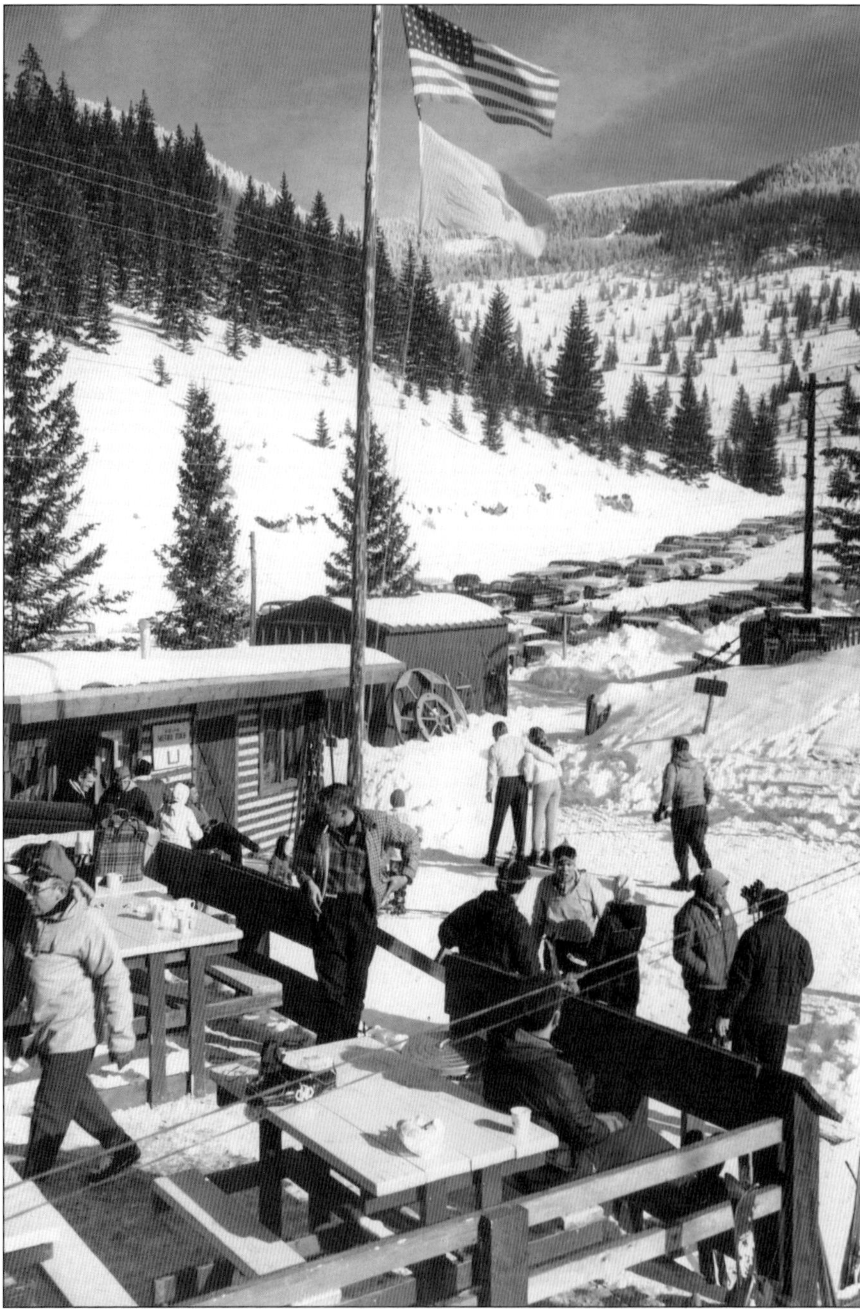

This fine photograph reveals the deck of the new Sierra Lodge at Santa Fe Basin in the early 1950s, looking east toward Lake Peak. The parking lot is where today's Tesuque Peak and Millennium chairs begin, with both running up to the highest slopes seen here. At the base of the flagpole sits the ski school office. The first chairlift began just out of frame to the right and ran up today's Thunderbird run. The ski area's brochure for 1949–1950 promised, "skiers can choose between pleasant, easy-to-ski slopes or a number of fast, daring downhill runs from the top." Graeme McGowan's prediction for grand skiing here was finally a reality. (Photograph by Starr Jenkins for the USFS, courtesy PFC.)

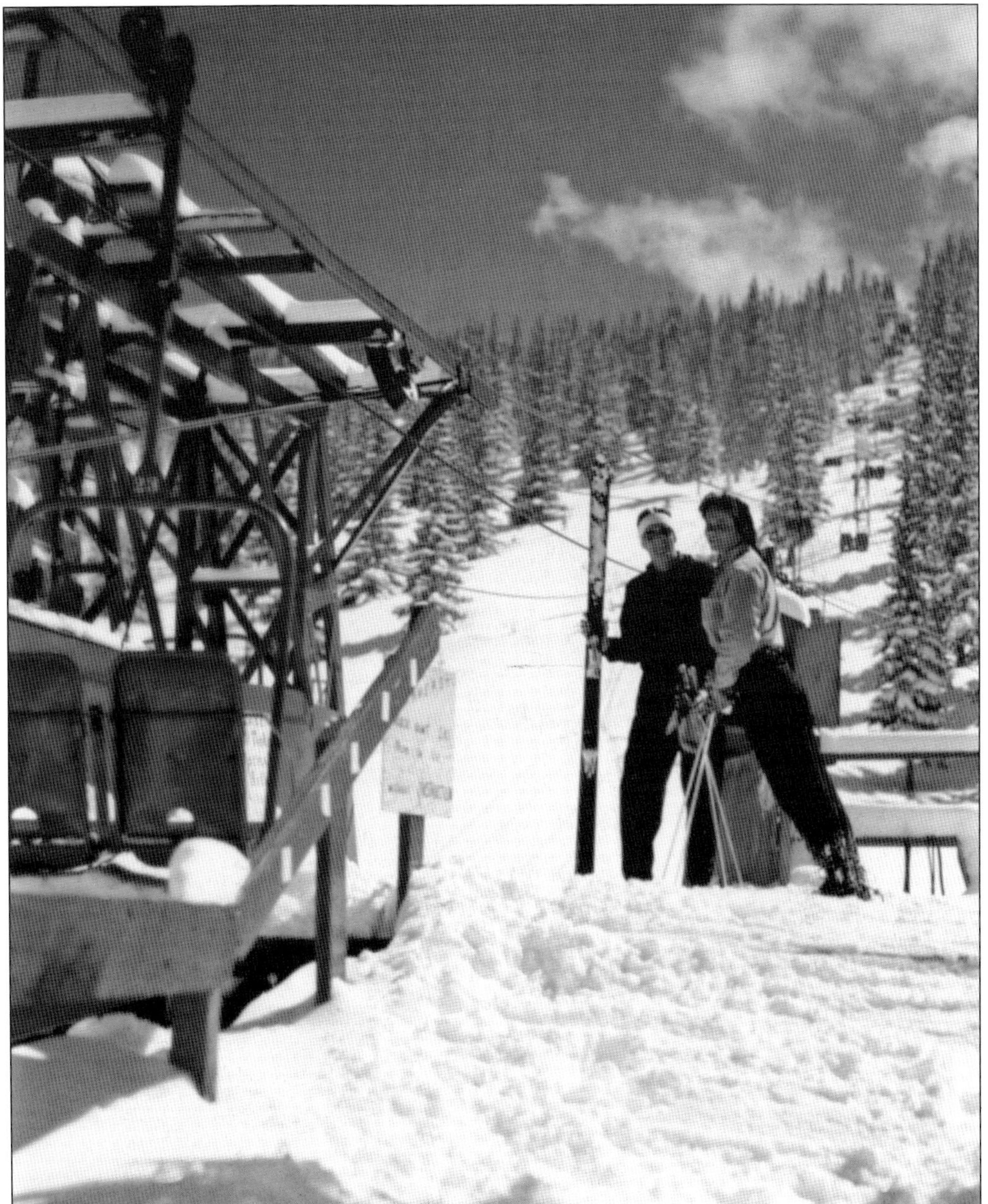

Here is a close-up of the base terminal of the first chairlift at Santa Fe Basin, the state's first, opened in 1950. A skier stretches her hamstrings before boarding the near-empty lift. Even though ticket prices were dropped in the lift's second year from $3 to $2, it was apparent that they were not being mobbed. Skiing at Hyde Park and at Tesuque Creek lower on the mountain was still ongoing, siphoning off some business. In a story in the 1948 issue of the *American Ski Annual*, Buzz Bainbridge reported, "Races were held almost every weekend, with local stores providing the prizes. Among the star racers were Ann and Marion Cunningham, the Spitz boys, Bob Wilson, Jack O'Hara, Ann Breese and Betty Wiley. Santa Fe's favorite skiing son, Kingsbury 'Pitch' Pitcher, went with his wife to Sun Valley to resume instructing in the ski school there." (Photograph by Boyer, courtesy PFC.)

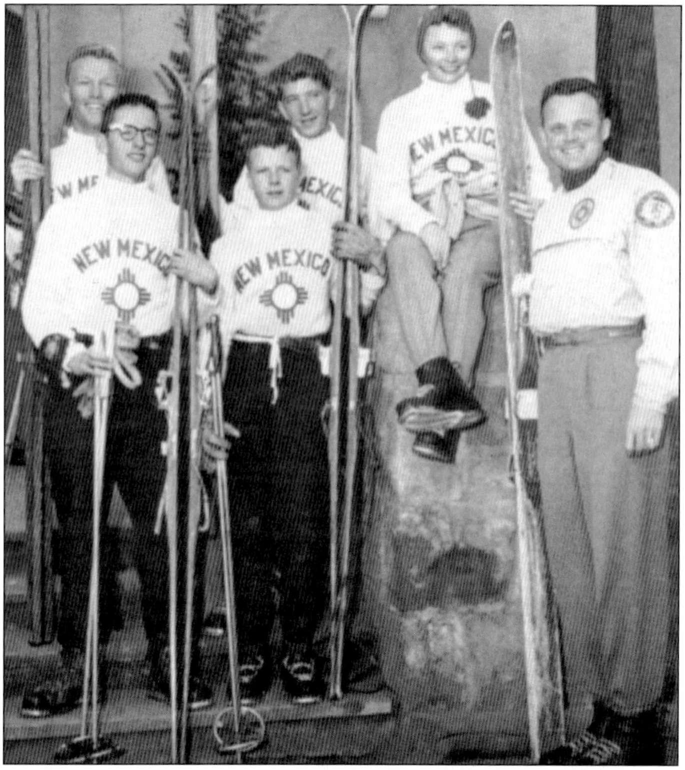

Members of the 1954 New Mexico Ski Team proudly represented the state at the Sun Valley championships. Team coach Buzz Bainbridge is on the right. Members that year included Mary Lind (seated), John Dendahl (front center), John Kinsolving (front left), Buster Quist, Dickie Nordhaus, Jim Jordan, and Tom Brennand. Bainbridge filled many roles in the state's ski community, including directing Hyde Park and Big Tesuque in the 1946–1947 season, managing the Santa Fe Basin for five years in the 1950s, directing La Madera at various times, and founding Red River Ski Area in 1960. (Courtesy NMSM.)

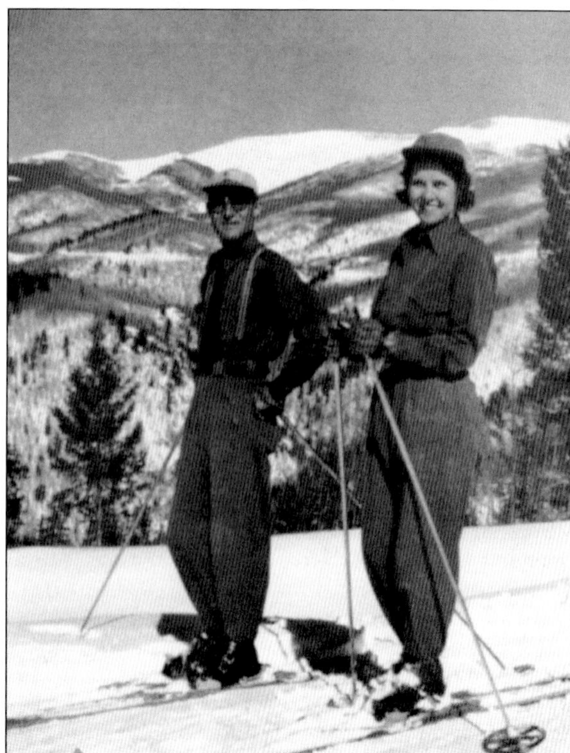

While there was still skiing at Hyde Park near Santa Fe, as seen in this shot of two winter enthusiasts published in 1953 in *Picturesque New Mexico*, it was winding down. Thousands of feet lower in elevation than the Santa Fe Basin, seen behind them, it received little snow some years, and the community's energy and interest was shifting to the higher terrain. The original caption for this image read, "New Mexico's high country is rapidly gaining fame for winter sports with more than a dozen areas in the state doing capacity business." (Photograph by New Mexico Highway Bureau, courtesy NMSM.)

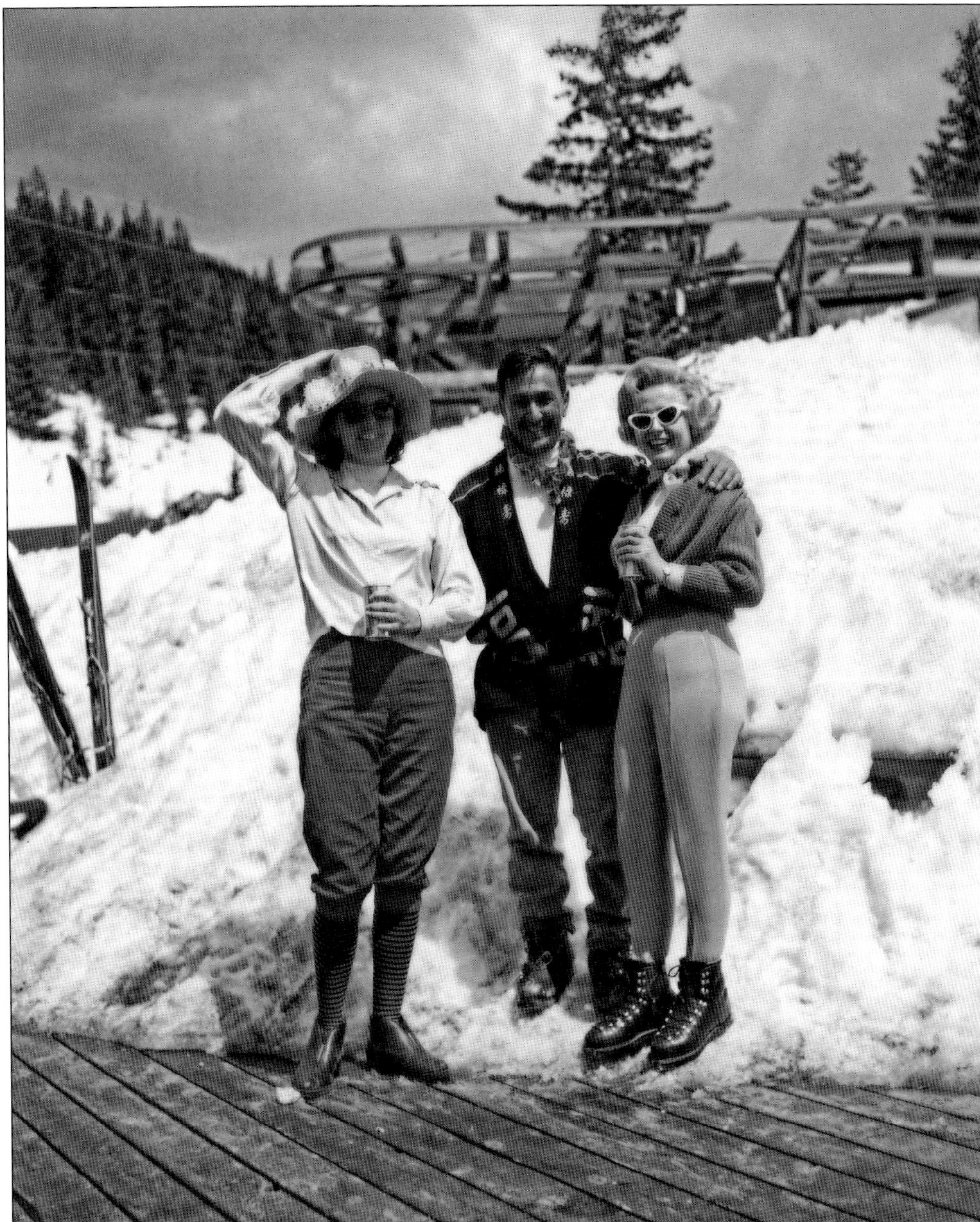

Sandwiched between two lively spirits is Pete Totemoff. A native Alaskan, he came to New Mexico in 1939 seeking respite from tuberculosis and ended up smack in the middle of the state's emerging ski industry. Here, he is seen at Santa Fe Basin sometime in the 1950s or early 1960s standing on the deck that would bear his name many years later. He was with Ernie Blake during the first explorations of the terrain that would become Taos Ski Valley and worked there off and on for years. He also held roles at Sierra Blanca, Sipapu, and La Madera, where his nemesis was a skating pond that would not hold water. A fun-loving individualist, he was among the most cherished of New Mexico's ski pioneers. "He was so sure he was going to die of TB when he came here that he immediately bought a cemetery plot," says Mickey Blake. Fortunately, it was not filled until 1990. (Courtesy PFC.)

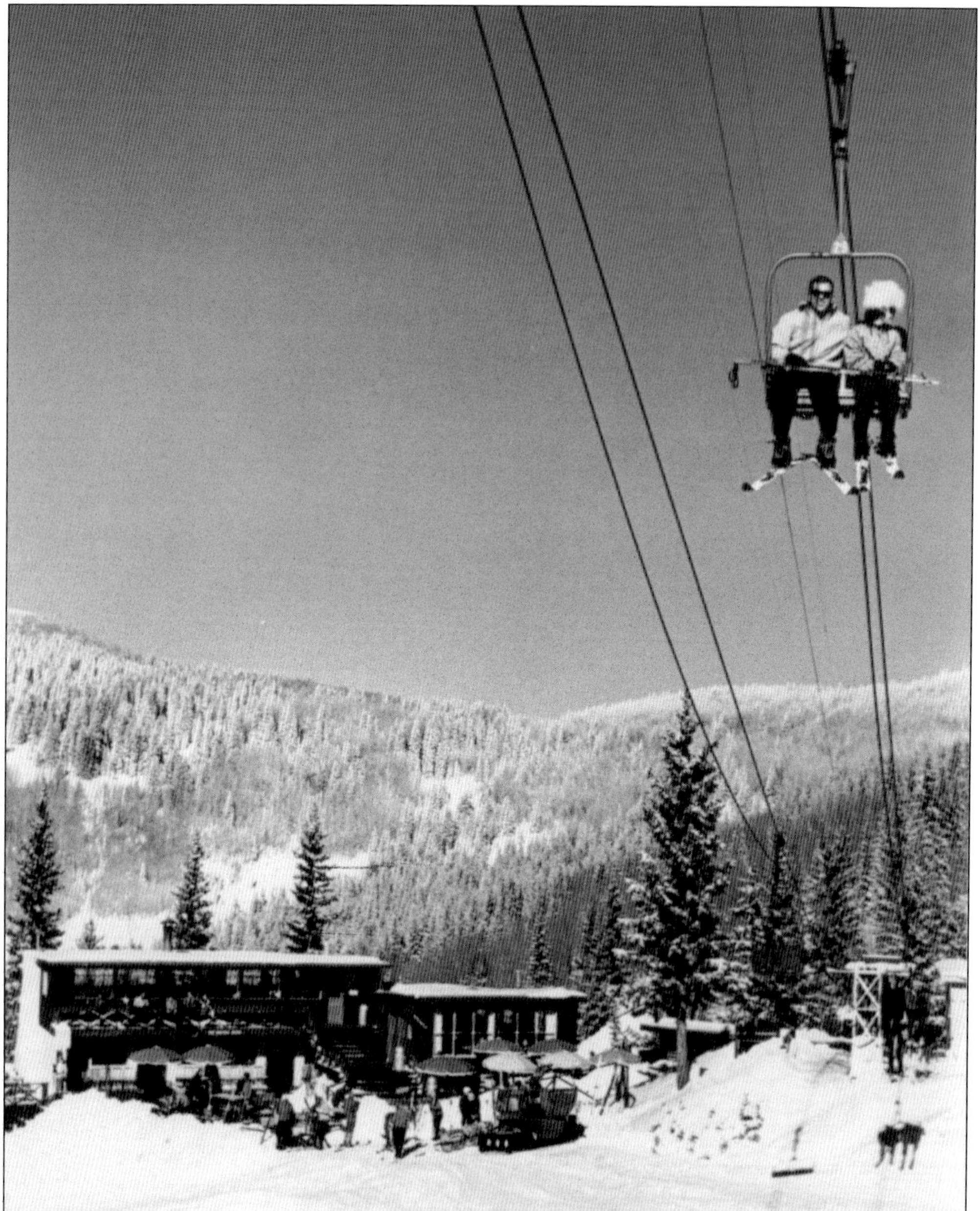

Here is another image of the so-called "Red Chair" at Santa Fe Basin, with the Sierra Lodge at its base. The lodge looks quite similar today, though it is called Totemoff's, with food and drink still served on its sunny deck. Its second floor used to serve as a changing area, where parents would coax kids into leather boots and scratchy wool sweaters. It also served as the ski rental shop until 1967. The lift was an odd contraption, with one cable pulling the chair along while it rested on wheels rolling along another cable. Made in 1888 of durable Sheffield steel, the rust was knocked off and the cables were tested for reliability, and voila—a chair on the cheap. One of these old chairs occupies a prominent spot on the deck today, bringing back fond memories for old-timers. The chair operated through the winter of 1963, when it was removed and its towers taken down. (Courtesy PFC.)

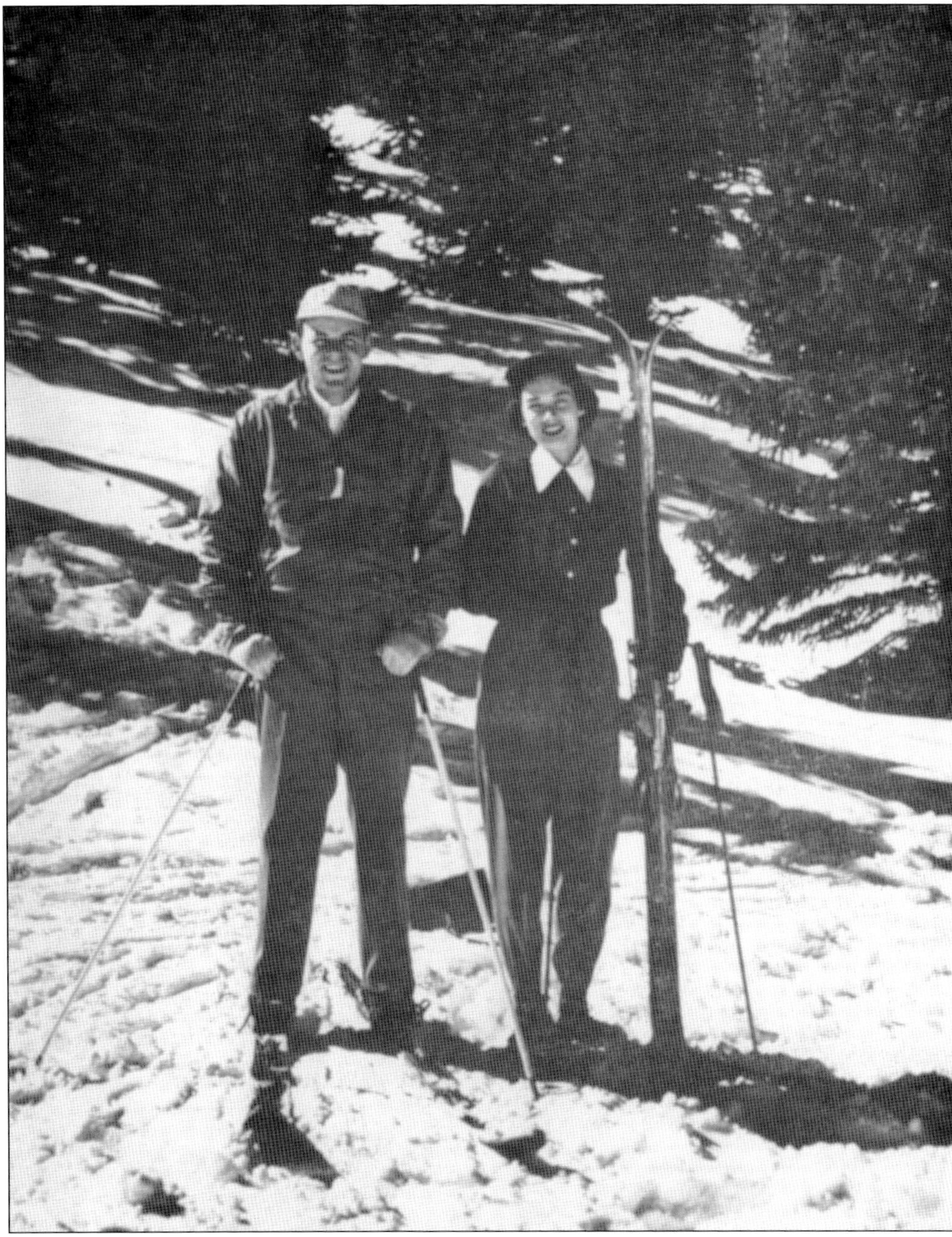

These skiers enjoy a sunny day in 1952 at Santa Fe Basin in a staged shot for the Santa Fe Chamber of Commerce. Buzz Bainbridge was busy forming clubs in the area in those days. In an article in the *Santa Fe New Mexican* in 1995, he noted, "All I wanted was bodies, and I was always working the lift lines forming ski clubs. I'd ask where a group was from and said I could give them each a 50¢ discount if they were a club. They'd elect a president right there on the snow." Sensing he was on to a good thing, he and his wife, Jean, began traveling to Texas, forming 28 clubs, which would compose the backbone of New Mexico ski growth over the next decades. Bainbridge also ran Santa Fe's ski school, and Ernie Blake worked under him—perhaps the only time Ernie took orders from anyone! (Photograph by Tyler Dingee, courtesy PFC.)

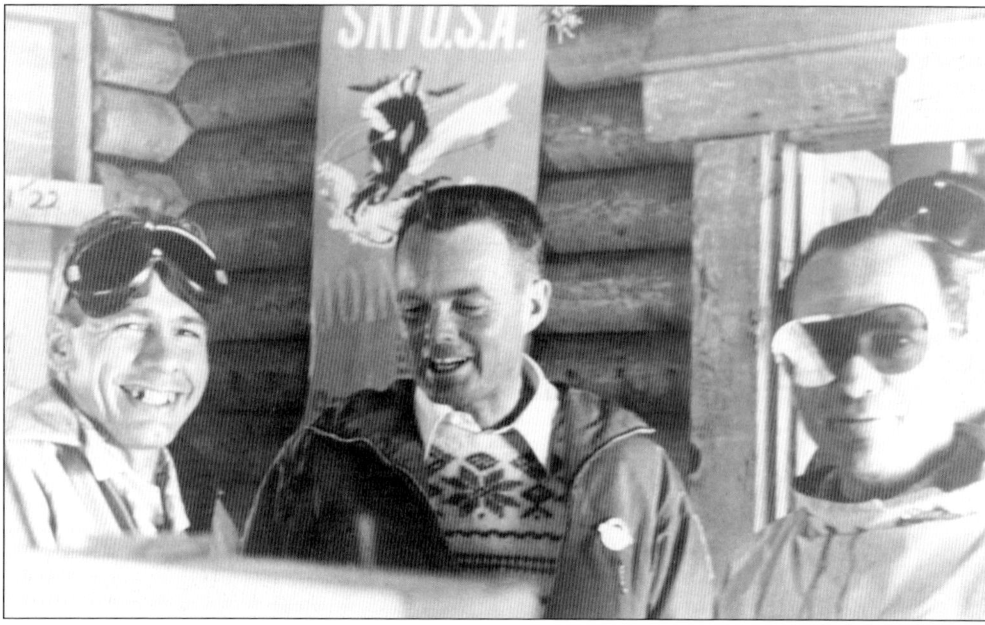

Elsewhere in New Mexico, the ski scene was blossoming, or at least holding its own. Seen here from left to right are Mal Wallis, Buzz Bainbridge, and Ernie Blake at Sawyer's Hill above Los Alamos. Wallis and his brother Hup were closely associated with Sawyer's Hill, but Blake and Bainbridge were visiting from Santa Fe Basin. New Mexico's ski founders were not so much competitors as coconspirators and fellow enthusiasts. Their willingness to share information, techniques, and even personnel continued for decades, more akin to a family than dueling corporations. (Courtesy LASC.)

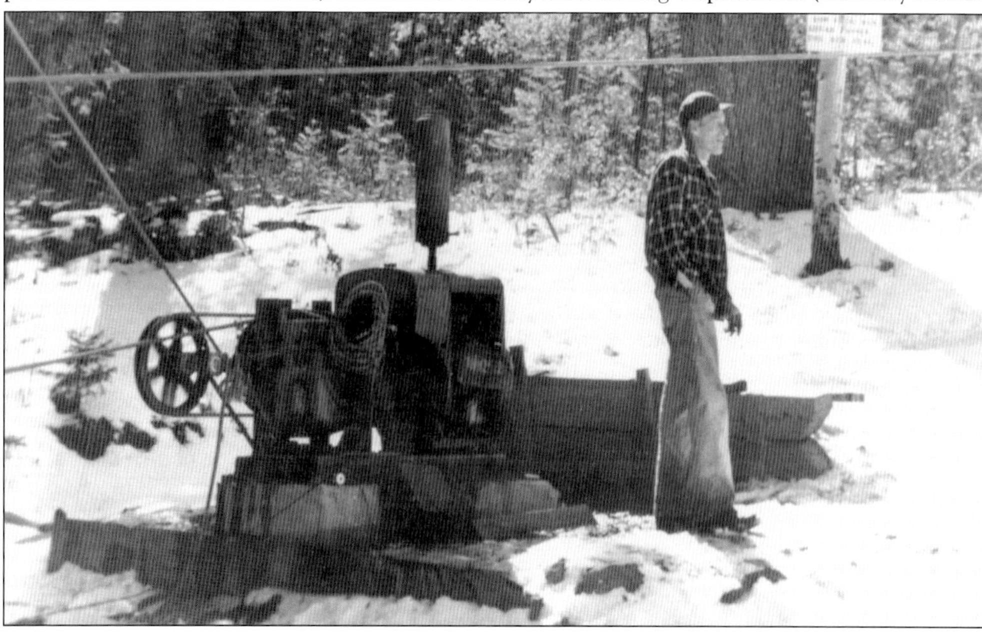

Luther Rickerson, rope tow operator at Sawyer's Hill in the 1950s, takes a smoke break on a warm, sunny afternoon. By the winter of 1943–1944, Sawyer's Hill had two rope tows with a 370-foot vertical and a small base lodge. The first ski slopes were cleared here by Hup Wallis, brother of Mal Wallis, for Los Alamos Ranch School students in 1937 or 1938. (Courtesy LASC.)

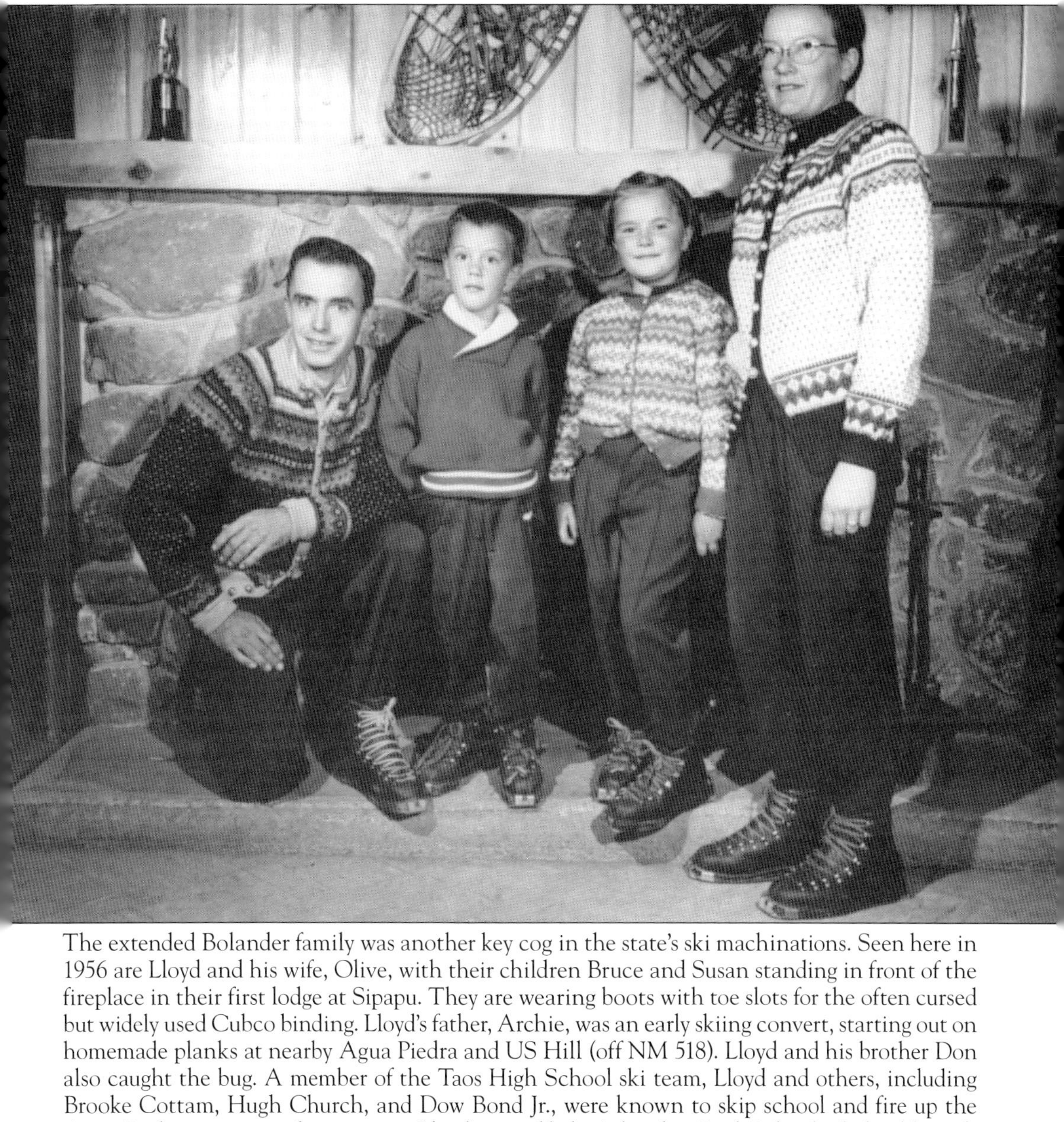

The extended Bolander family was another key cog in the state's ski machinations. Seen here in 1956 are Lloyd and his wife, Olive, with their children Bruce and Susan standing in front of the fireplace in their first lodge at Sipapu. They are wearing boots with toe slots for the often cursed but widely used Cubco binding. Lloyd's father, Archie, was an early skiing convert, starting out on homemade planks at nearby Agua Piedra and US Hill (off NM 518). Lloyd and his brother Don also caught the bug. A member of the Taos High School ski team, Lloyd and others, including Brooke Cottam, Hugh Church, and Dow Bond Jr., were known to skip school and fire up the Agua Piedra rope tow after a storm. Lloyd's grandfather's brother Paul Bolander helped launch Agua Piedra. The family acquired their Sipapu property in 1950, opened a Texaco gas station and a store, and built a series of small cabins. In 1952, they erected their first rope tow at Sipapu, and the ski area continues to operate today. (Photograph by Fred Nobs of Brownwood, Texas, courtesy Bolander family.)

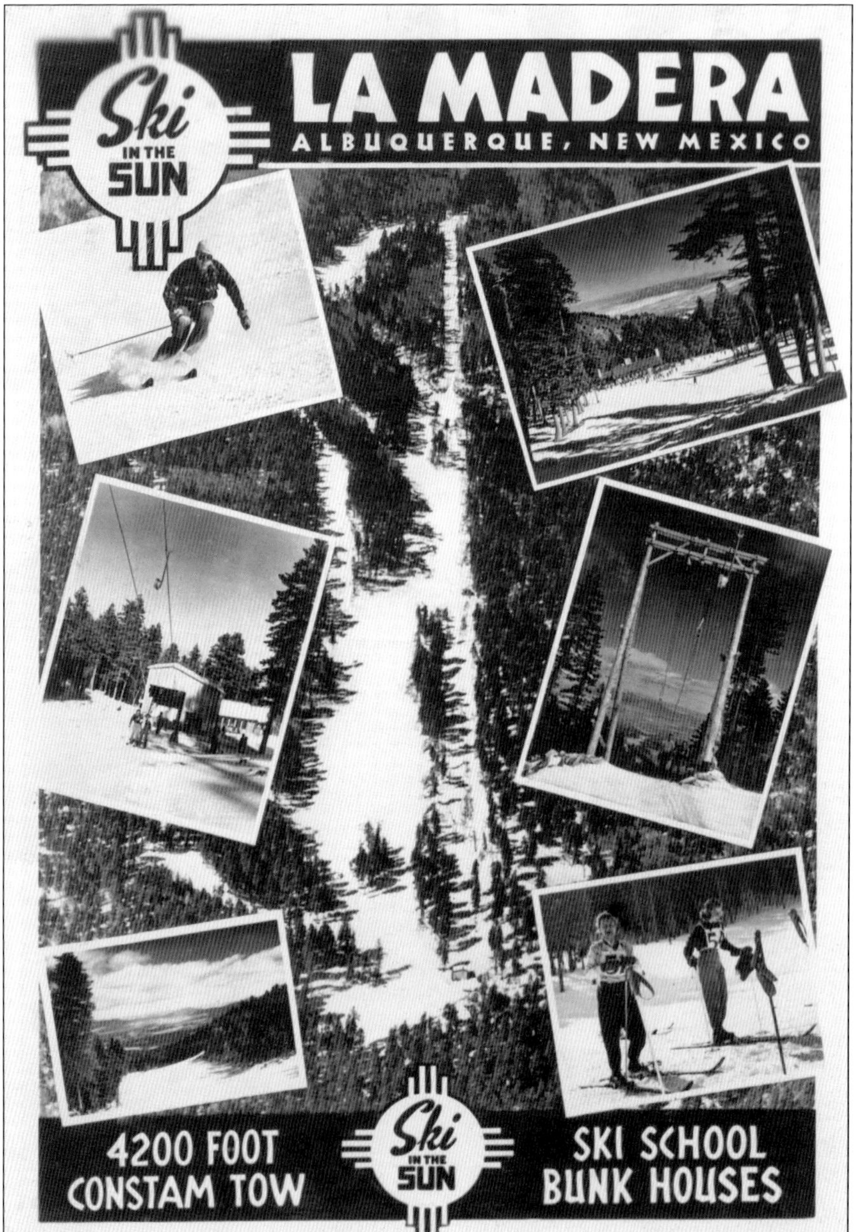

Postwar Albuquerque went on a growth spurt, and nearby La Madera followed suit. Ski area consultant Graeme McGowan was commissioned by the Albuquerque Chamber of Commerce and the club to survey the Sandia Mountains for future development. He found the mountain's eastern slope eminently suitable. In 1946, Robert Nordhaus returned to Albuquerque after serving in the 10th Mountain Division, bought the assets of the Albuquerque Ski Club, and formed the La Madera Company. A 4,200-foot Constam T-bar was installed that year at La Madera, which was the longest in the United States at the time. An ice rink, bunkhouse, and restaurant were built in the base area, and daily operations began. A ski patrol was organized, and several club members ran the area. This late 1940s poster highlights some of the newly added amenities and the "Ski in the Sun" logo. (Courtesy NMSM.)

The cover of the December 1946 *Albuquerque Progress*, a publication of Albuquerque National Bank, featured a couple of skiers at La Madera near Duke City, which was undergoing a transformation into a significant ski area as America accelerated out of World War II. The 1946–1947 season here was a good one, with skiing from Thanksgiving to April, and attendance of 16,000 people. It hosted lots of races, a ski ball, and chuck wagon suppers. Both high school and the University of New Mexico ski teams trained here. (Photograph by John Barnes, courtesy NMSM.)

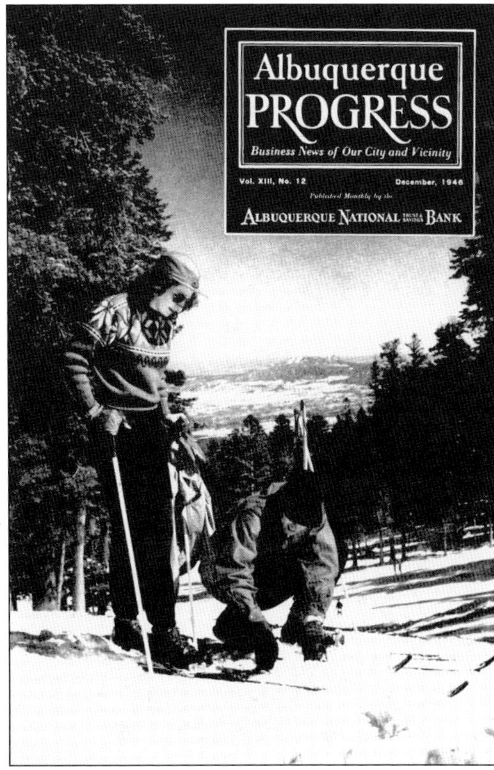

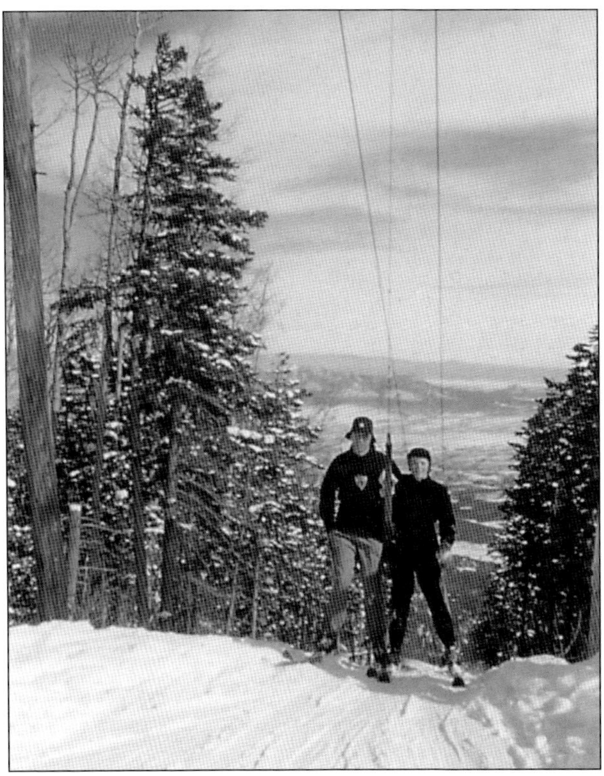

Two riders on the La Madera T-bar approach the terminus of the remarkable lift in 1952. Behind them, and several thousand feet below, rest the Ortiz Mountains and the Sangre de Cristos. From the top of the Sandias, one can see east to the westernmost edge of the Great Plains and look the opposite direction into Arizona and south and north for more than a hundred miles. The Constam T-bar was dismantled in 1973. The ski area's first chair, a double Stadeli, arose in 1963, luring away most of the T-bar riders. (Photograph by Robert Nordhaus, courtesy SP.)

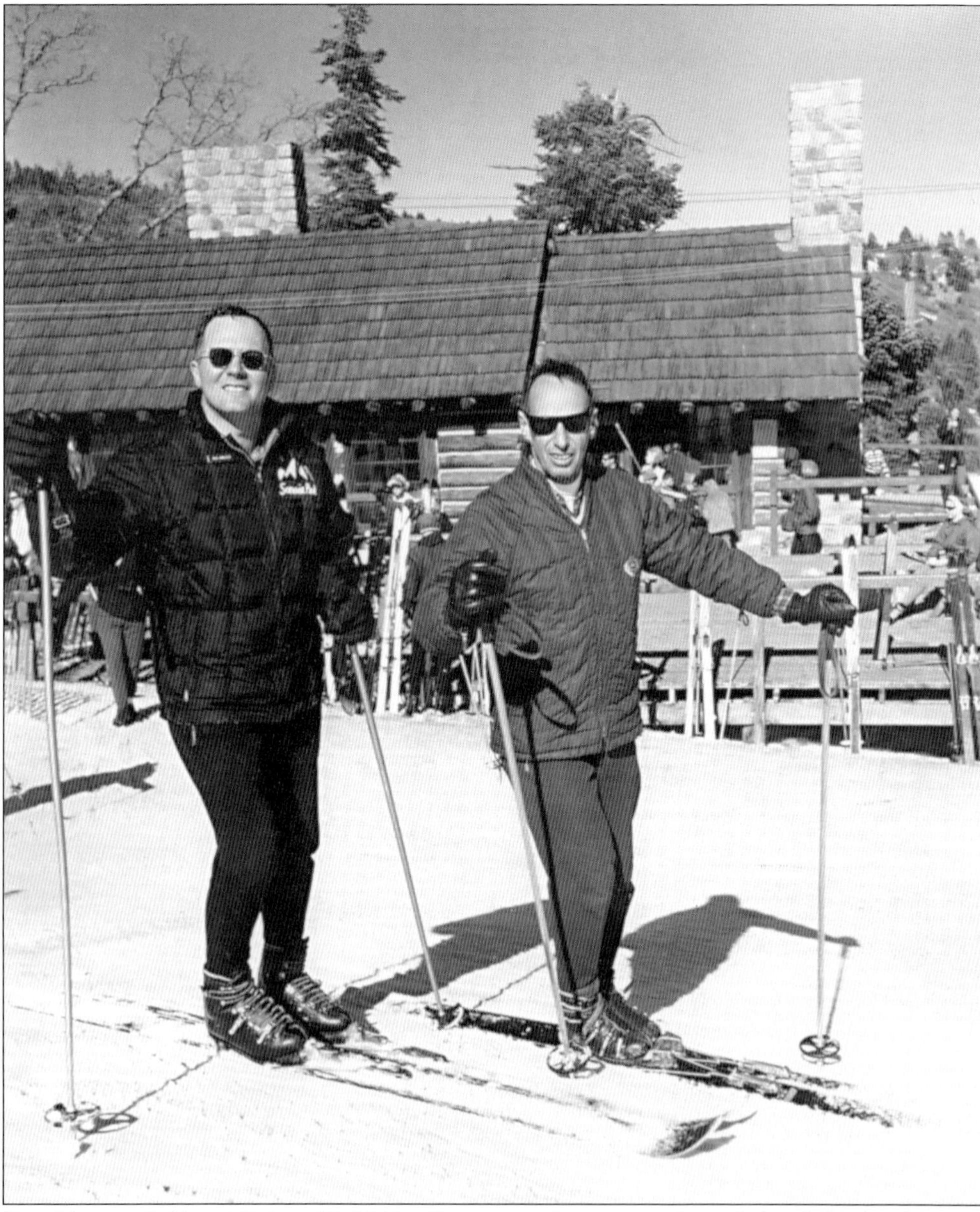

Ben Abruzzo (left) and Robert "Bob" Nordhaus were the primary forces behind the development of La Madera into today's Sandia Peak. They are seen here at the base of La Madera in 1962. Nordhaus was a New Mexico native, born and raised in the original Las Vegas. He obtained a law degree from Yale University in 1935 and became the founding president of the Albuquerque Ski Club in 1936. His wife, Virginia, first suggested they try out this new sport of skiing. He once told author Daniel Gibson, "We began to learn—no one really knew anything about it." Low snow years in the early 1950s led him to turn over operations to the City of Albuquerque, but in 1952, he and a group of investors resumed management. Both men were inducted into the New Mexico Ski Hall of Fame's first class in 2003 along with Ernie Blake. (Courtesy SP.)

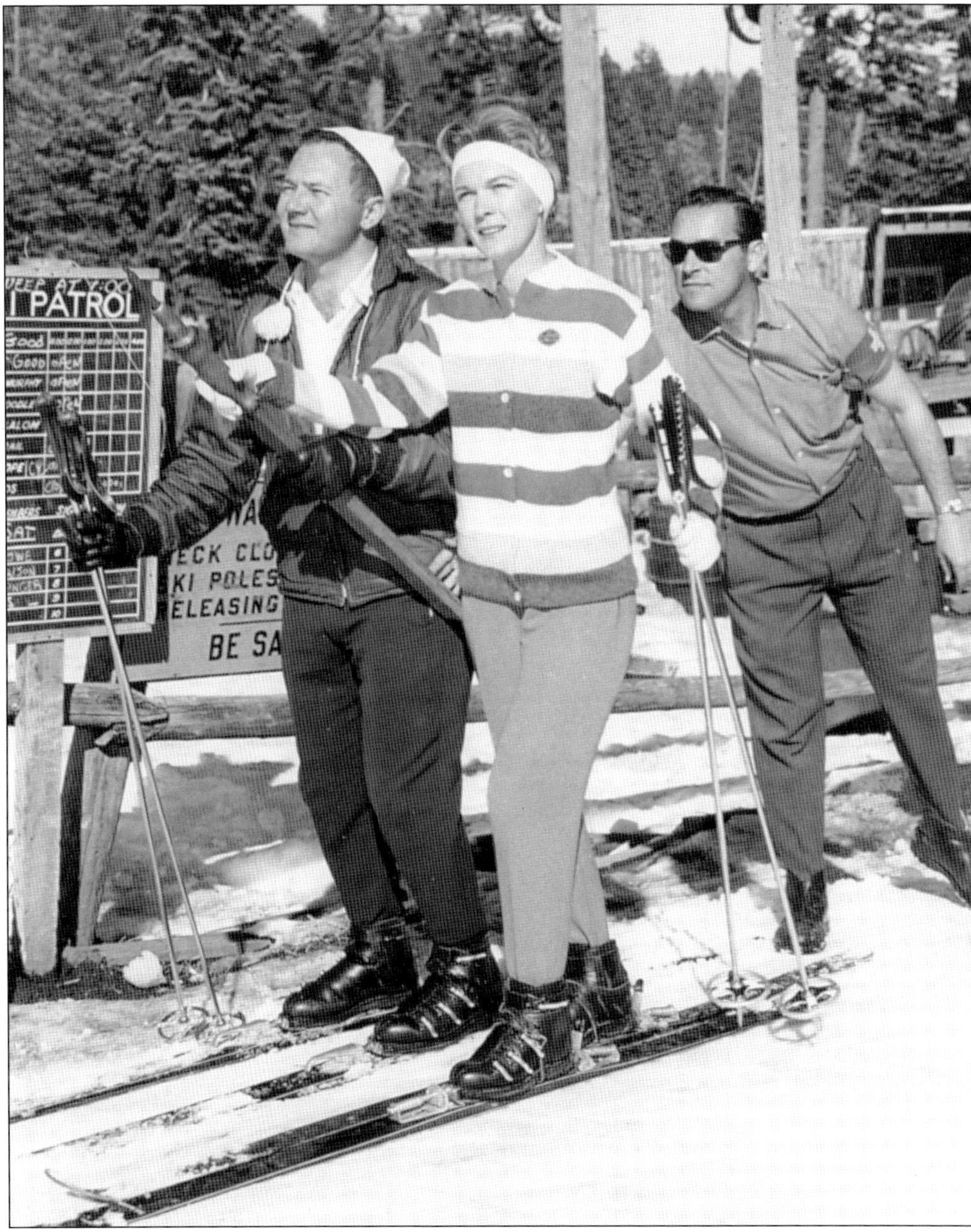

Ben and Pat Abruzzo catch the T-bar in 1952 at La Madera, today's Sandia Peak Ski Area, on a lovely spring day. Ben played a major role in the development of La Madera and the construction in the 1960s of Sandia Peak Tram. The couple settled in Albuquerque in 1952 and got stuck in the mud on the access road on their first visit to the ski area but were charmed nevertheless. He became manager in 1957 and bought half an ownership share in 1958 from Nordhaus. Abruzzo ran the area for several years before forming the Sandia Peak Ski and Tram Company with Nordhaus. Pat raised a handful of children, several of whom went on to fill major roles in New Mexico's ski scene, including Benny Abruzzo, the longtime manager of Ski Santa Fe and Sandia Peak, whose son Ben Abruzzo oversees both today. Access to La Madera was greatly improved in 1959 when the US Forest Service paved the road. (Courtesy SP.)

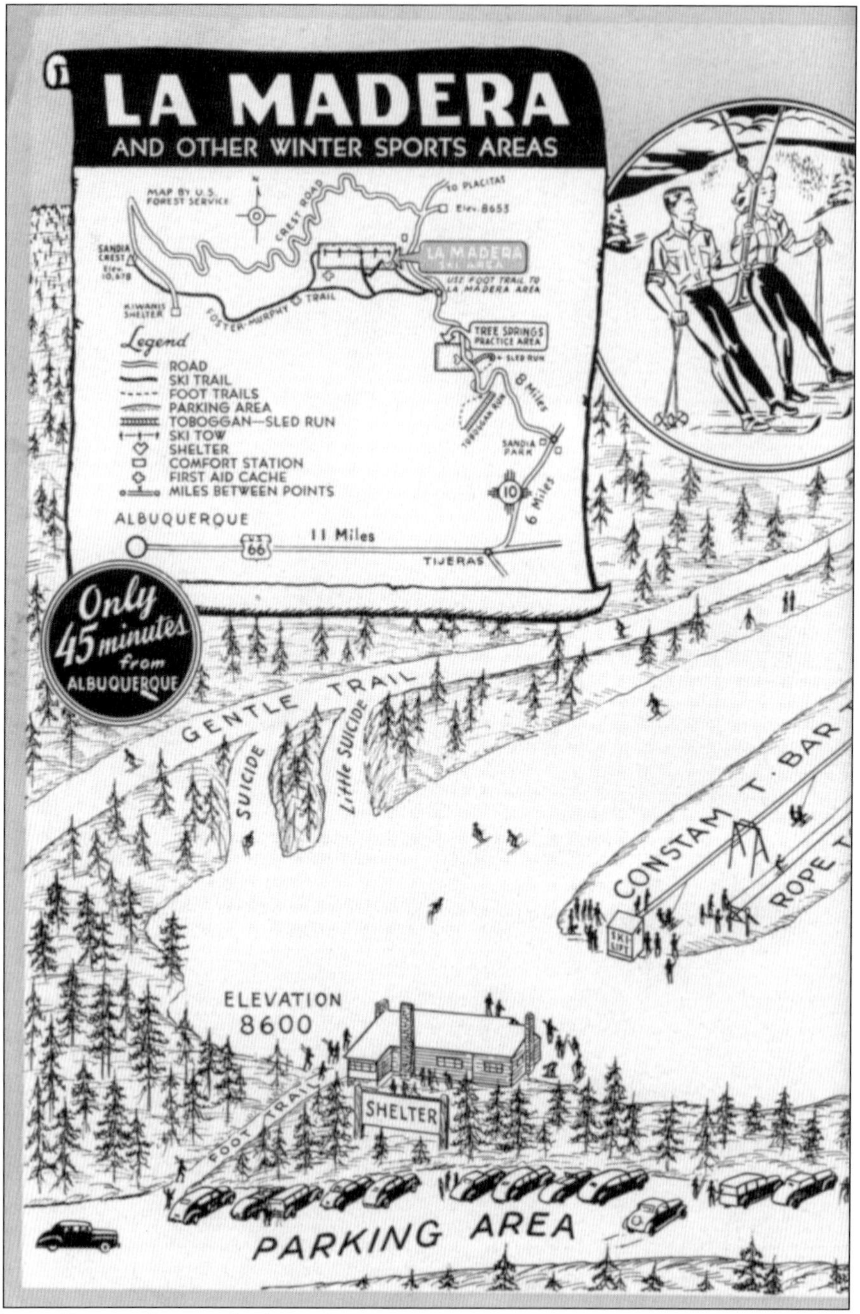

This classic illustrated map is both a delight to the eye and a very accurate depiction of the Sandia Mountains and La Madera Winter Sports Area. The US Forest Service provided the inset map at upper left. It shows the roads from Albuquerque past the ski area to Sandia Crest above it, at 10,678 feet. En route, one would pass Tree Springs, where members of the Albuquerque Ski Club first cleared some runs with the aid of the Forest Service and engaged in some old-fashioned uphill climbing and downhill skiing. The claim that it was only 45 minutes from Albuquerque only applied on rare days when roads were clear and dry; snowdrifts and mud made for many a harrowing outing. The short, but very steep, runs Suicide and Little Suicide still terrify novices today. (Courtesy SP.)

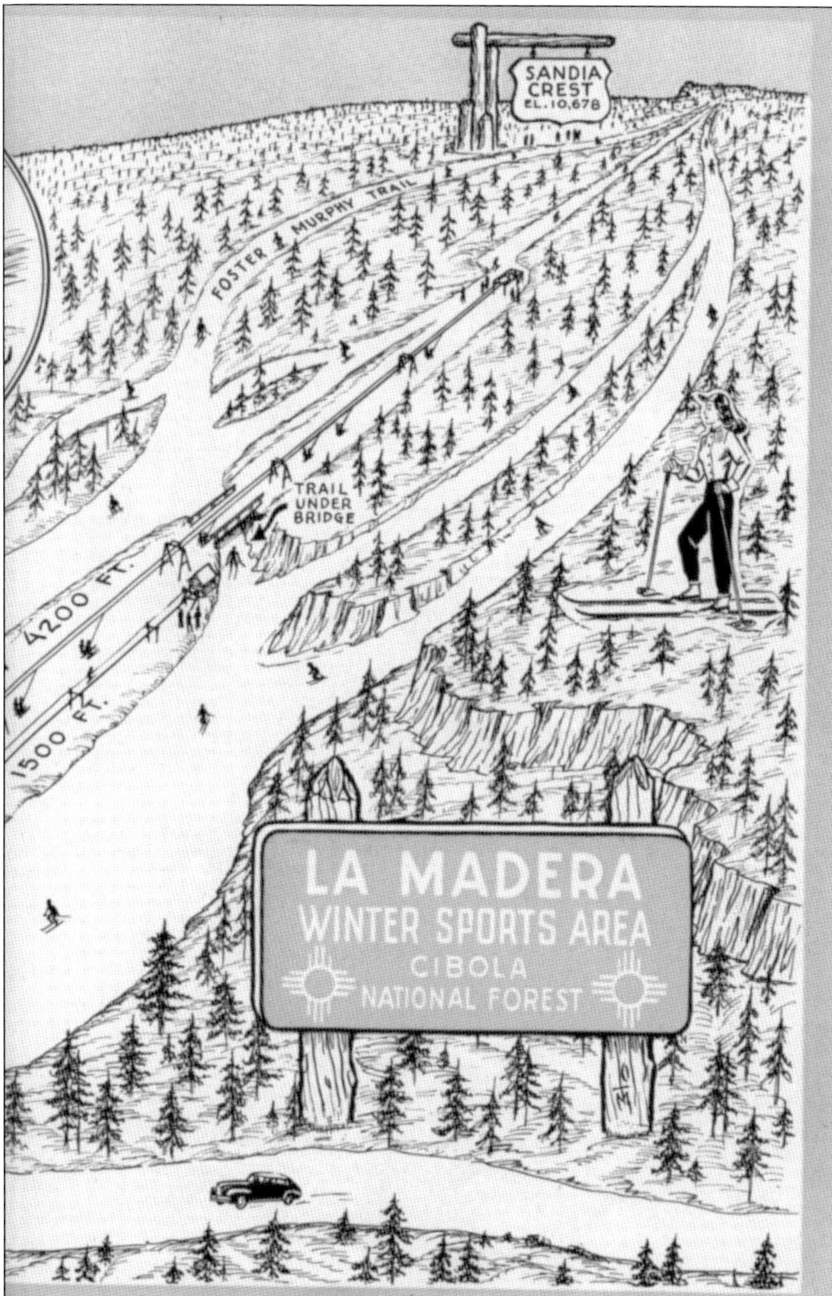

The center of this map promoting La Madera shows the summit of the Constam T-bar, which was the remarkable heart of the fledgling ski area. At 4,200 feet in length, complete with bridge, it was the longest such lift in the nation when installed in 1946. For the super adventurous, one run, the two-mile Foster-Murphy Trail, descended from the Crest to the ski area. A short platter-pull lift was later added that reached near the Crest rim, and eventually, a chairlift replaced both. The Cibola National Forest was named after the Spanish word, acquired from the people of Isleta Pueblo, for buffalo, which used to roam the high southern plains to the east of the Sandia Mountains. (Courtesy SP.)

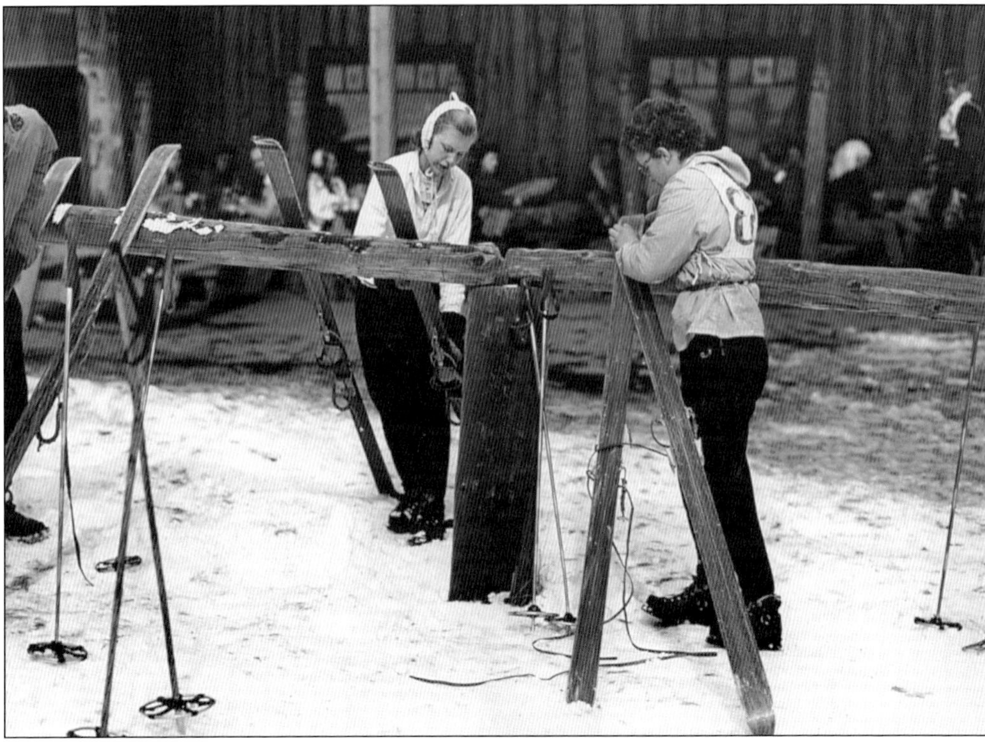

Two young women apply wax to their skis at La Madera in the 1950s prior to heading out. The hitching post was helpful for waxing and for keeping errant skiers from plowing right onto the café's porch. For wood skis to slide over snow without sticking, the appropriate wax needed to be applied according to the snow consistency and temperature. Picking the right wax was an art as much as anything. The invention of durable, always-slick synthetic base materials was a huge step forward in skiing evolution. (Courtesy SP.)

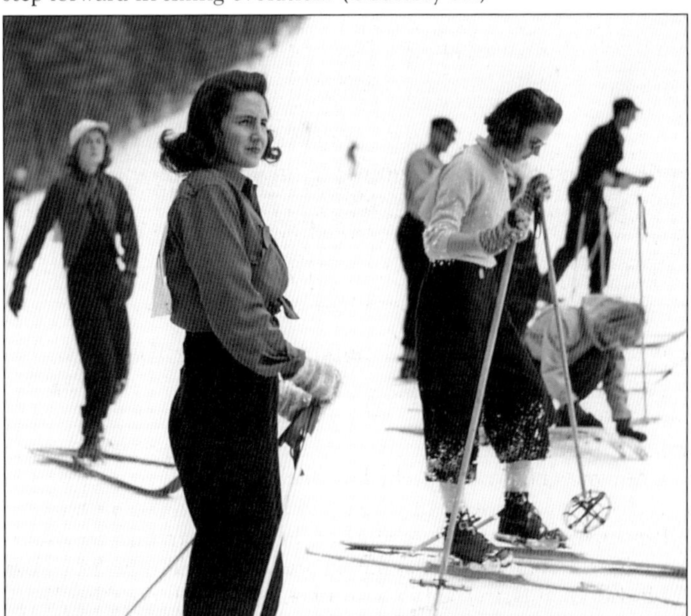

Seen here are possibly some of the Albuquerque High School or University of New Mexico students who frequented the ski area in its early days, enrolled in the La Madera program in the 1950s. One is shuffling along without poles. They would have been headed to the area's infamous long and challenging T-bar. When riding the T-bar, it was helpful to have two people of about the same height riding. A kid with an adult, or two mismatched friends, was a disaster in the making. (Courtesy SP.)

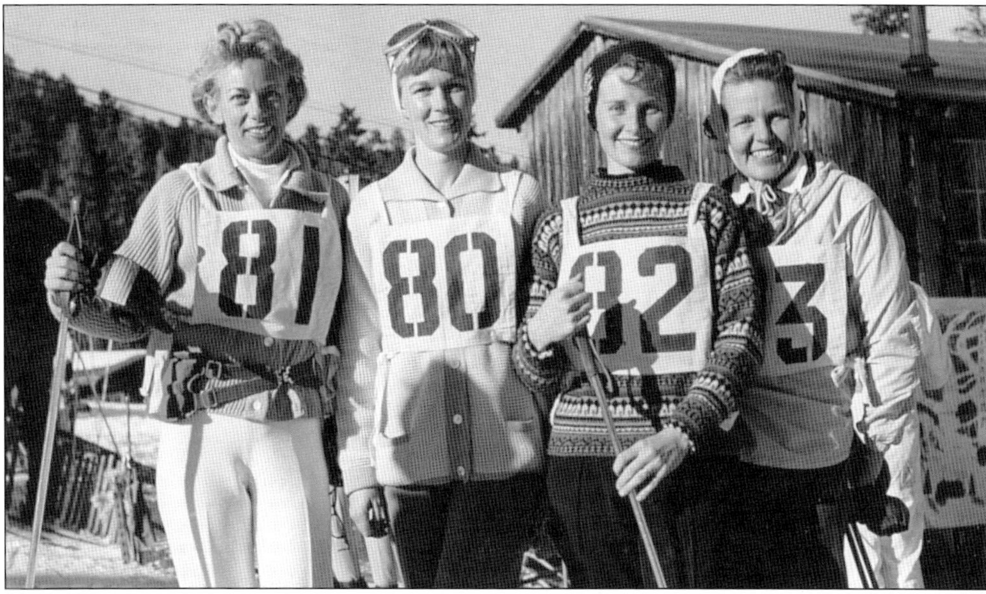

From left to right, Billie Cotter, Pat Abruzzo, Katie Eckert, and Donna Boyden pose before a competition at La Madera in the 1950s. While they skied hard, they were good friends on and off the slopes. Both the Abruzzo family and Boyden family played key roles here. George Boyden, Donna's son, helped build and manage the Sandia Peak Tram for many years, which included hundreds of perilous climbs up its towers and out onto the tram cables. (Courtesy SP.)

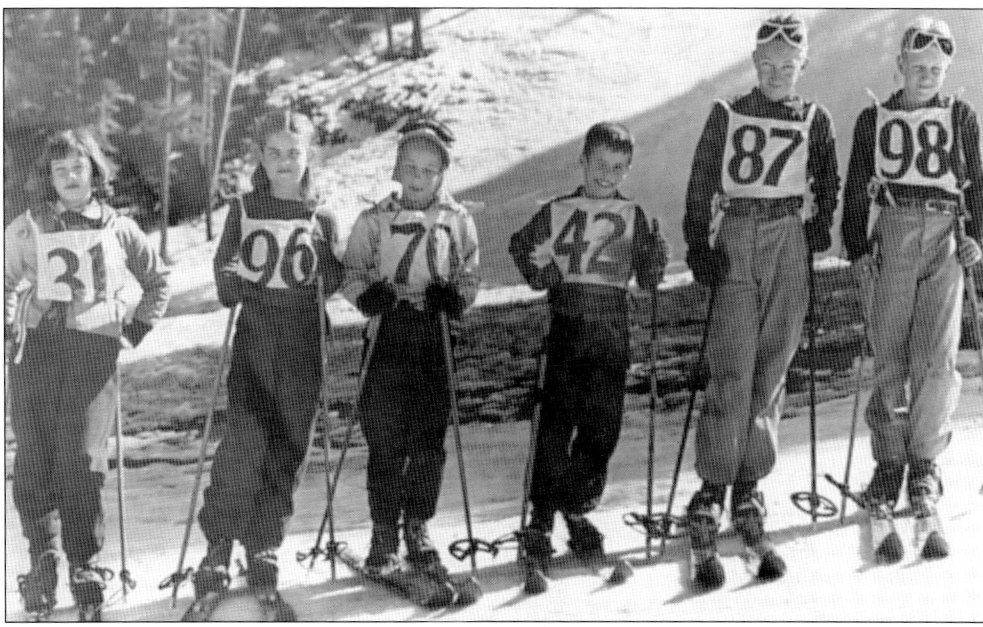

Kids were an integral part of La Madera's busy racing schedule, including this group of rippers in the 1950s. Albuquerque High School held a student program on Friday afternoons directed and coached by Tony Wilson. Participants received discounts on lift tickets and lessons. With bunkhouses and a few other overnight accommodations, the ski area even held New Year's Eve ski parties, with runs partially lit by floodlights, in the 1950s. In 1954, a blizzard hit on New Year's Eve, and many participants showed up on foot after their cars were marooned below. (Courtesy SP.)

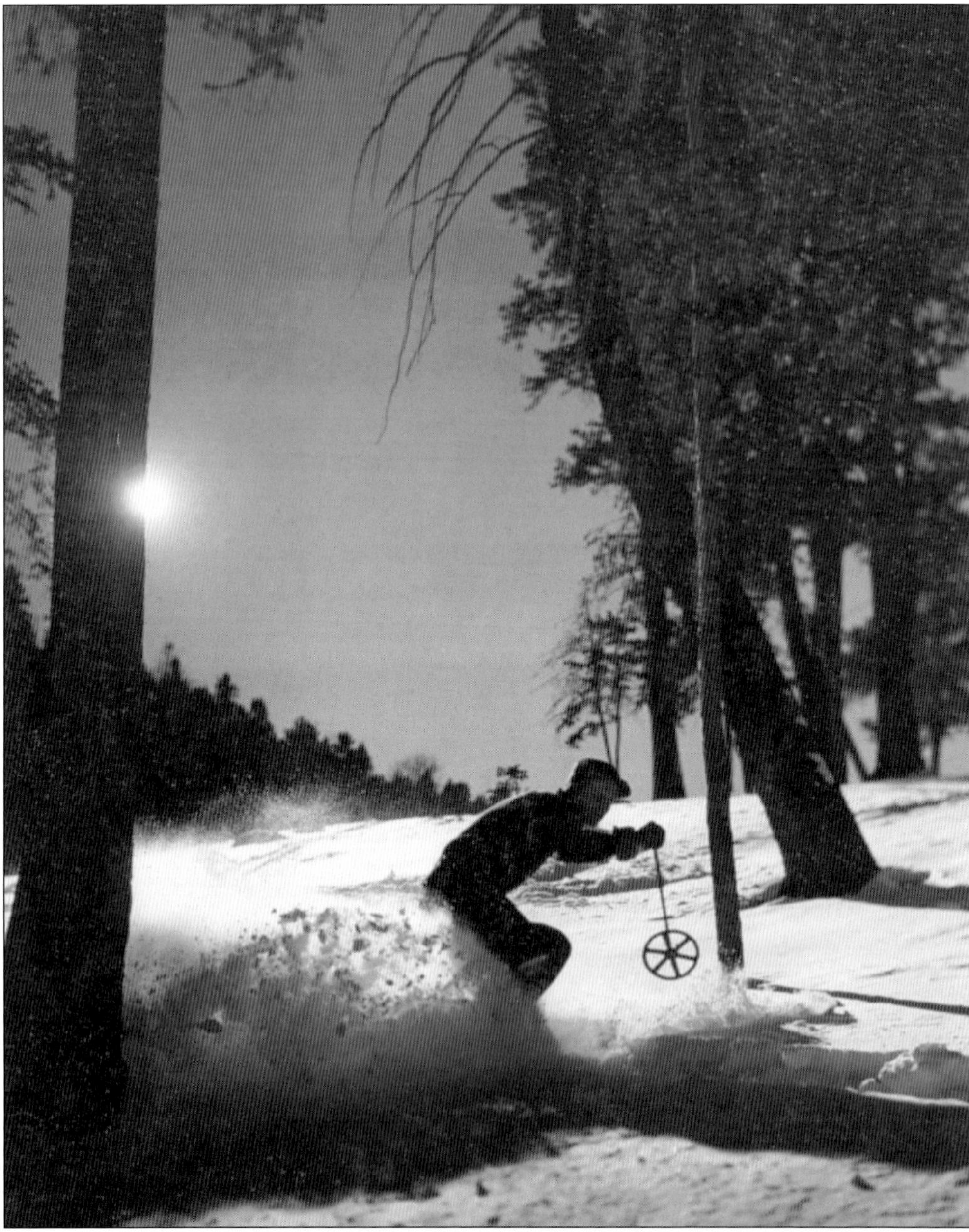

This skier at La Madera in the 1950s shows the huge ski pole baskets that were common until the mid-1960s. The spray of snow indicates a good powder day on the slopes above Albuquerque. La Madera's first rope tow, an impressive 1,500 feet long, was installed in 1937, and by 1947, the *Albuquerque Tribune* reported that more than $100,000 had been invested in the fledgling ski area, including the 4,200-foot Constam T-bar, a day lodge, and a skating rink. Low snow years in 1950 and 1951 challenged the ski area financially and led to the nickname "La Mudera." But good snow returned, and under Robert Nordhaus and Ben Abruzzo, the area flourished. As Jerry Martin stated in Pamela Salmon's book *Sandia Peak*, "Bob was the dreamer who said, 'This is what I want.' Ben was the doer. He made sure everything worked. And I was the builder, the task man." Together, they formed a great team. (Courtesy SP.)

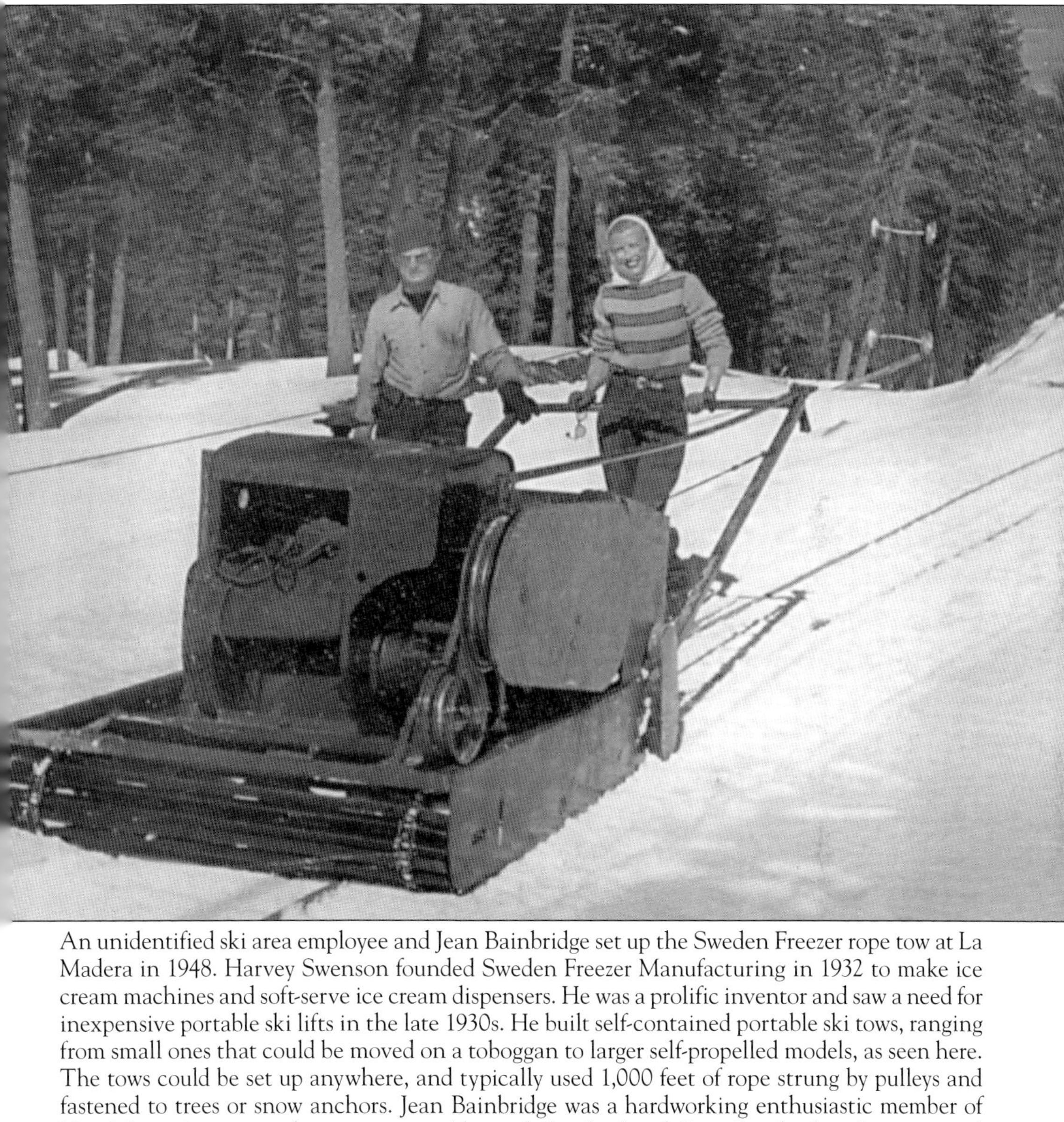

An unidentified ski area employee and Jean Bainbridge set up the Sweden Freezer rope tow at La Madera in 1948. Harvey Swenson founded Sweden Freezer Manufacturing in 1932 to make ice cream machines and soft-serve ice cream dispensers. He was a prolific inventor and saw a need for inexpensive portable ski lifts in the late 1930s. He built self-contained portable ski tows, ranging from small ones that could be moved on a toboggan to larger self-propelled models, as seen here. The tows could be set up anywhere, and typically used 1,000 feet of rope strung by pulleys and fastened to trees or snow anchors. Jean Bainbridge was a hardworking enthusiastic member of New Mexico's nascent ski community. Alongside her husband, Buzz Bainbridge, she organized and taught hundreds of ski classes, helped write and produce promotional literature, and was key to the formation of dozens of ski clubs in Texas, whose members skied here. Plus, apparently, she could run a Sweden Freezer. (Courtesy SP.)

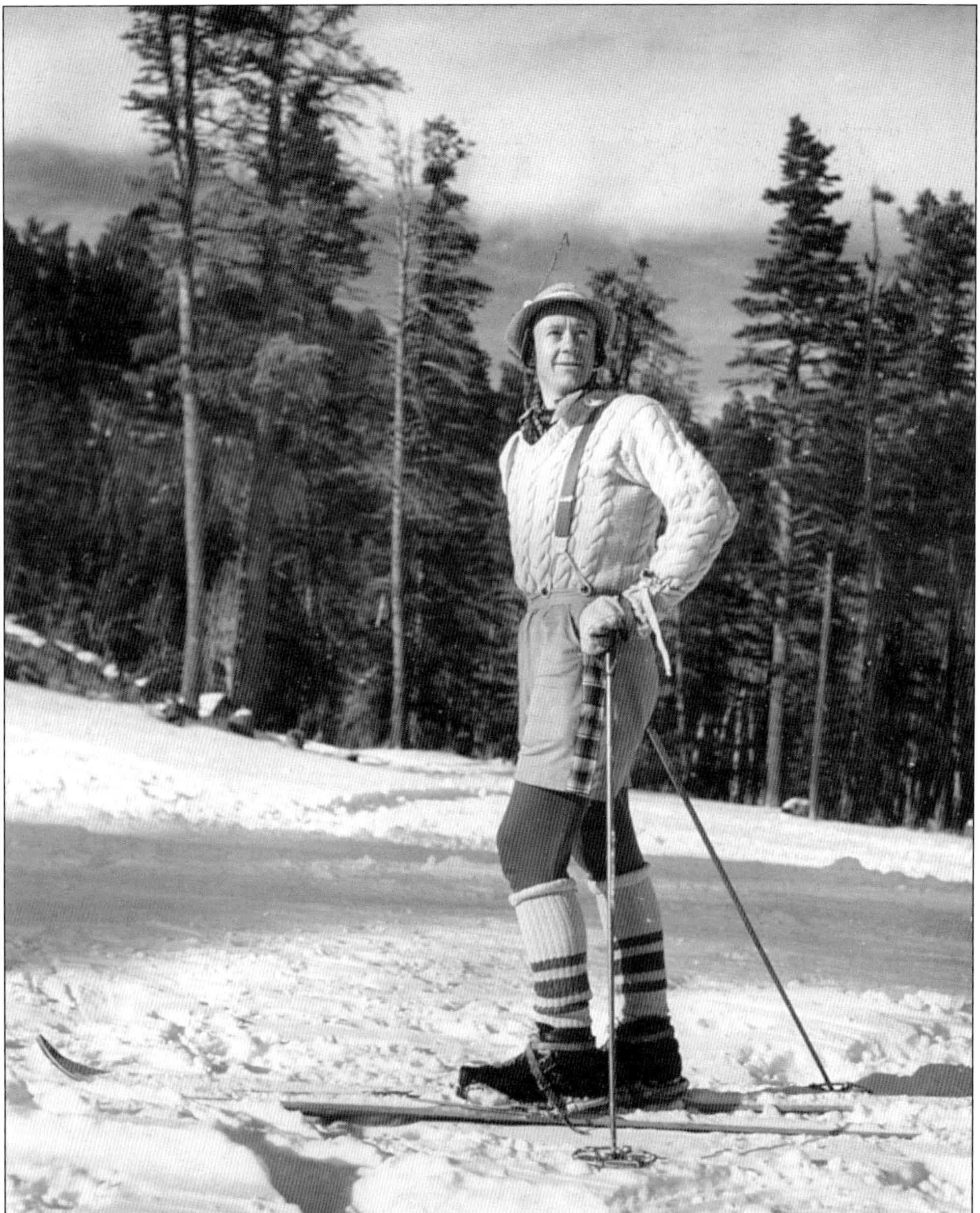

Uelo Begini sports traditional European Alpine attire, including lederhosen with suspenders, high socks, and a wool cable-knit sweater, at La Madera in the 1950s. There were a handful of experienced European skiers among the packs of New Mexicans flailing around them. They often served as instructors and, certainly, role models on how to behave on and off the slopes. Ernie Blake, when he was managing the Santa Fe area, spoke of another European immigrant skier, La Madera instructor Giuseppi Olmi, in the *American Ski Annual* of 1953: "Seppi would come over from Albuquerque to play the guitar and sing the stirring mountain songs of the Tyrol." He added, "Being a community venture, the Santa Fe Ski Basin made a conscious effort to make visiting skiers feel at home—hardly a Saturday passed that they were not invited to a 'Gluehwein' party at a private home or to a square dance." (Courtesy SP.)

La Madera instructor Giuseppi Olmi dictates the finer points of the basic snowplow to a striving novice in this classic photograph. From all the side-cut marks on the slope, it looks like the pair has been up and down this hill many times already! Olmi, an Italian artist, came to New Mexico on a visitor's visa and was "hired" by Robert Nordhaus. As a foreign visitor, he could not earn a salary, but he could sell paintings. So, Nordhaus became the owner of an Olmi Madonna painting, and Seppi went to work. (Courtesy SP.)

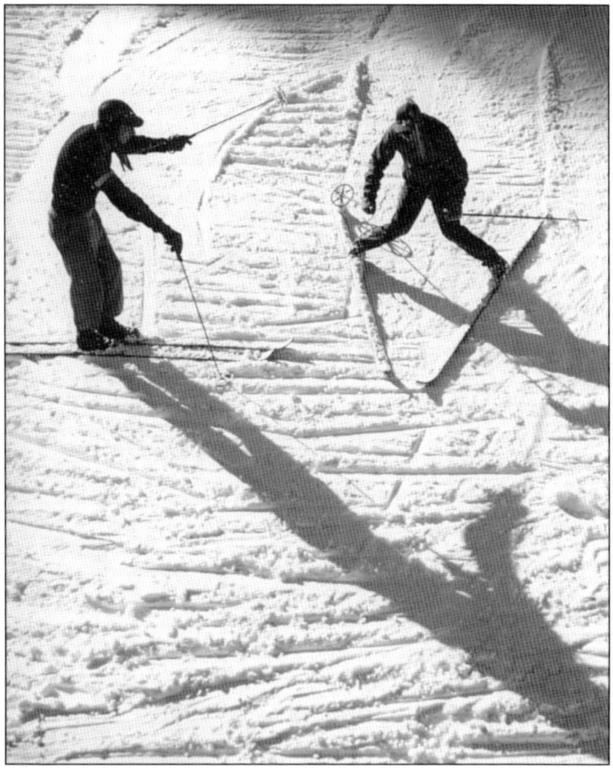

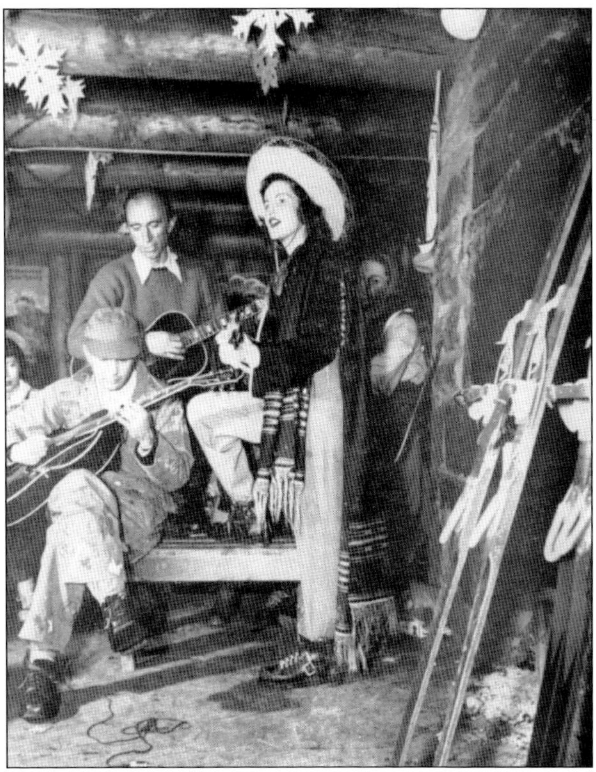

This scene may be staged, as the same woman appears in another promotional image used as the frontispiece of this book, or perhaps she just felt inspired to join these two local troubadours inside the La Madera Lodge in 1952. La Madera ("The Woods") was launched in 1937 by New Mexico's own Robert Nordhaus and other Duke City families, making it among the oldest ski areas in the western United States. The 30-member club was able to get the US Forest Service to clear a ski hill at Tree Springs the prior year as people learned how to maneuver these strange new contraptions called skis. (Courtesy SP.)

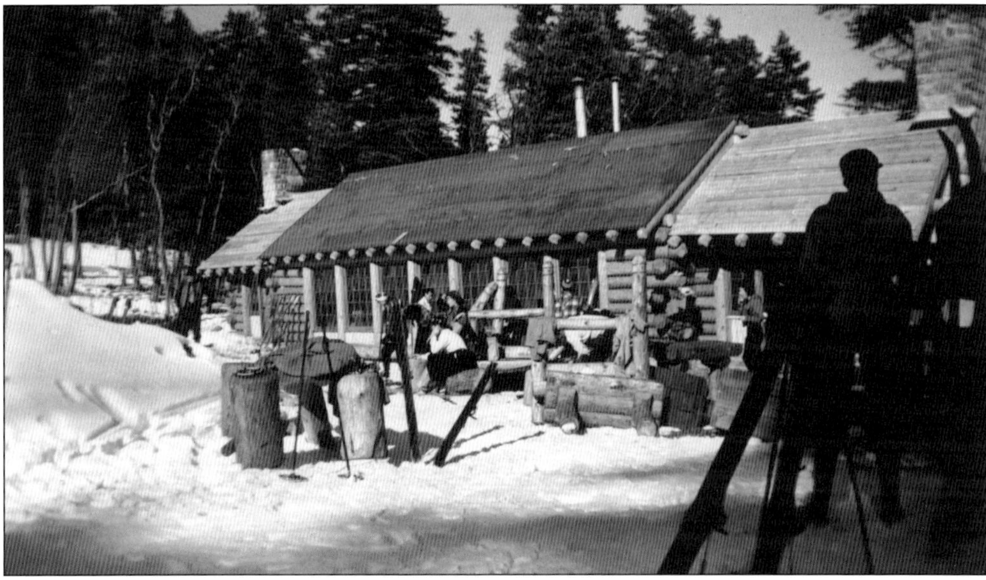

The log cabin–style main day lodge at La Madera was built by the CCC in 1938. It was dismantled in 1983 and replaced by a much larger facility that still stands. Its stone fireplace was a favorite spot in the ski area's early decades where one could steam up wet wool socks and pants. The CCC worked throughout the state and played a major role in providing well-built facilities, from lodges, roads, and trails to bridges and picnic areas in state and federal parks and forests. (Courtesy SP.)

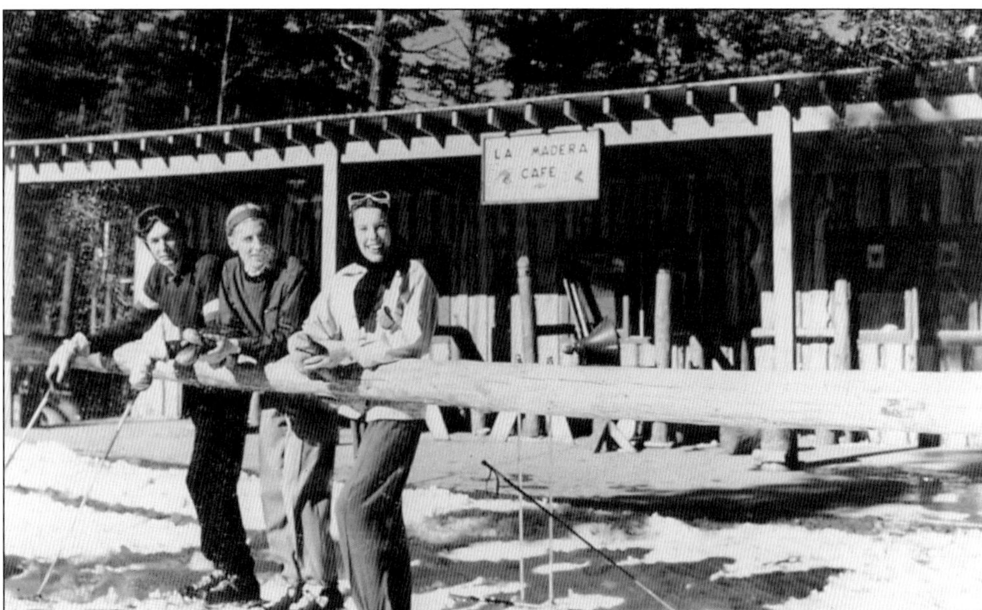

Three skiers are seen at the hitching post of the La Madera Café, the place for food and drink in the 1950s. From left to right are unidentified; Jimmie Doolittle, a notable young racer who went on to direct his family-owned Albuquerque Lumber Company; and Joan Stromberg, whose family owned a prominent clothing store in Albuquerque. The café served up everything from club sandwiches and fried chicken to T-bone steaks, juices, and coffee for 10¢ and doughnuts for a nickel. (Courtesy SP.)

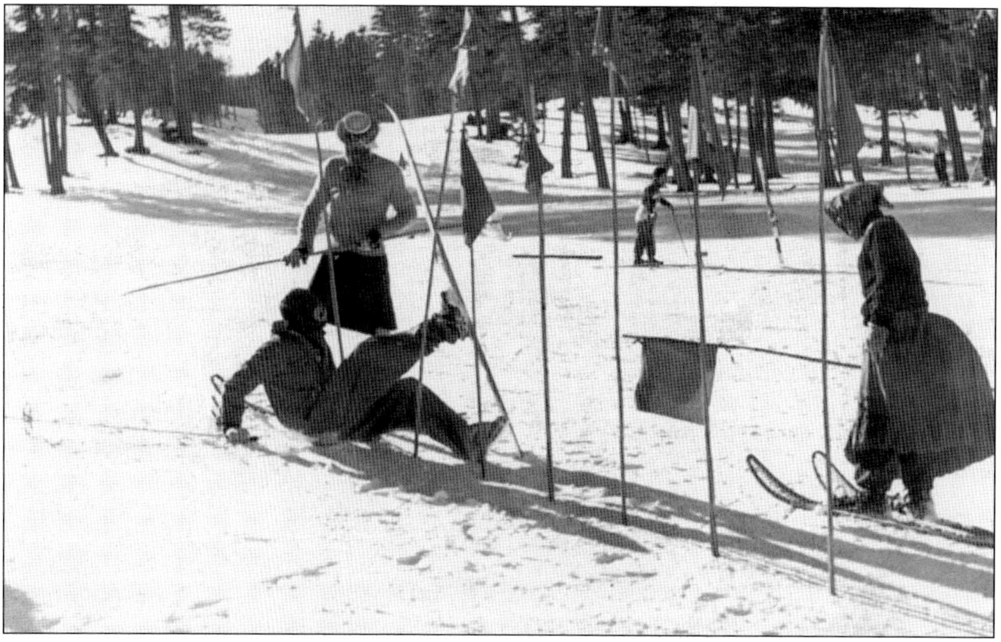

Boys, or grown men, will have their fun, as seen in this image taken at La Madera in the 1950s during one of their annual snow carnivals. On the right, in the skirt and large snowshoes, is Pete Totemoff; he was always one for a practical joke, some ribbing, and a lot of laughs. Here, he is serving as some kind of referee in a bizarre race. Having an audience, or not, seemed to matter little, but two skeptical onlookers can be seen at upper right. (Courtesy SP.)

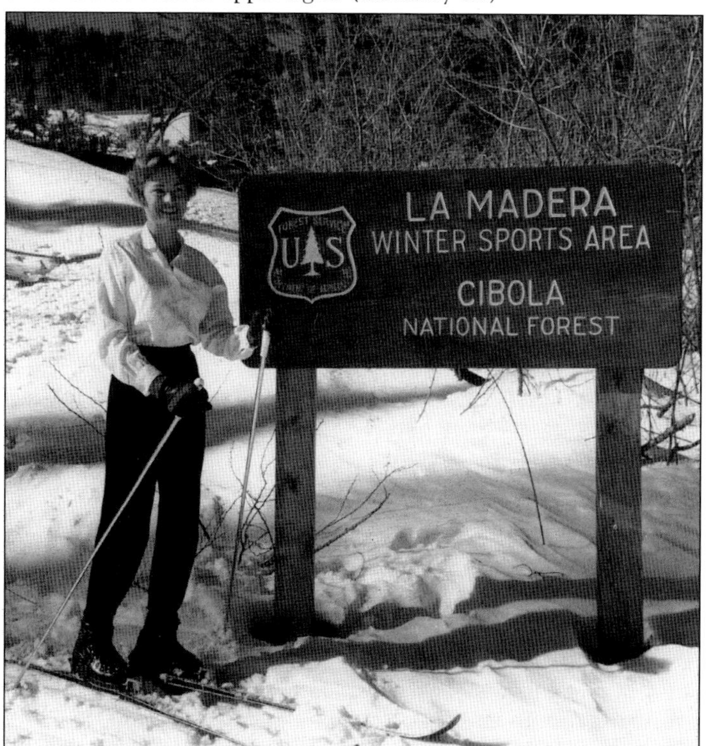

One could hardly ask for a more perfect image to promote skiing's wholesomeness than Mrs. Fletcher Brown standing at the entry sign to La Madera. In the 1930s, Graeme McGowan determined that a canyon called La Madera would be suitable for a ski area. The Cibola National Forest, home to the Sandias, invited the infant Albuquerque Ski Club to move its operations here, and history was made. (Courtesy SP.)

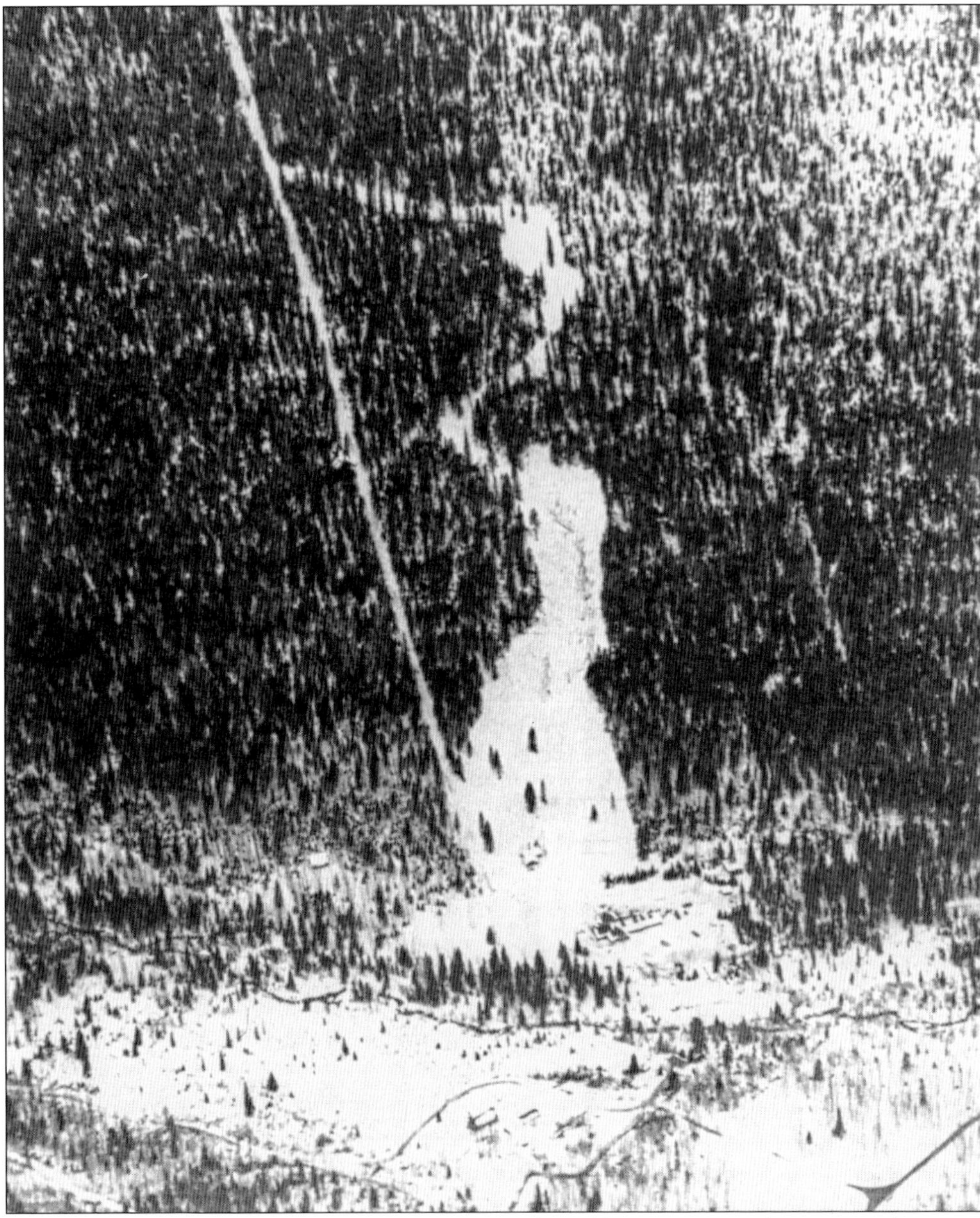

Taos Ski Valley in the narrow and steep Rio Hondo Valley begins to take form in this aerial photograph taken in late 1956 or early 1957. The thin line was the cut made for the area's first lift, a Bridger Boseman T-bar salvaged from Agua Piedra. The liftline was eventually extended up through the top of the frame, where it ended and widened to become the famed Al's Run. In the first few years, the only way down was Snakedance, writhing down through heavy timber—woe to beginners! This was the first section of the area to be developed. The so-called frontside today features a slew of tough mogul and tree runs, including Al's (ranked in the nation's top 10 in numerous articles and polls), Inferno, Spencer's Bowl, Rhoda's and Edelweiss Glade, and more recently, North American and Ernie's cutting through the old Burroughs property. Lake Fork Creek winds along the valley floor, which would over time become the heart of the Village of Taos Ski Valley. (Courtesy TSV.)

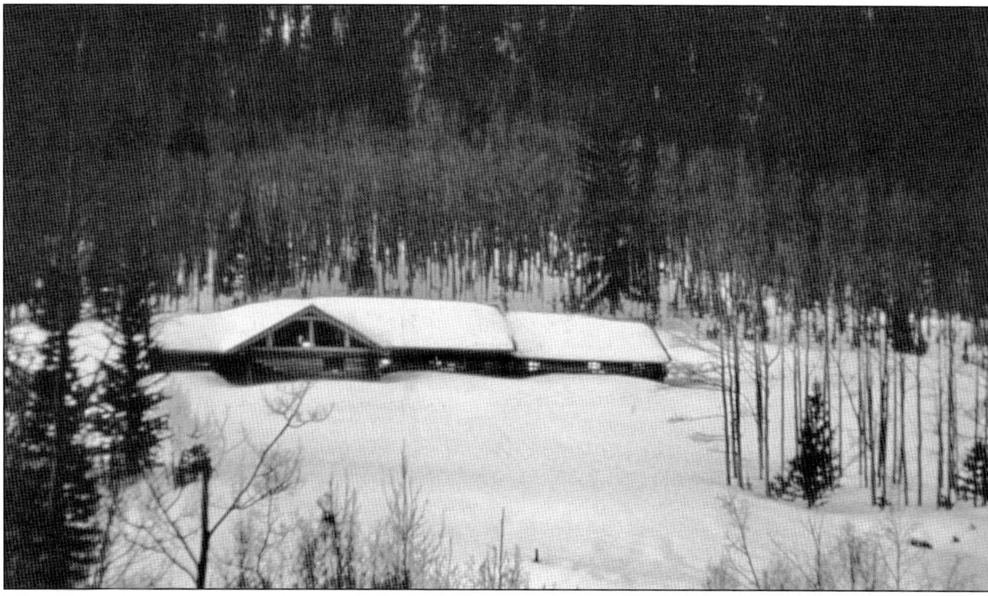

The unfinished Hondo Lodge, intended to be a hunting hideout, was one of the few buildings that greeted Ernie Blake and company when they first fought their way into the future site of Taos Ski Valley in 1954. It became home base over the next few years for staff and the occasional guest. With their children, the Blakes spent the first year in an 11-foot trailer before moving into the Hondo. Here, Rhoda cooked large crew and family meals, despite the lack of electricity, which finally arrived in 1963. This view is toward the future ski slopes. (Courtesy BFC.)

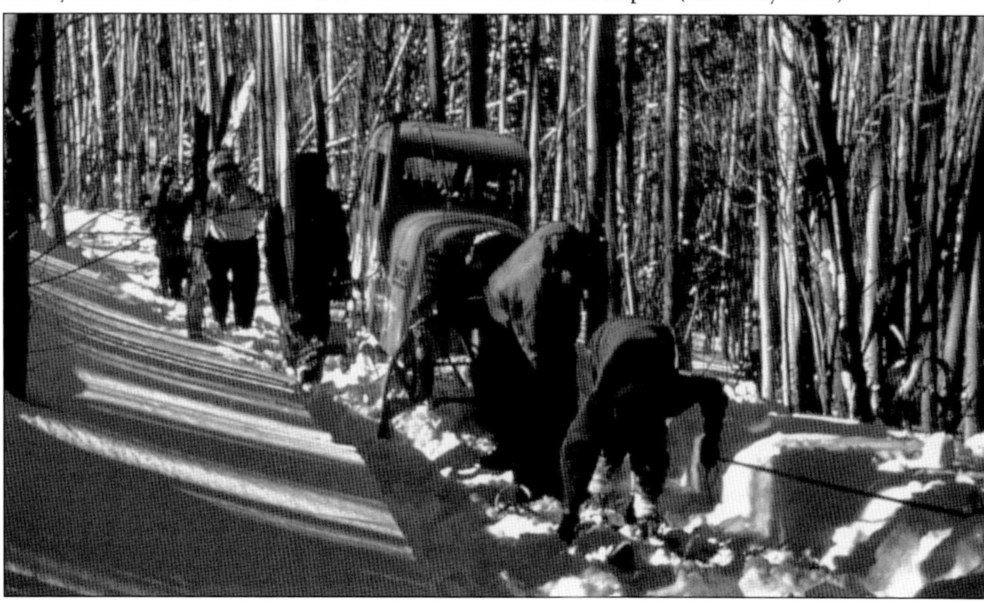

A Sno-Cat has towed intrepid skiers hanging onto long ropes up the Burroughs Trail near Taos Ski Valley in its earliest years, 1956 or 1957. From here, they would either hike up farther or turn tail and ski back down the track to the base. The route was named for a former New Mexico governor who owned land the trail briefly cut through and would decades later become Rubezahl when the ski area topped the frontside and skiers could descend into the backside and Kachina Basin, and eventually home, on just the seven-mile-long Rubezahl. (Courtesy BFC.)

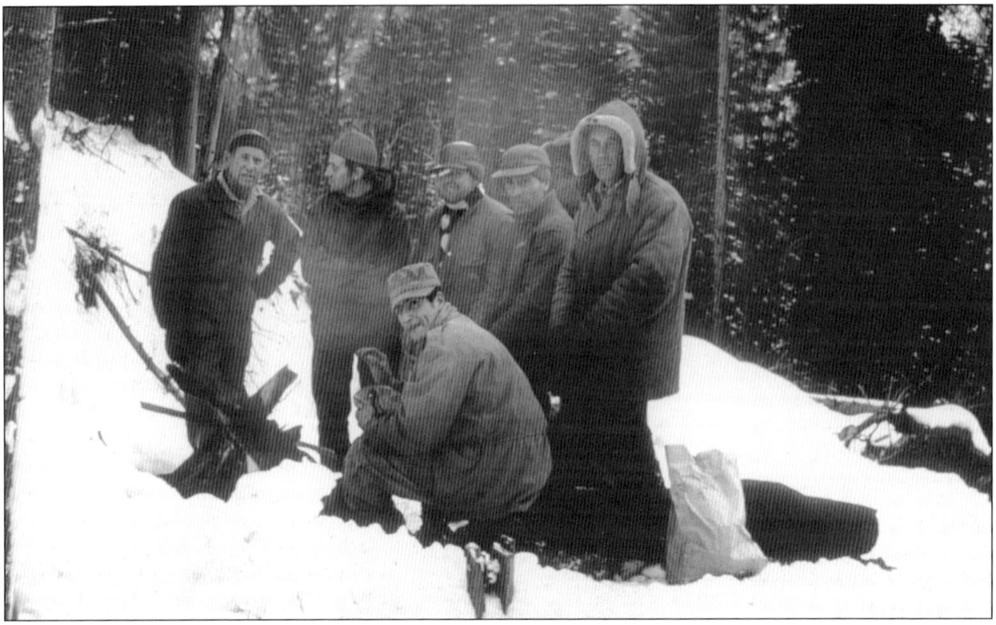

A crew warms up around a fire in 1961 in early snow while digging the big poma tower footings at Taos Ski Valley on what would become Al's Run. From left to right are a member of the Bolton family that launched Red River Ski Area; Hans Reiger, who spoke only German; Phil Sanchez (in front); Lee Varoz, who had only one good eye; Eloy Montoya, an original employee; possibly Jake Herrera, partially obscured; and Andres Montoya of Taos, who spoke no English. (Courtesy BFC.)

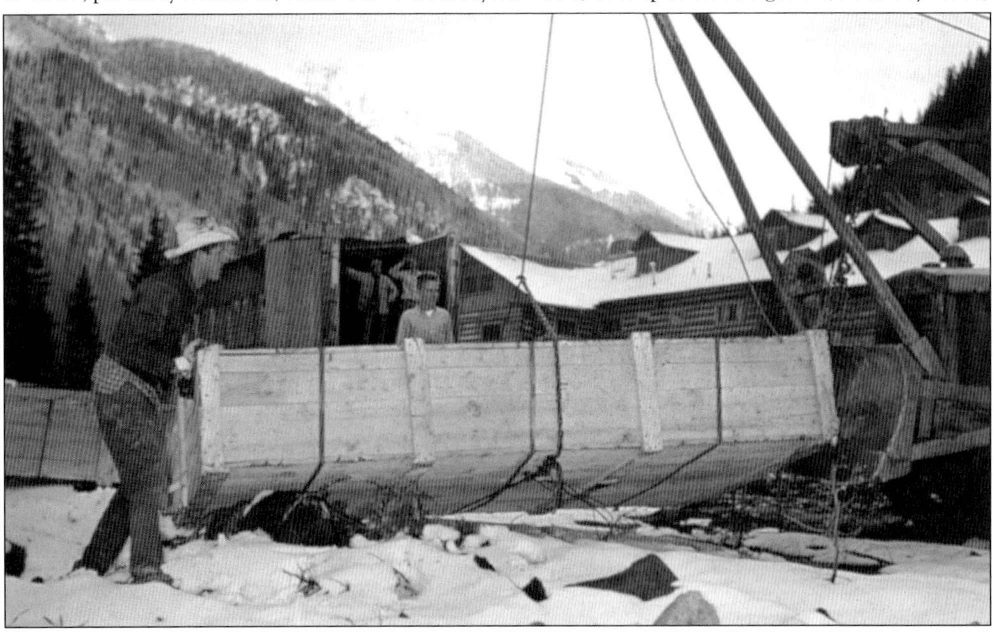

Chilton Anderson oversees, and a young Mickey Blake watches as the crates for the big poma are unloaded in fall 1957 in front of the Hondo Lodge at TSV. The poma parts were laid out on the ground, and a second early storm dumped two feet of snow on them. "We got the poma installed, but all winter and spring people keep finding pieces and bringing them to us," reports Mickey. He was associated with TSV for decades and wore many hats. (Courtesy BFC.)

Ernie Blake preps for a flight in 1953 or 1954 in his Cessna 170. In 1953–1954, he taught himself to fly, as he was simultaneously managing the Santa Fe Basin and Sunlight ski area in Glenwood, Colorado, and it was the only possible way to successfully do so. On his many flights north and south, he would fly over mountain ranges looking for the perfect spot to create his own ski area. He noticed how long into spring, and even summer, the high alpine terrain of the Lake Fork and Hondo valleys outside of the town of Taos held snow. (Courtesy TSV.)

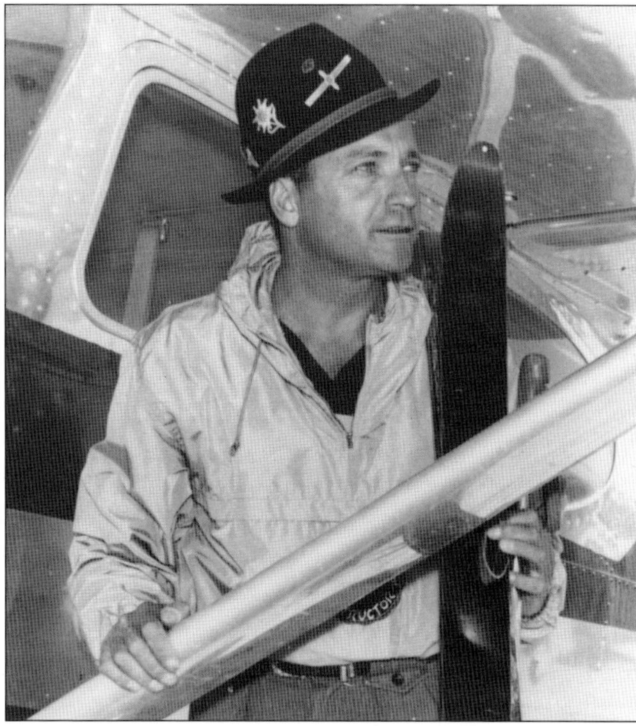

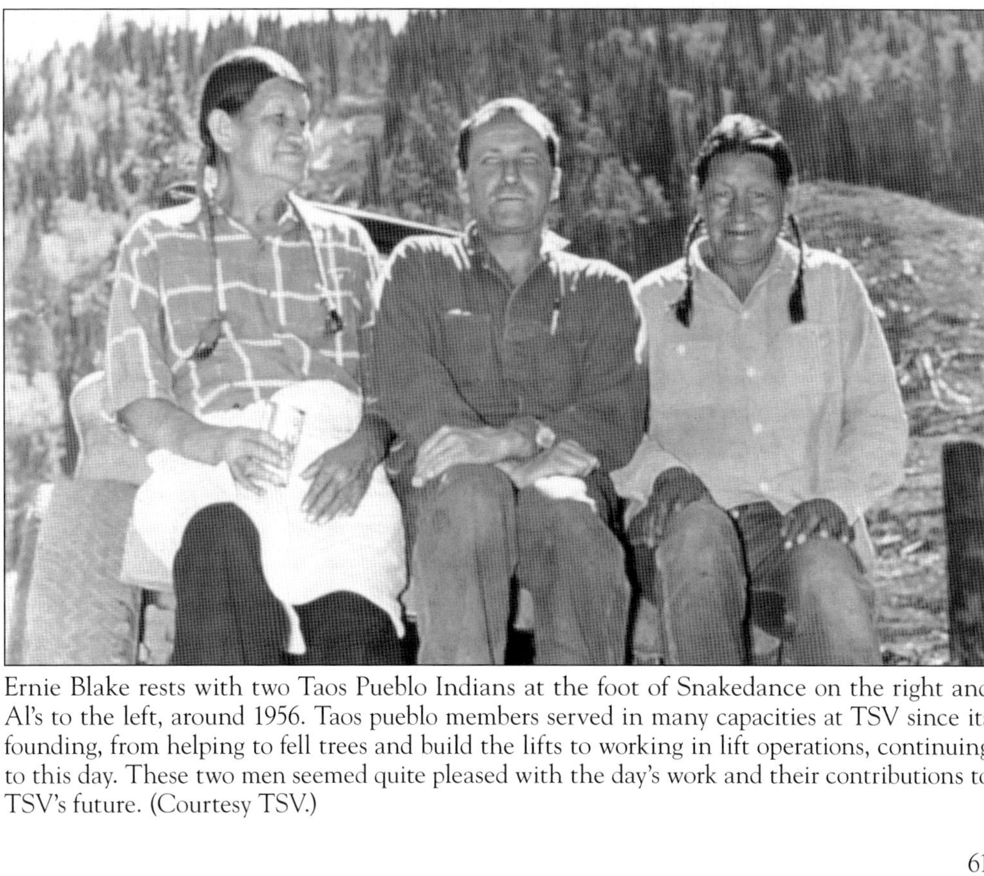

Ernie Blake rests with two Taos Pueblo Indians at the foot of Snakedance on the right and Al's to the left, around 1956. Taos pueblo members served in many capacities at TSV since its founding, from helping to fell trees and build the lifts to working in lift operations, continuing to this day. These two men seemed quite pleased with the day's work and their contributions to TSV's future. (Courtesy TSV.)

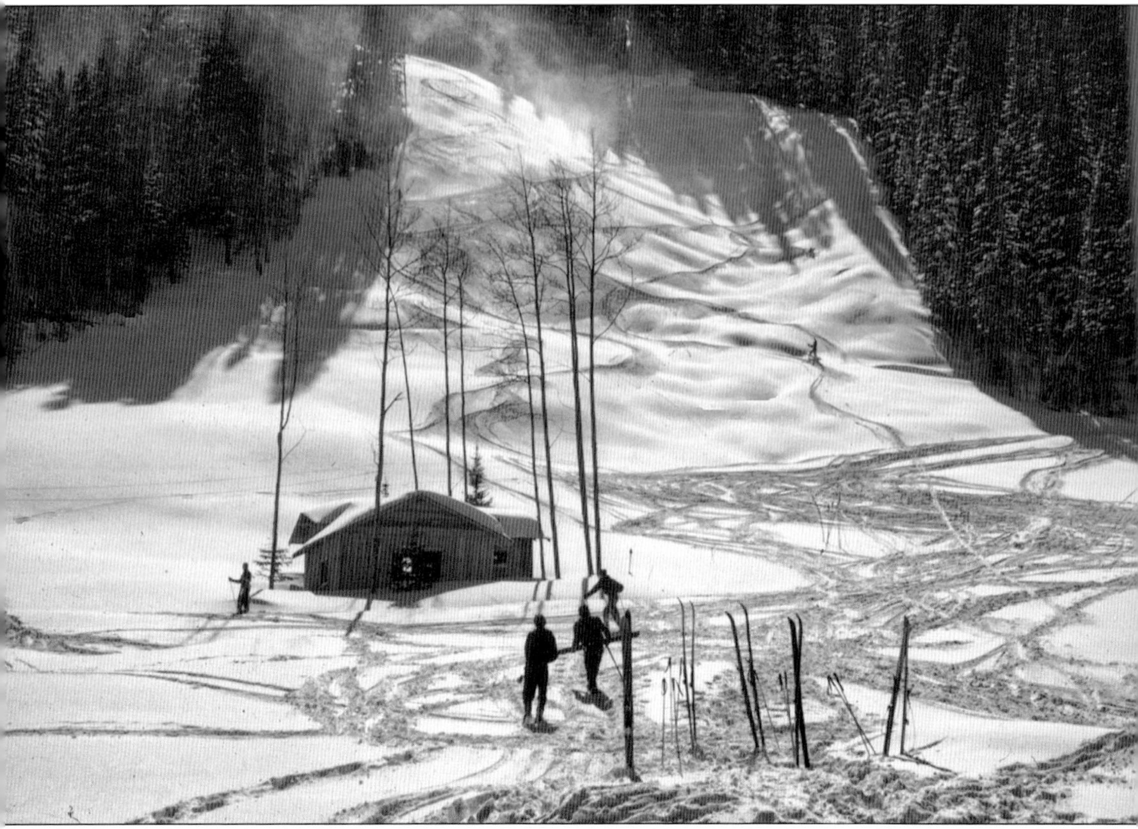

Pictured is a typical sunny but cold day at the base of Taos Ski Valley looking up Snakedance with snow drifting off the pines. Note the tracks of a few lucky skiers etched in the super-light powder. In those days, around 1957, one could find untouched powder days after a storm, with skier numbers in the hundreds. The small building is the Chalet Alpina. Ernie Blake bought TSV's portion of the base area without knowing the structure was there; it was hidden in thick forest. It went on to be employee housing. The Killingers, the Zaps, Walter Widmer, Walter Ruegg, and many more lived there over the years. "My daughter Adriana fell out of Chair One, which later ran above it, onto its roof at age three," recalls Mickey Blake. "I can't remember the name of the kid who liked to dance naked in the front window, much to the amusement of guests riding the chair." (Courtesy TSV.)

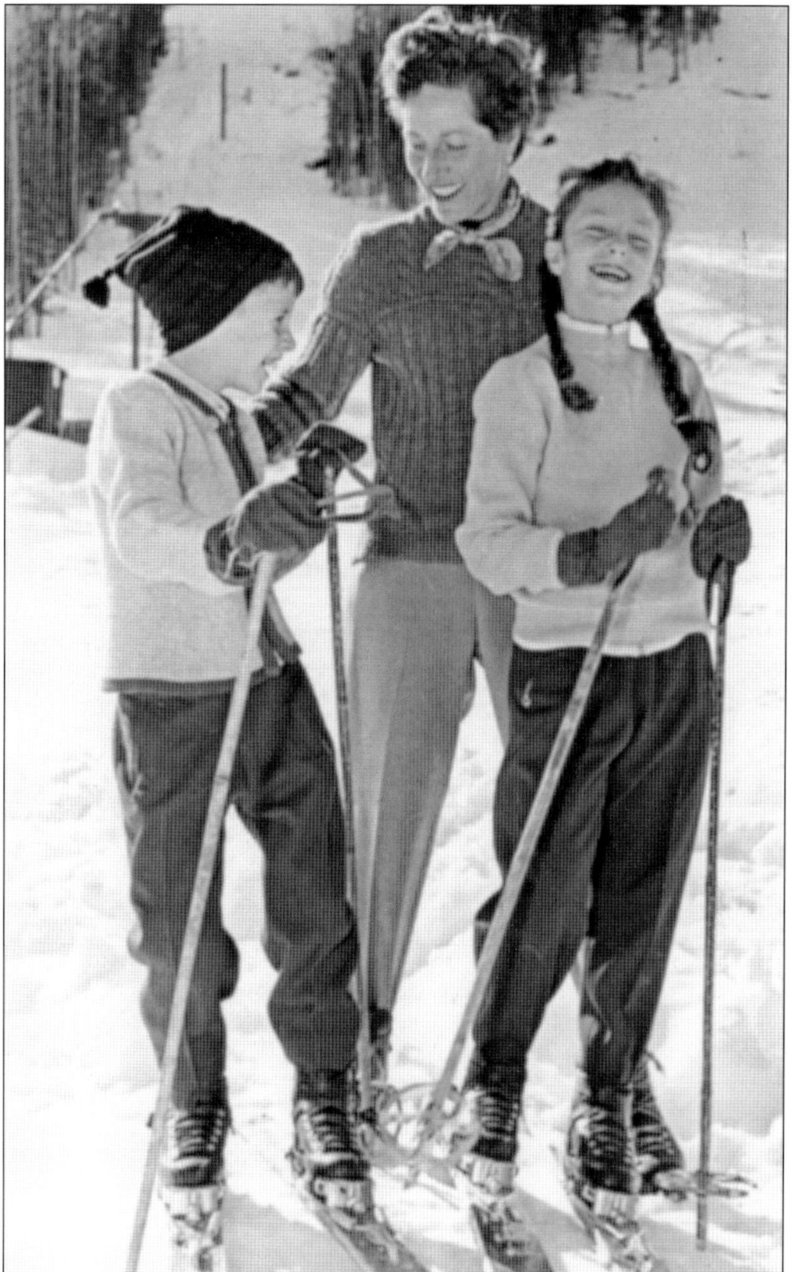

Rhoda Blake stands at the base of Snakedance at TSV around 1957 with younger son Peter and daughter Wendy. The towers for the big poma can be seen on Al's Run on the left; it became operational in 1957. In addition to raising three kids in the ski valley, Rhoda also mounted rental ski bindings, cooked massive staff meals, helped administratively, sold tickets, instructed, and helped select and design most of the early intermediate ski runs. The kids grew up skiing, and Peter, after a long absence, returned to resume the role of instructor. Wendy married locally and remains in Taos to this day. Eldest son Mickey went on to direct the area for many years after his father died. (Courtesy BFC and TSV.)

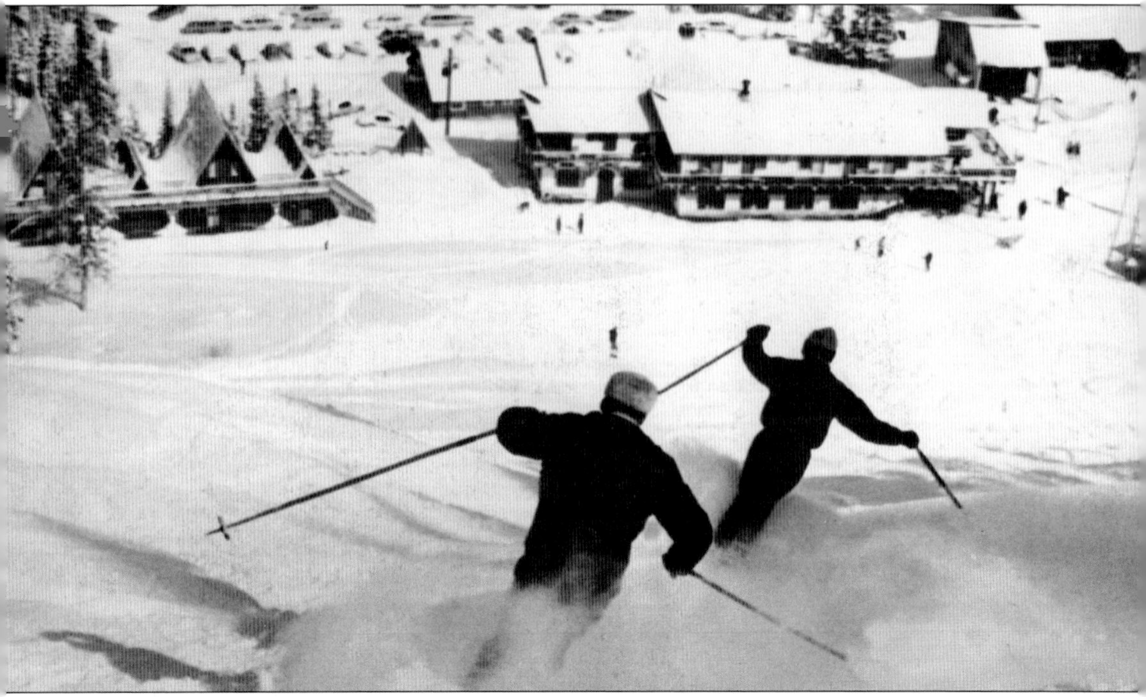

Two of Taos Ski Valley's legendary founders, brothers Jean and Dadou Mayer—who built and ran the famed Hotel St. Bernard at the foot of this slope—make the huge moguls and double fall line of Snakedance seem like a stroll in the park in this photograph taken between 1962 and 1964. Jean arrived for the 1957–1958 season to manage the Hondo Lodge and the TSV Ski School. He opened his hotel in 1960, and its excellent food along with his charming style and hospitality were essential aspects of Taos's early and subsequent success. Dadou went on to found and operate the Edelweiss Lodge for many decades, which initially sat right next to the St. Bernard before a much larger, more contemporary version was built a few hundred yards away. The St. Bernard still sits at the foot of the slopes; however, with Jean Mayer's passing in 2020, its future is uncertain. (Courtesy TSV.)

Four

Budding Out
1960s and 1970s

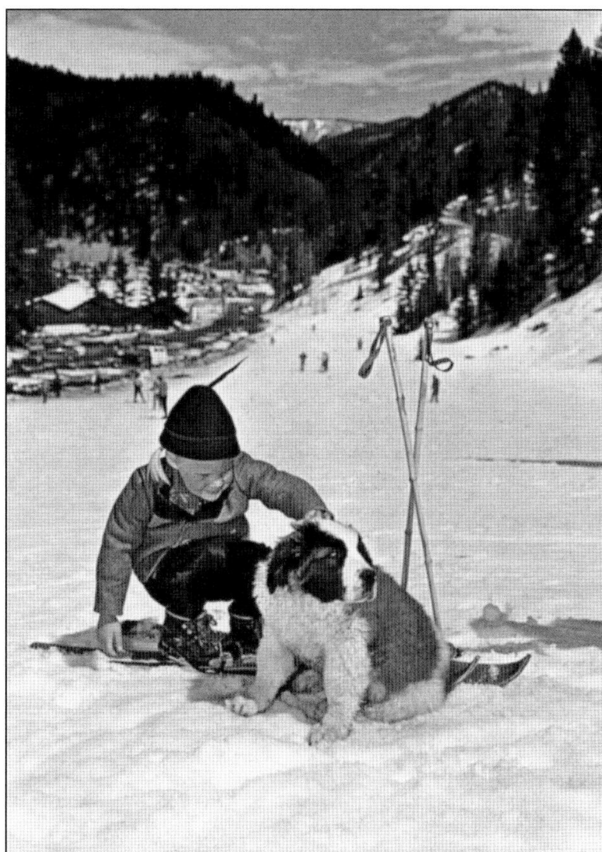

By the early 1960s, several other New Mexico ski areas had been recently launched, as seen in this photograph taken in Red River that graced the inside cover of the November 1960 *New Mexico* magazine. By 1960, it had a double chair running an impressive 5,800 feet, with a 1,524-foot vertical drop. (Photograph by Harvey Caplin, courtesy NMSM.)

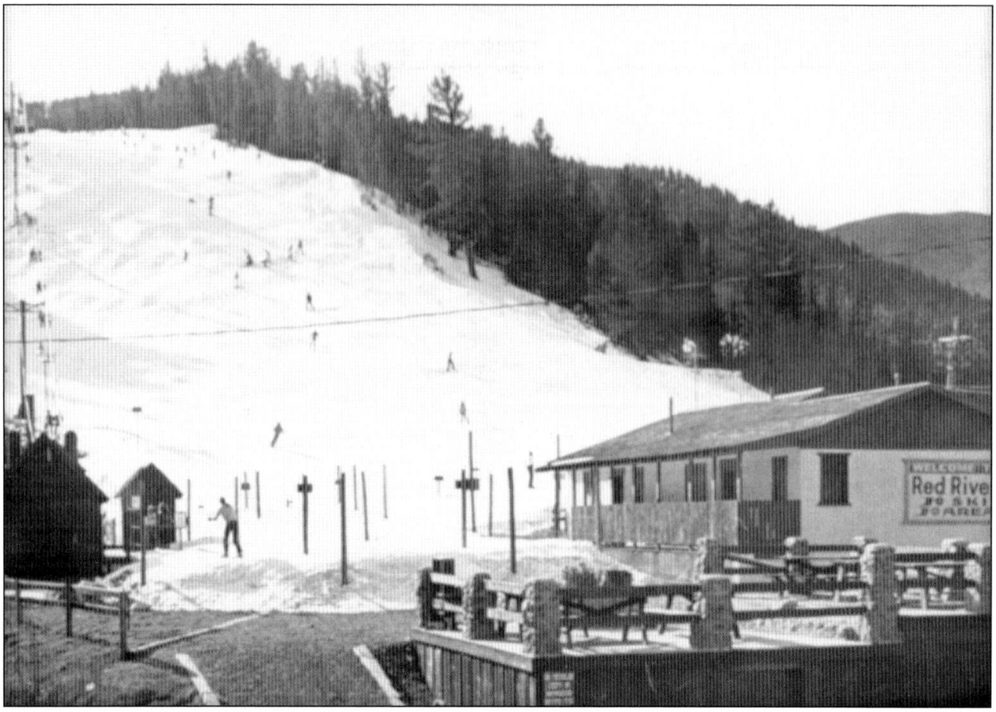

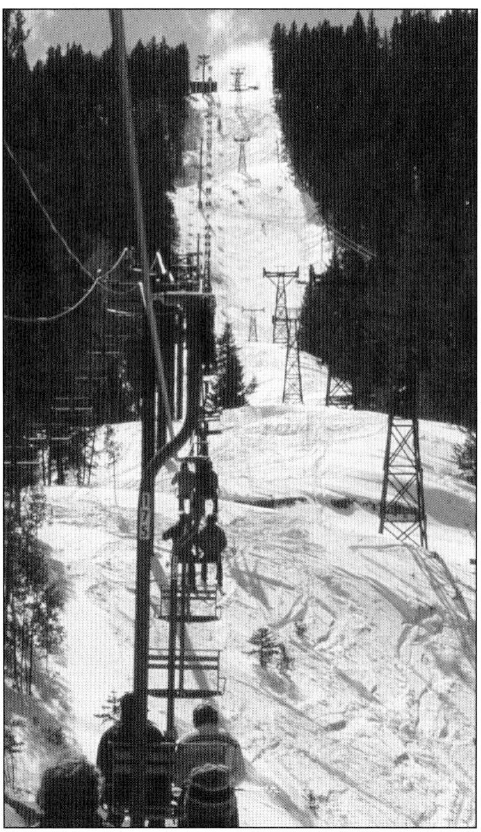

This image from the 1960s shows Red River's base area and the bottom pitch, called the Face, the nemesis of many beginners. The building, which housed ski patrol and a few apartments, is gone, having been replaced by a two-story restaurant/bar named the Lift House. Red River's first lift, a rope tow made from salvaged Texas oilrig parts by L.S. Lewis, is said to have opened December 6, 1941, and closed the next day following the Pearl Harbor attack. In 1959, members of the Bolton family of Oklahoma erected its first chair and other "modern" lifts. (Courtesy RRSA.)

In the 1950s, Oklahoma businessman Stokes Bolton and his wife, Billie, determined that a local ski area would be a good way to draw winter visitors to their Red River motel. Using surplus steel from Texas oil derricks, he built a chairlift and several short tows. He convinced Buzz Bainbridge to move from the Santa Fe Ski Basin to manage his new area, along with German-born skier Toni Woerndle to head up the ski school. The new area opened in 1959. The photograph shows the original chairlift towers at right after the lift was decommissioned, and the new Riblet double chair that replaced it in 1974. (Courtesy RR.)

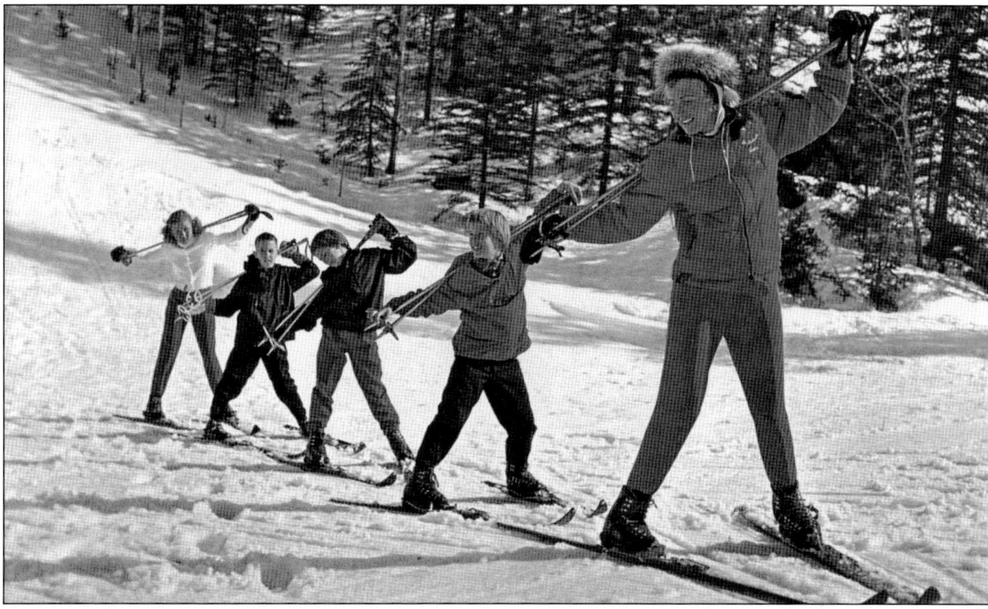

This instructor at Red River, thought to be Jean Bainbridge, leads a warm-up exercise for her ski school students, as seen in the November 1960 issue of *New Mexico* magazine. If God had given Texas or Oklahoma a ski area, it would be called Red River. The flatlanders to the east of New Mexico have flocked here since its opening day, charmed by its easy-going manner, relatively tame slopes, and old-timey Western feel. The town was born as a mining camp in the 1860s and still retains a "Wild West" flavor. (Courtesy RRSA.)

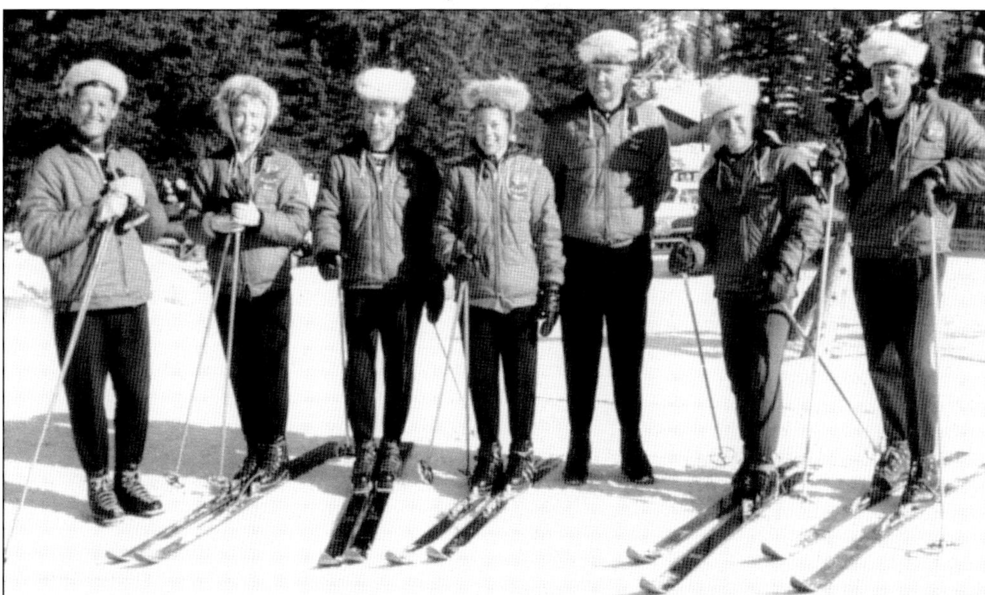

Given the many raw beginners who showed up at Red River in its early days (and continue to arrive today), having a strong ski school was very important. Sigi Klein directed it in the early 1960s. Coonskin caps were popular local headgear in those days. From right to left are Toni Woerndle, Jean Bainbridge, Carl Sverre, Marie Winterhaler, Admiral Winterhaler, Dadou Mayer, and Jochen Freund. (Courtesy RRSA.)

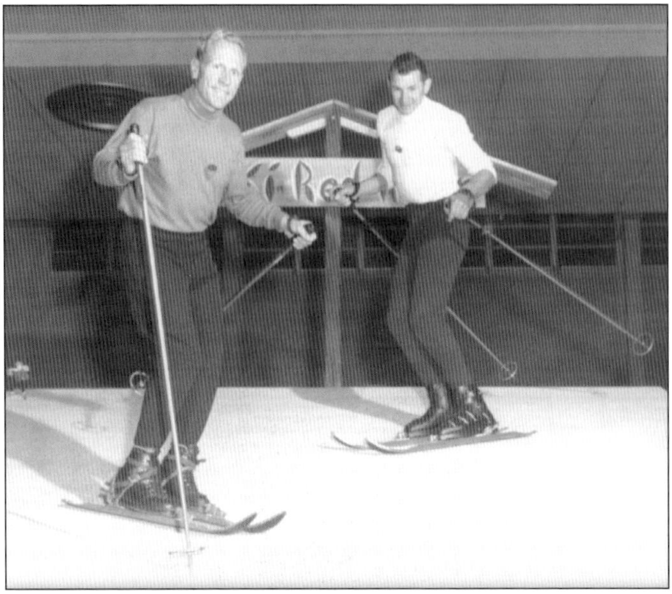

Red River made a huge effort to reach out to potential skiers in Texas and Oklahoma and sent out a crew led by Wally Dobbs, its "ambassador-at-large," for many years to meet with local ski clubs and attend ski swaps. Seen here are two Red River representatives demonstrating a brief rage, shorty skis, sometime in the 1960s. Dobbs, who died in 2015 after induction into the New Mexico Ski Hall of Fame, once said of Red River's popularity, "The thing is, once you've been here three days, you're a native." (Courtesy RRSA.)

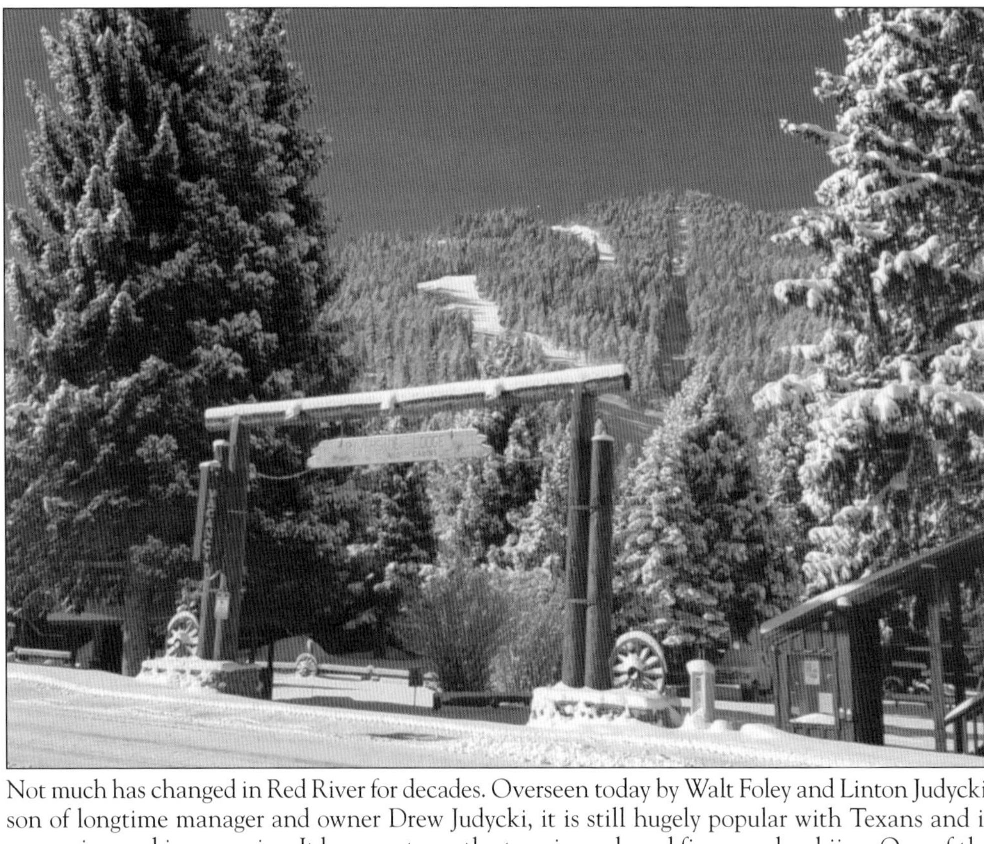

Not much has changed in Red River for decades. Overseen today by Walt Foley and Linton Judycki, son of longtime manager and owner Drew Judycki, it is still hugely popular with Texans and is easy-going and inexpensive. It has a noteworthy terrain park and fine powder skiing. One of the coolest features about the "Ski Town of the Southwest" is the fact that guests can ski almost to their lodging on Main Street, as seen in this photograph taken around 2000. (Photograph by Daniel Gibson.)

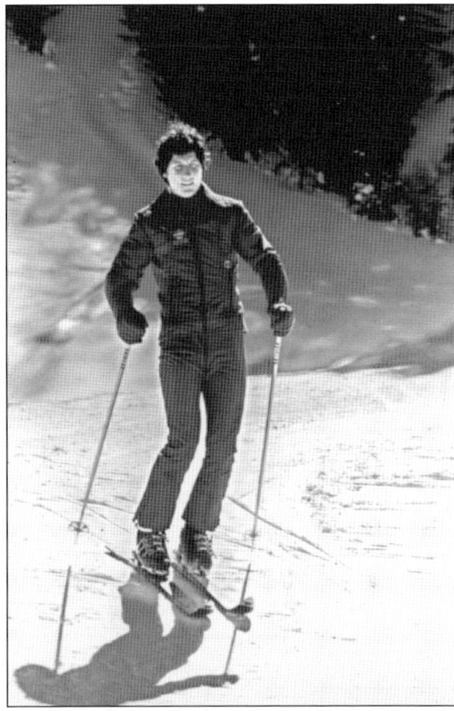

Among Red River's various managers over the years, few have been as singularly important as Drew Judycki. He arrived in 1968 as a college student and began instructing. He rose to ski school director, then marketing director, and then general manager before buying it with investors in 1984. Raised in Athol, Massachusetts, he was taught to ski by his father. He turned down football scholarship offers to attend Highlands University in Las Vegas, New Mexico, to be close to the Rocky Mountains and skiing. He passed away in 2008. (Courtesy RR.)

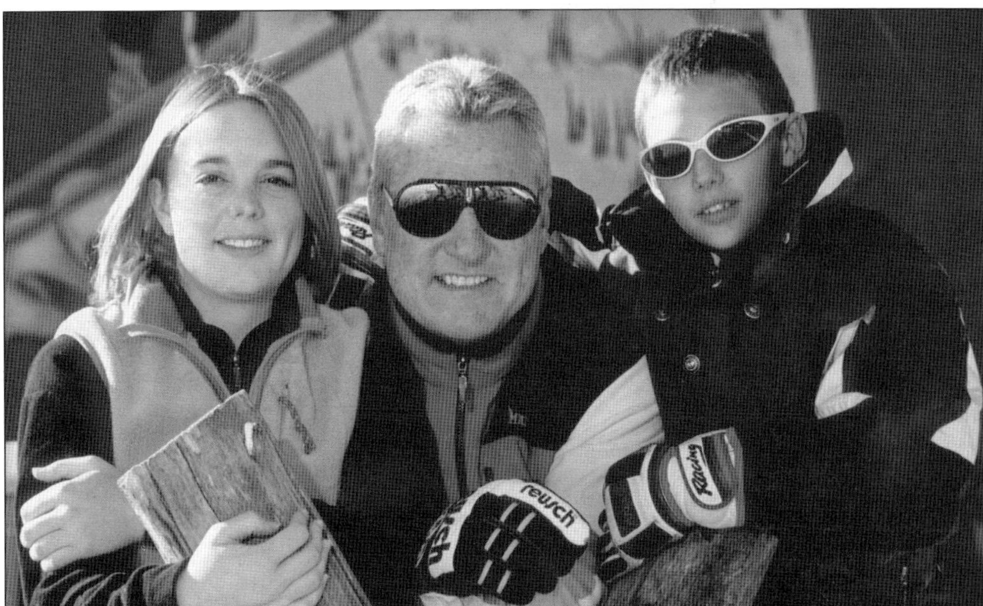

Longtime Red River manager Drew Judycki is seen here with his kids Lauren and Linton during the 1995–1996 season. After his father's unexpected passing in 2008, Linton gradually assumed management duties and was joined by Walt Foley in 2011. The duo oversees it today. Linton grew up on the Red River slopes and recalls, "When I was in second or third grade, I got an award for being the kid who wore their ski pants the most to school. When we were let out, I could get in an hour or so on the mountain." He was training with the US Ski Team when his father died. (Courtesy RR.)

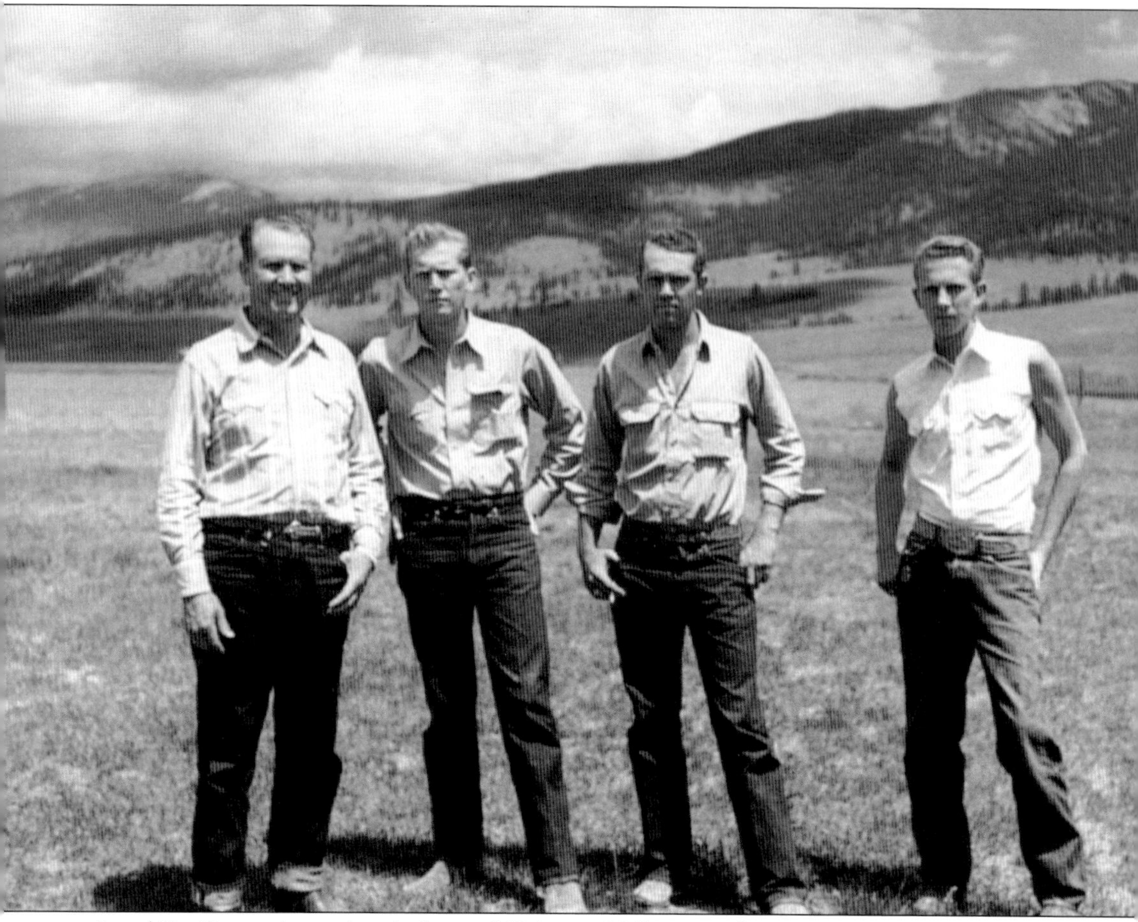

Angel Fire Resort, located in the beautiful Moreno Valley east of Taos, was originally conceived of as a summer retreat for heat-beaten Texans. Members of the Lebus family of Wichita Falls, Texas, pictured here in the late 1960s, first built a golf course and lake. After visiting Vail, they realized Angel Fire's winter snow could be white gold, and they decided to get into the ski business. They welcomed their first skiers for Christmas in 1966 and sold their interest in 1972. From left to right are Roy H. Lebus, Roy T. Lebus, George Lebus, and Tommy Lebus. (Courtesy AFR.)

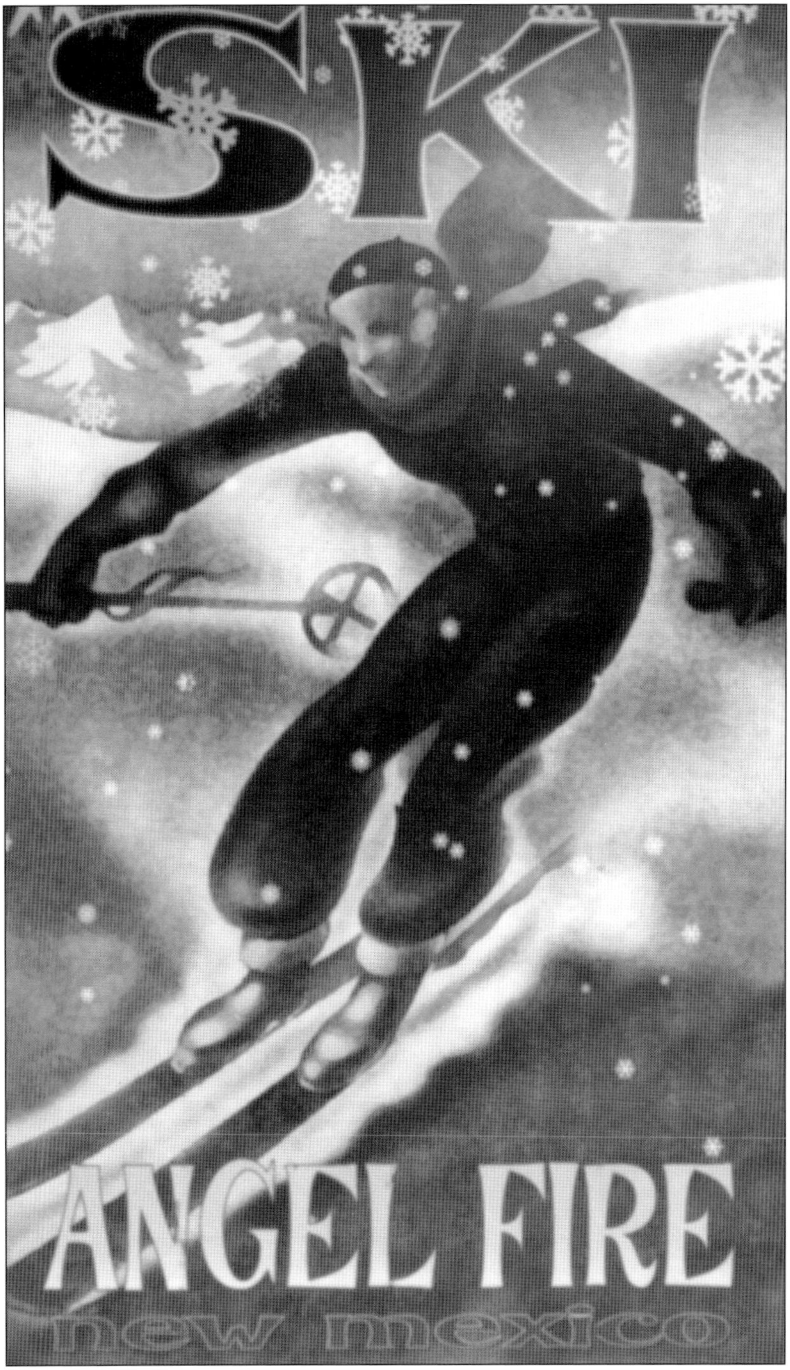

This classic 1960s poster graces the hallway of the Lodge at Angel Fire Resort today. It was widely distributed and helped promote the sport and resort in its early days. Angel Fire had a bumpy grand opening at Christmas 1966 when its frontside lifts quit running. Guests were bussed to the backside, where a Thikol Spryte snowcat towed them uphill for short runs. Despite the technical difficulties, everyone had a great time and enjoyed free hotdogs and burgers cooked over a huge bonfire. (Courtesy AFR.)

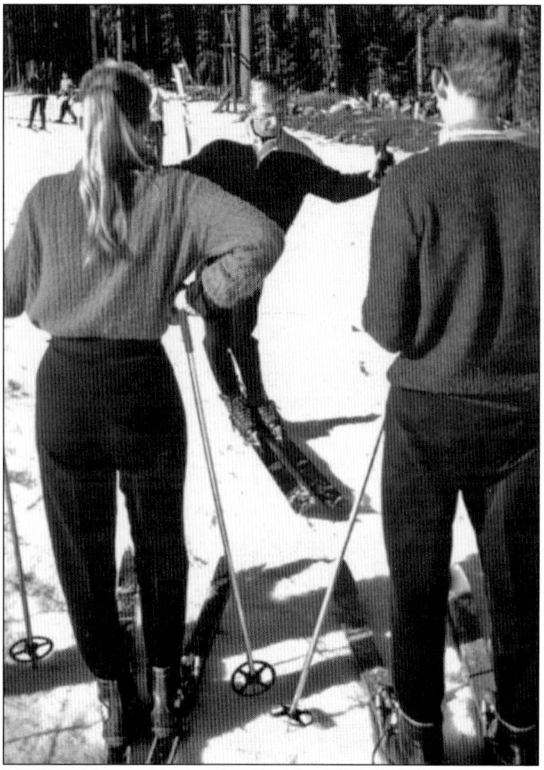

Bill Burgess, originally from California, arrived in Angel Fire in 1966 as an instructor. Teaching was his lifelong passion. He went on to spend more than 60 years in the local industry, ending his career as director of the Angel Fire Ski School. Over the years, he also served as a marketing director, the first elected president of Ski New Mexico, president of the Rocky Mountain Ski Instructors Association, and an organizer of the ESPN X Games shovel race competition. He died in 2018 and is a member of the New Mexico Ski Hall of Fame. (Courtesy AFR.)

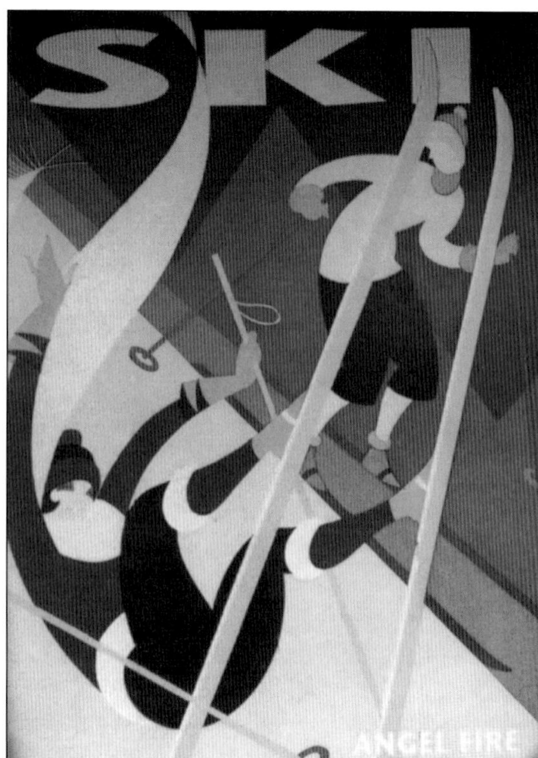

Here is another of Angel Fire's excellent posters produced in its early years. The 1967–1968 season was a bust with financial problems, but operations smoothed out for the 1968–1969 season, and it has run ever since. The resort went on to install the state's first high-speed detachable quad chair in 1996, the Chile Express, one of the nation's longest at 2.5 miles with a vertical rise of 2,060 feet. (Courtesy AFR.)

Another new ski area to emerge in the 1960s was Pajarito Mountain, located on the same ground the Los Alamos Ranch School students used to so laboriously climb and ski decades earlier above today's town of Los Alamos. It had long been eyed and skied by Los Alamos natives drawn to its deep snows, but poor road access remained a huge impediment. Finally, a road was notched in, the first runs cut, and lifts erected. Seen here is the first poma, 1,109 feet long, to reach the summit. It was replaced by a triple chair in 1984. (Courtesy LASC.)

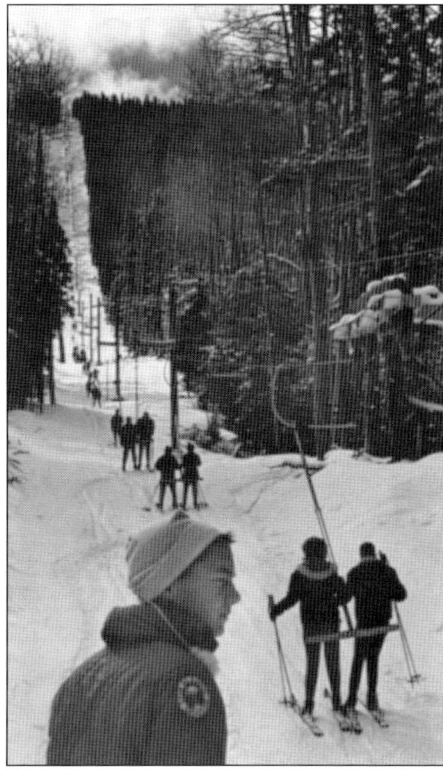

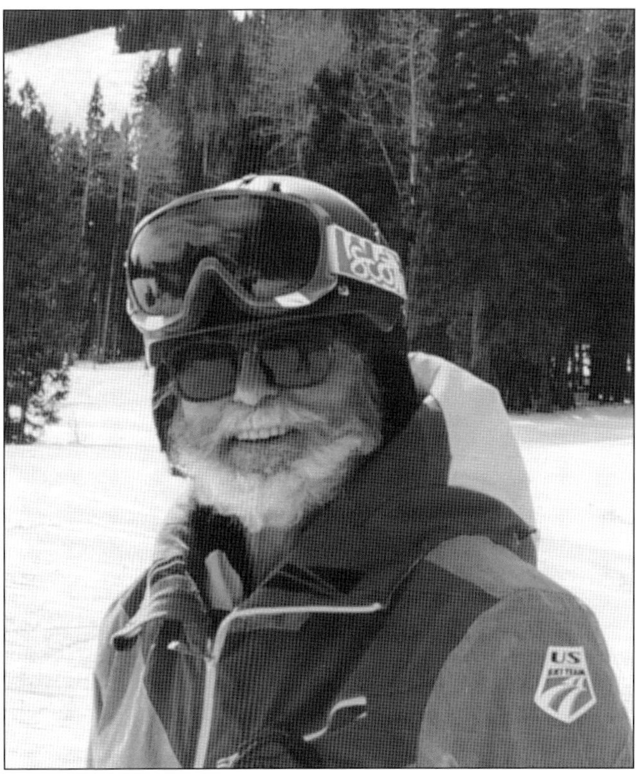

Tom Long, raised in Albuquerque, was hired by Sandia Peak Tram in 1966 for his electronic skills after serving many years at the ski area as a volunteer. He began skiing at age four in his backyard in Boston. Two years later his family moved to Albuquerque, and his father took him to ski at Tree Springs. He has been general manager of Pajarito Mountain since 2004. His father, Ed Long, was a skiing instructor for the 10th Mountain Division in World War II and also taught at La Madera. Tom is seen here in 2021 at Pajarito. (Courtesy the Long family.)

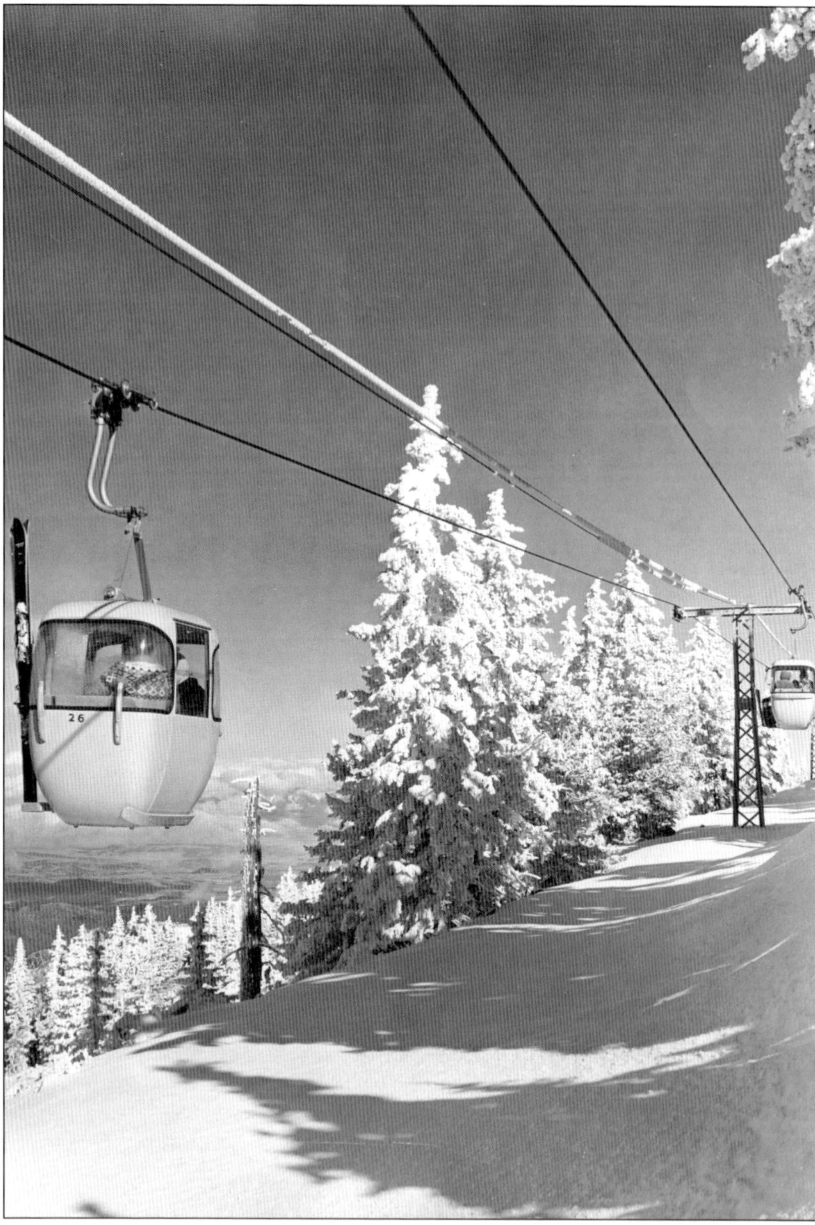

Yet another ski area, Sierra Blanca, in south-central New Mexico near Ruidoso, was birthed in the roaring 1960s. It opened for Christmas 1961 under the direction of Pitch Pitcher, whose resume in ski development landed him in the ski halls of fame of both New Mexico and Colorado. He died in 2018 at age 98 after a stellar life. With the aid of Pete Totemoff—him again—Roger Pope, and Buzz Bainbridge, the state's first gondola arose in 1962 here on the former hunting grounds of the Mescalero Apache. It was the first monocable four-person gondola in the United States and the only gondola in New Mexico for five decades. Financed by oilman Robert O. Anderson, chairman of Atlantic-Richfield Corporation, the ski area was carved from the flanks of 11,981-foot Sierra Blanca Peak. First, a crazy road that climbs almost 3,000 feet from nearby Ruidoso had to be built. Weeklong explorations on foot and skis in 1958 and 1959 to survey the terrain, with air drops of food and equipment, are epic tales. (Courtesy PFC.)

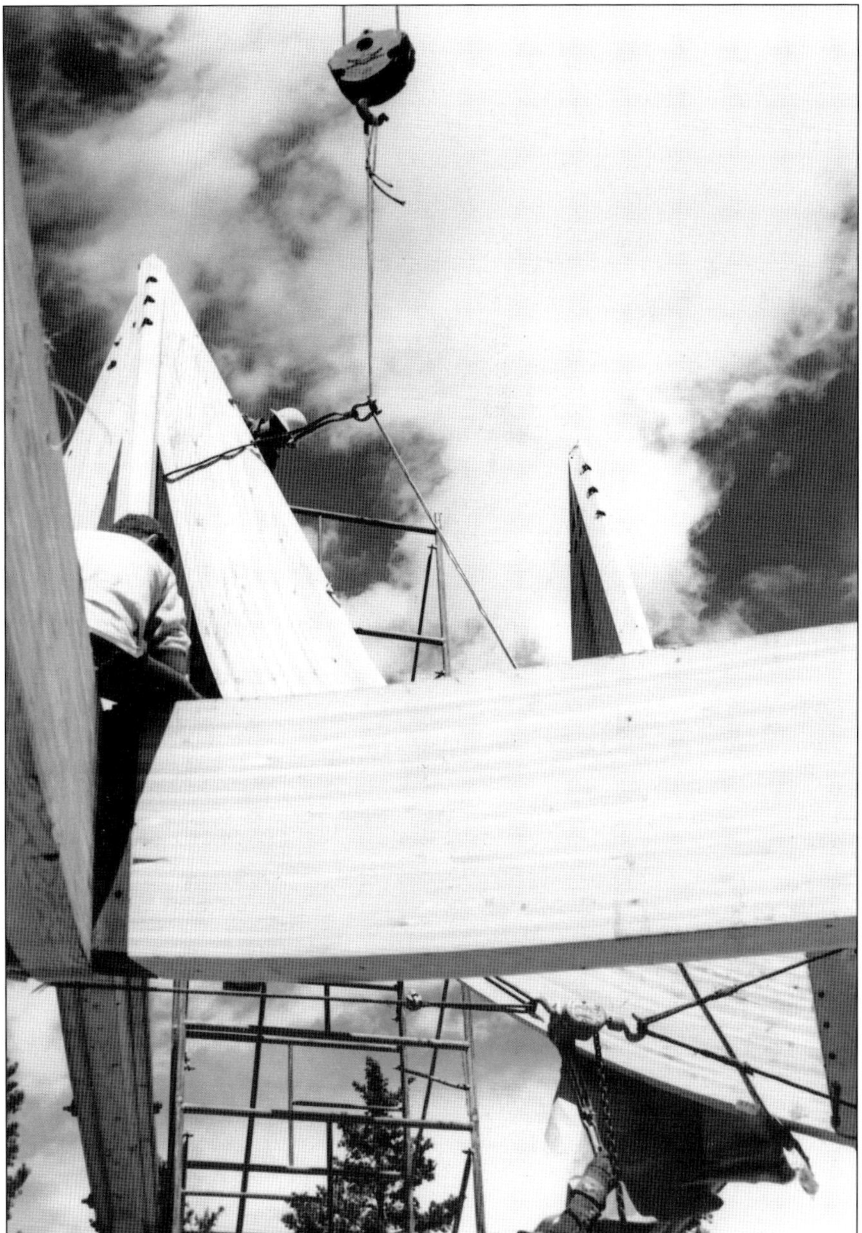

The distinctive modernist-style main lodge at Sierra Blanca, with its soaring laminated wood beams provided by the Gibson Lumber Company of Albuquerque, was designed by award-winning architect Victor Lundy. In an article in the *Santa Fean* magazine of January–February 1980, Pitch said about R.O. Anderson, "He's an interesting man. He said to me, 'You come down and build it.' And I said, 'Who else?' And he said, 'Just you. You do it. You're the president. You design and build it.' What an unparalleled opportunity! In the summers of 1960 and 1961, we spent $3 million and built a first-class resort." But this was hardly Pitch's first foray in the ski industry. As he noted in his induction to the New Mexico Ski Hall of Fame, "My first real job in the ski business was teaching at Sun Valley while waiting to join the Air Force in 1942. Mentors were Friedl Phiefer and Fred Iselin [Aspen's founders], names I suspect are unfamiliar to today's skiers." (Courtesy PFC.)

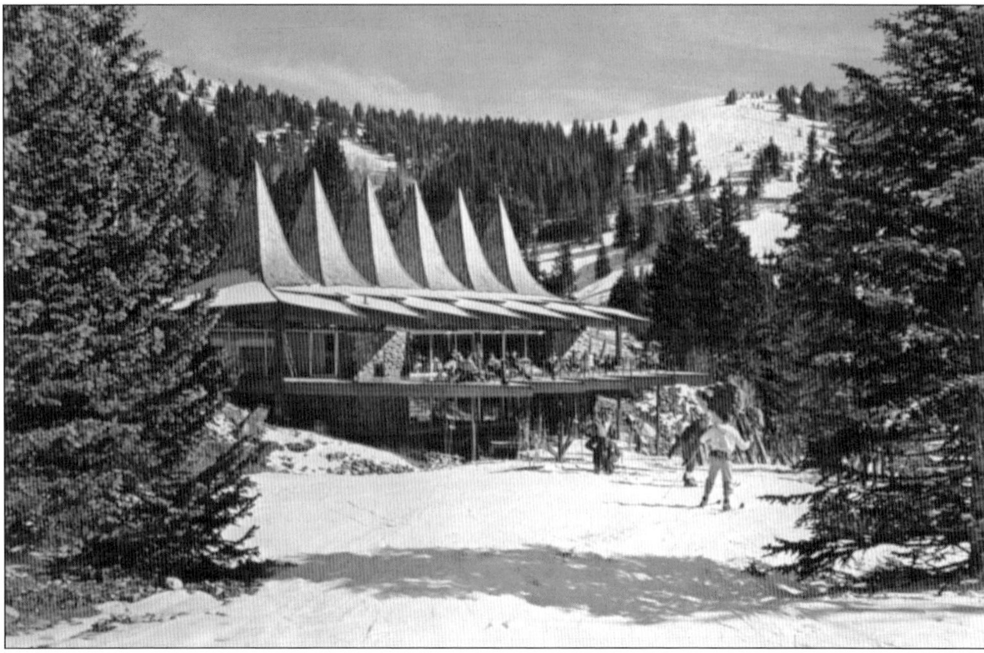

The Sierra Blanca Lodge with its peaked roof looks today just as it did in this postcard of 1968 from the Schaaf Post Card Co. It sits at the base of today's Ski Apache. Pitch's involvement in New Mexico's ski community had actually begun years earlier. In his hall of fame notes, he reports, "Here in New Mexico my first project was running a rope tow at Hyde Park. My job was to sell tickets, run the rope tow, fix the Ford motor on top of the slope when it quit, and once in a while teach." (Courtesy PFC.)

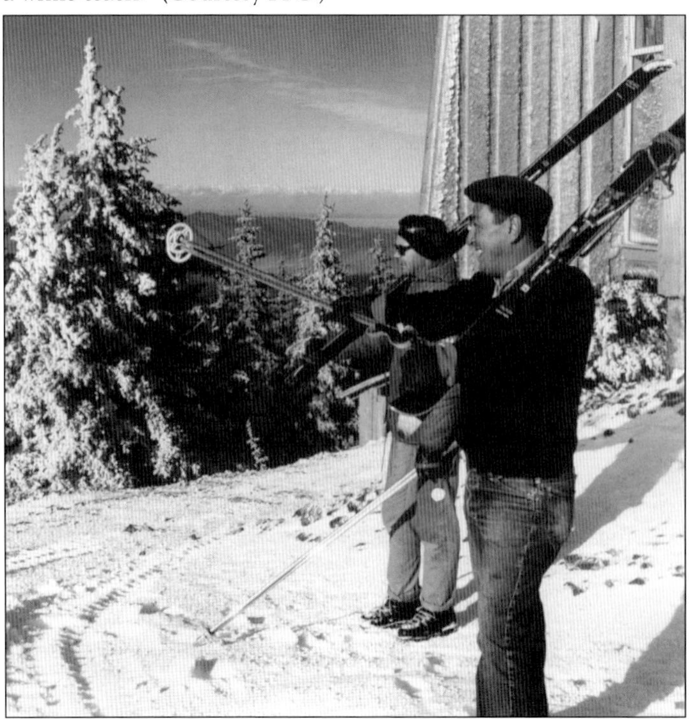

Pete Totemoff stands at the summit of the Sierra Blanca ski area. He is looking down onto shimmering White Sands, then a national monument, some 7,000 feet below. To the west rises the snowcapped Gila high country. Arriving in New Mexico from Cordova, Alaska, where he had won a state ski championship, Totemoff had only one lung, but it never seemed to slow him down. He was first hired in 1946 to manage La Madera for Robert Nordhaus. He later was one of the first snow rangers for the US Forest Service. (Courtesy PFC.)

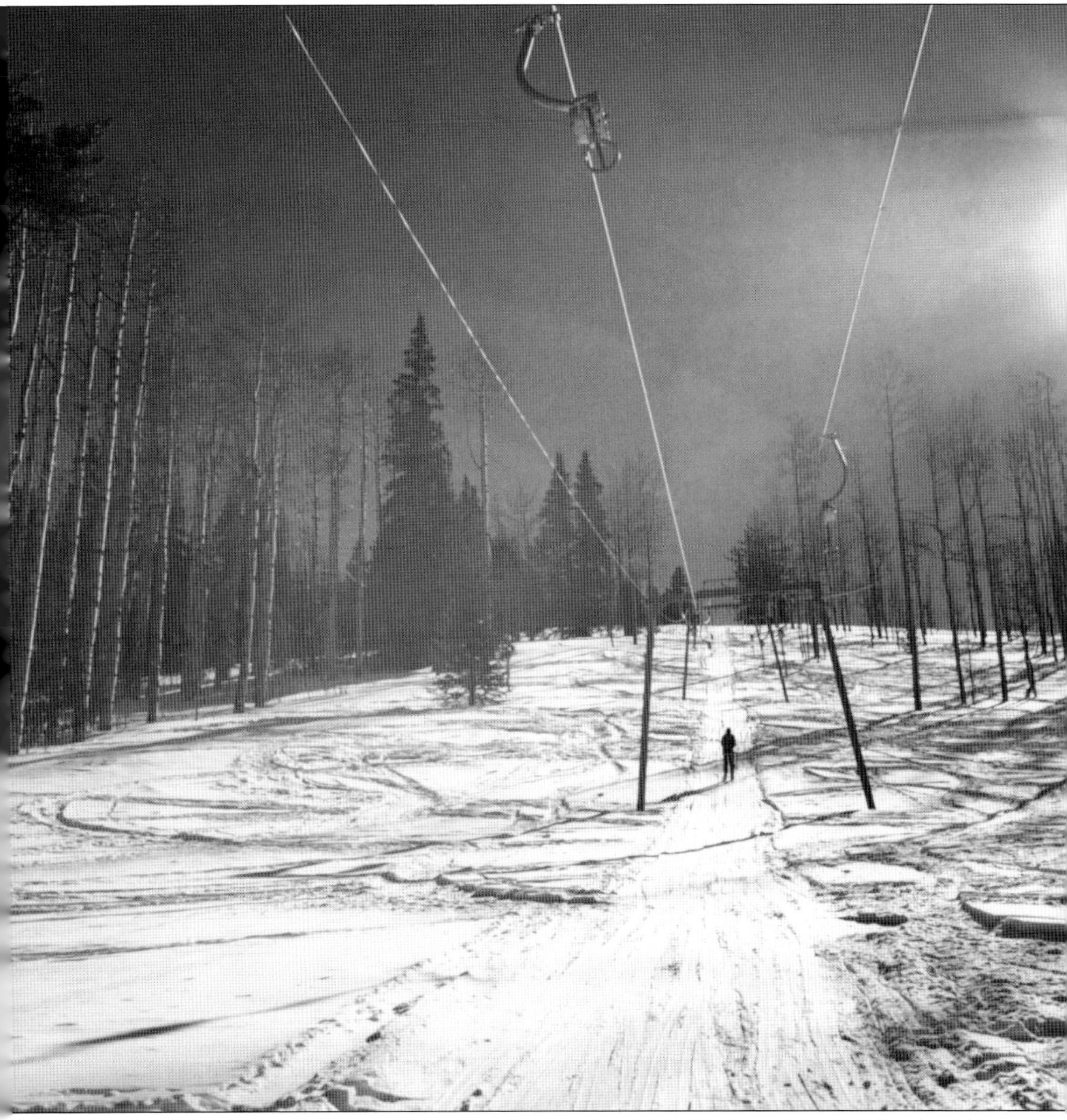

This T-bar lift at Sierra Blanca, the Lincoln, climbed 750 vertical feet over its 2,000-foot length. It was put up by Pitch and company to open the area in 1961 on a limited basis. It almost did not happen. He noted in a *Ski* magazine article in December 1963, "We had a real photograph finish. A hundred and ten inches of snow fell just before the opening date, and many of the crew refused to work in the heavy snows. The night before we opened, our delayed German T-bars had only reached El Paso. By goading truck drivers, we got them into the parking lot in time to uncrate them by the light of two great bonfires. We started putting them on the cables at seven in the morning. By eight o'clock, skiers were standing in line, and by nine we were in business." (Courtesy PFC.)

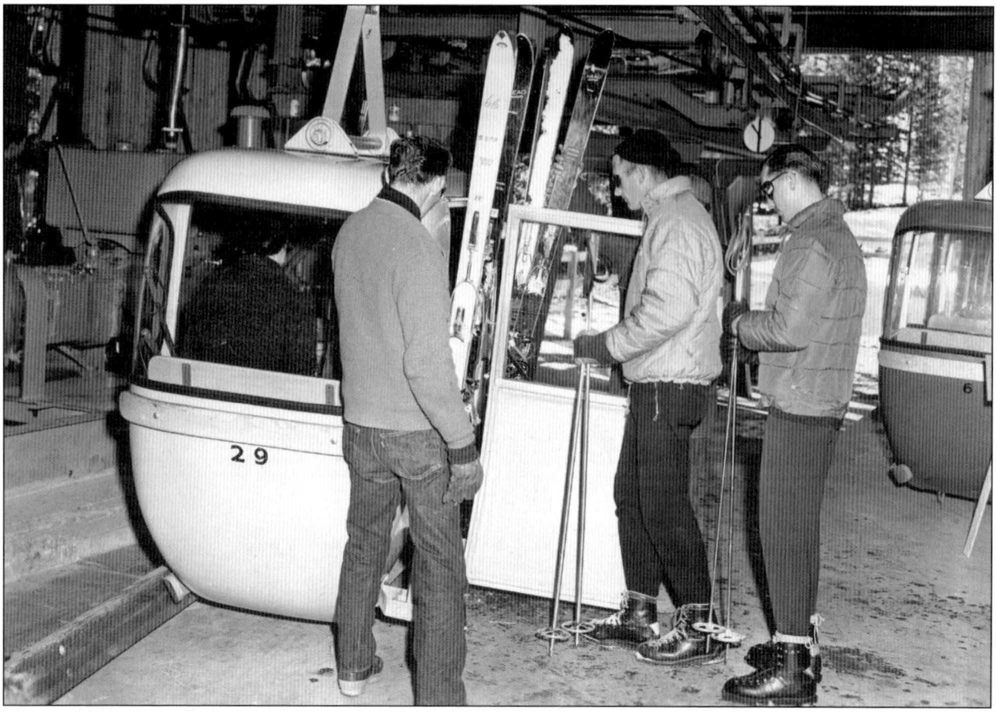

Sierra Blanca's gondola, seen here in the early 1960s, was a state-of-the-art lift when installed for the 1962–1963 season—a four-person Pohlig. Amazingly, it remained in operation until 2012, when it was destroyed in a wildfire. It climbed 1,700 vertical feet over its 8,000-foot length. Note in the rack the three sets of Head skis—a top-of-the-line ski that revolutionized ski making. Along with the Lincoln T-bar, the Capitan T-bar that opened here in 1961, and a few smaller lifts, by 1969 it had a 5,000-people-per-hour capacity—the state's greatest. (Courtesy PFC.)

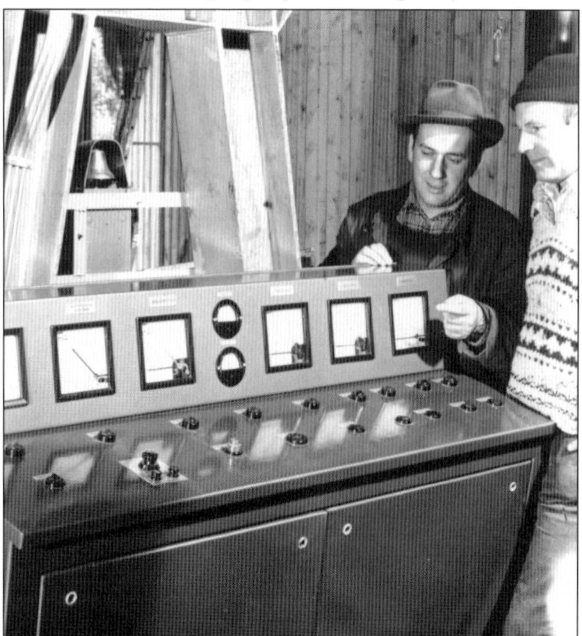

Pitch Pitcher (right) and Lawrence Peebles check out the controls for Sierra Blanca's gondola. Peebles was among the first crews to explore the terrain here and plan its development. It was sort of up Pitch's alley. After World War II, he and his wife settled first in Santa Fe where he ran an aviation company. Next came ranching in Taos, where he met Ernie Blake, followed by running a larger ranch near Aspen. There, he renewed his association with Aspen's founders and taught some skiing while helping to get Snowmass at Aspen underway. (Courtesy PFC.)

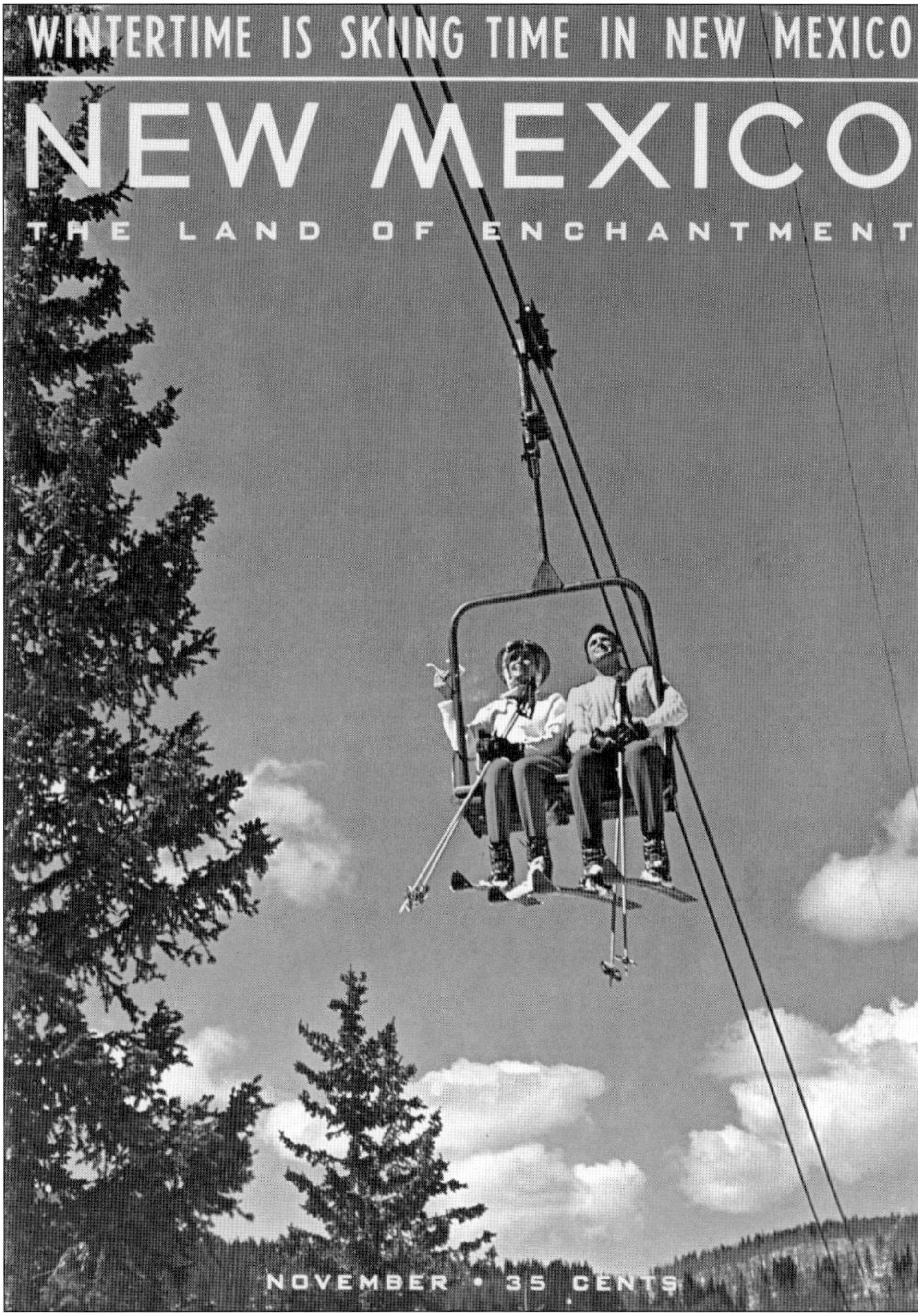

The cover of the November 1960 issue of *New Mexico* magazine presaged decades of continual growth of the state's ski areas. It features an image of the old "red chair" at the Santa Fe Ski Basin, the state's first. In 1963, Pitch Pitcher assumed control of the ski area after Sierra Blanca was sold to the Mescalero Apache tribe. Pitch helped the tribe hire a new, skilled manager, Roy Parker, and remained as a consultant, but immediately focused his prodigious energies and organizational skills on another ski area he could call his own. He set his sights north on Santa Fe. (Courtesy NMSM.)

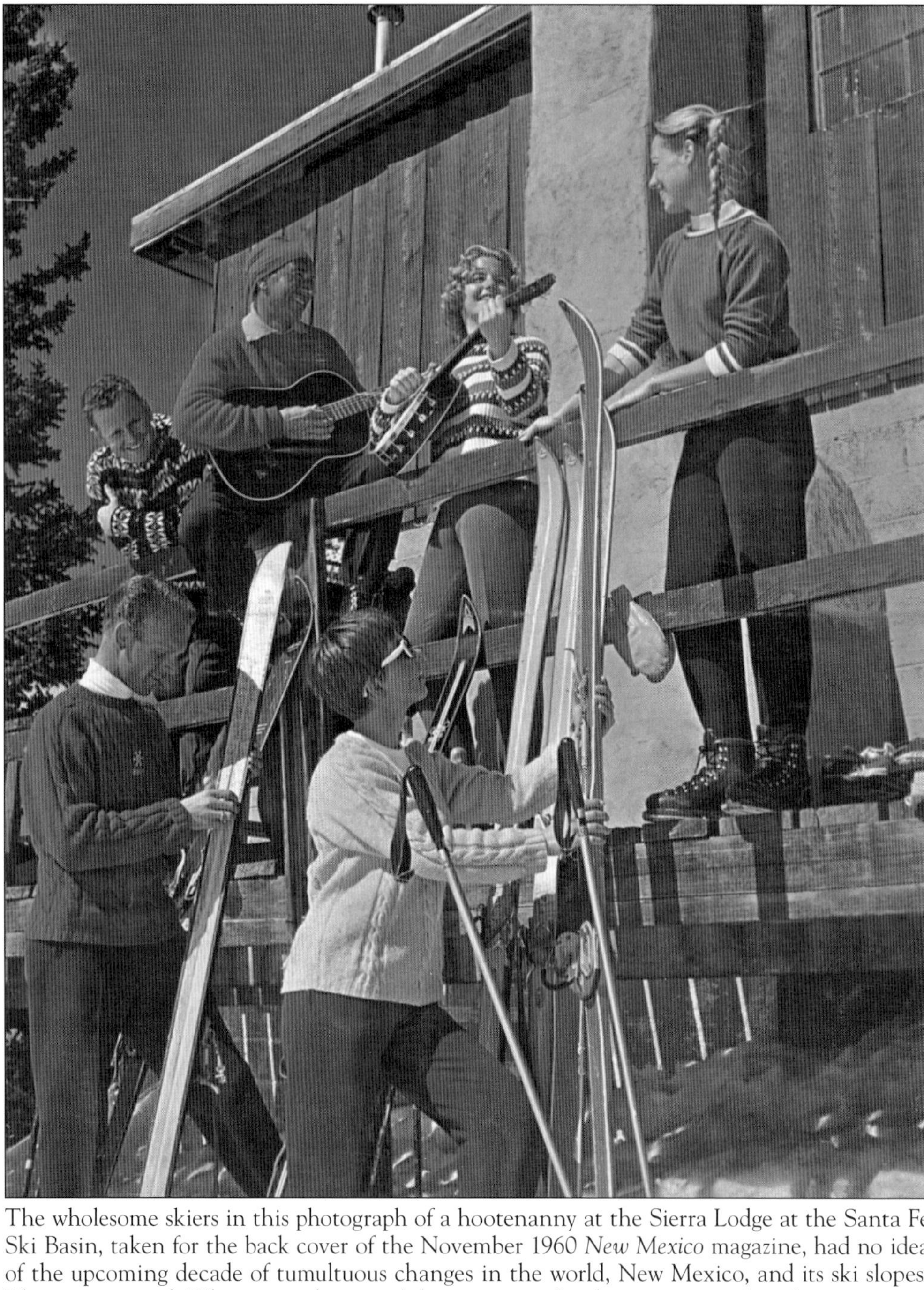

The wholesome skiers in this photograph of a hootenanny at the Sierra Lodge at the Santa Fe Ski Basin, taken for the back cover of the November 1960 *New Mexico* magazine, had no idea of the upcoming decade of tumultuous changes in the world, New Mexico, and its ski slopes. The caption read, "Skiing is only part of the activities, for the companionship that is enjoyed by gathering around a roaring fireplace or on a porch of the lodge in pleasant weather for a song and conversation add to the merriment and enjoyment of skiing." At bottom are Harvey and Reserl Chalker, who managed the ski area for a handful of years in the late 1950s and early 1960s. Playing guitar is Giuseppi Olmi, Santa Fe's head ski instructor at the time. (Photograph by Harvey Caplin, courtesy NMSM.)

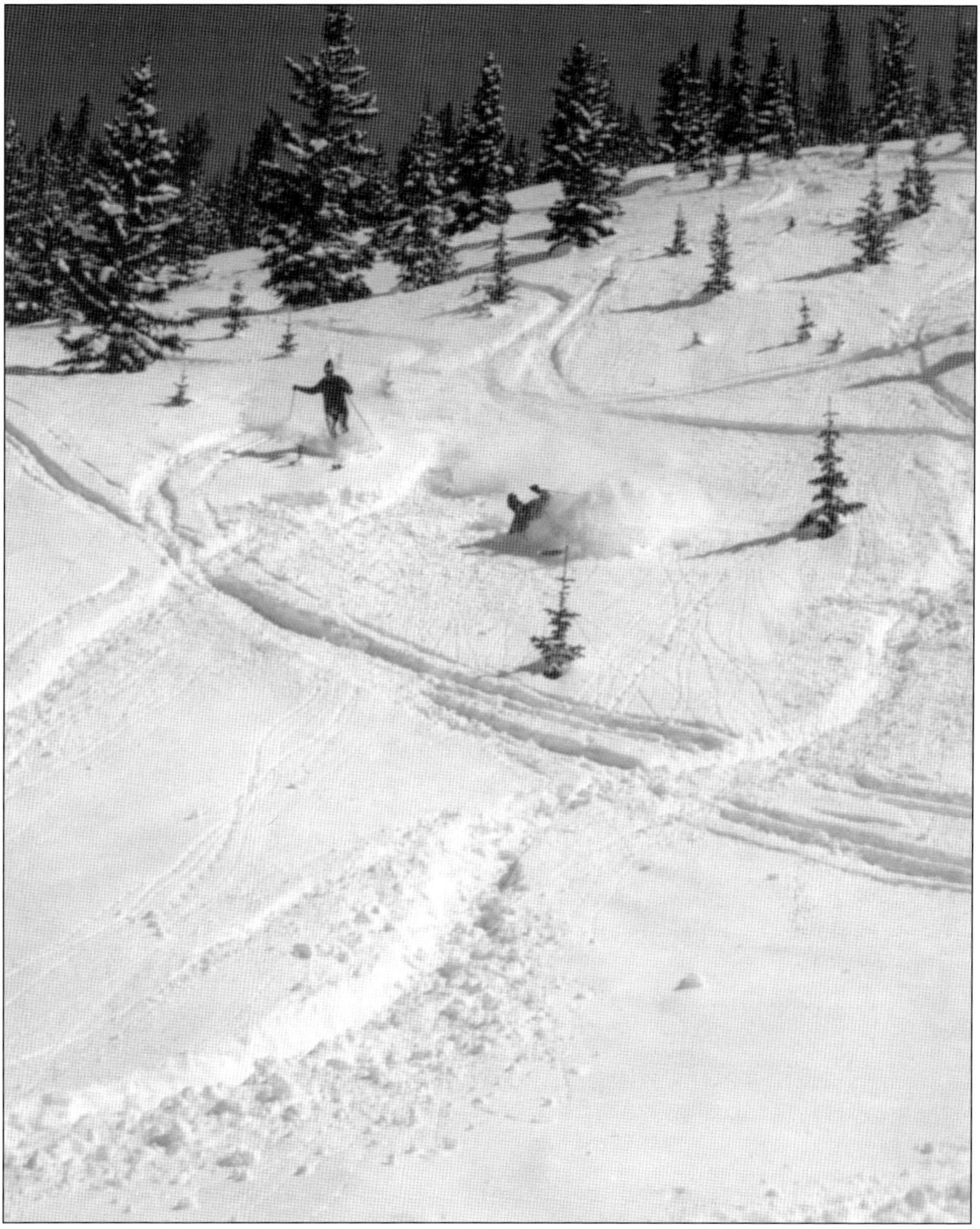

Todd and Peter Pitcher sample the powder at the Santa Fe Ski Basin sometime in the 1960s or early 1970s after the Pitcher family, led by Pitch, assumed control of the area in August 1963 and extended a poma to the basin's summit. The whole family was eventually involved; by 1980, Peter was the operations manager, daughter Noel ran the Noel Sport Shop and cafeteria, Alix worked in the ski school, and Davey worked with the ski patrol. Eldest son Todd was mountain manager at Wolf Creek, Colorado. The Pitchers had spent a few years in Santa Fe after World War II, and Pitch had gotten to know Ernie Blake. Ernie asked him to join him developing Taos Ski Valley, but he passed. Pitch explained to Marian Love in the *Santa Fean* magazine of January–February 1980: "I refused because I foresaw immense difficulties, but I have to hand it to him, he turned them all to advantages." (Courtesy PFC.)

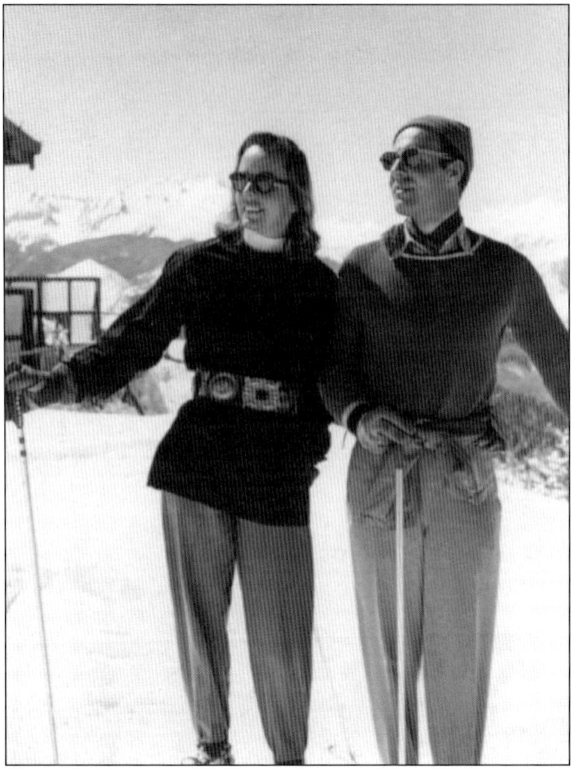

Pitch Pitcher and his lovely wife, Charity Jane, are looking good in this photograph most likely taken in the early 1960s in Colorado. The couple had lived on a ranch near Aspen in the 1950s and maintained friends there throughout their lives. Charity Jane raised six children but also loved to ski. The newest chairlift at Wolf Creek, Colorado, is named the Charity Jane Express in her honor. She is representing New Mexico with her Navajo-made silver *concho* belt. She died in 2013 in Santa Fe. (Courtesy PFC.)

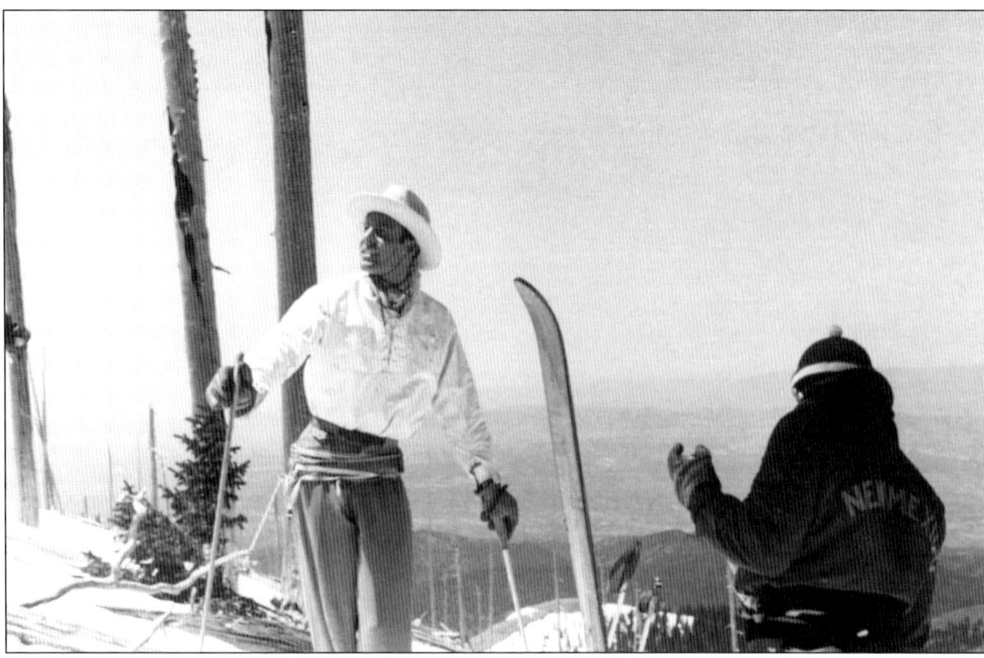

Pitch Pitcher is looking pretty stylish in this photograph taken at the Santa Fe Ski Basin not long after he assumed control of the operation in 1963. This image looks southwest, with the town of Santa Fe to the left. Some of the dead, standing Engelmann spruce trees that covered the upper mountain rise around him. (Courtesy PFC.)

The first major lift Pitch Pitcher and associate Roger Pope erected at the Santa Fe Ski Basin in 1963 was the so-called "Big Poma." And it was big! It rose 1,300 vertical feet, placing skiers almost at 12,000 feet near the summit of Tesuque Peak. At the time, it was the nation's highest poma, a notable distinction. Very powerful, it would launch kids off their feet, and its skier track would often become entrenched. Initially it served one lone run, Burro Alley, flanked by thick forests and slopes dotted with unmarked cliffs and chutes. Woe to anyone who fell off! The photograph at right, taken in 1964, is of its base. The photograph below was taken about halfway up the route where it clears the trees. It was replaced in 1973 but was basically a standby after the Tesuque Peak triple chair was built in 1983. Pope spent some 20 years working here, and a run, Pope's Nose, is named after him. (Both, courtesy PFC.)

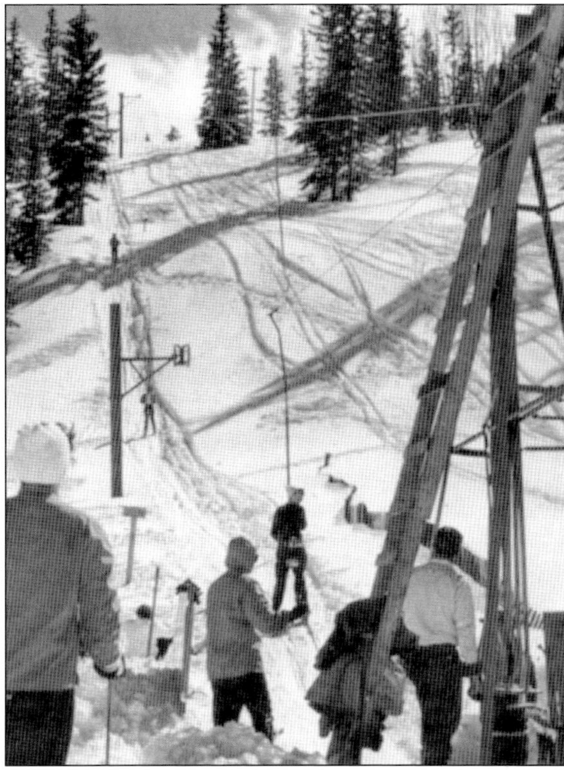

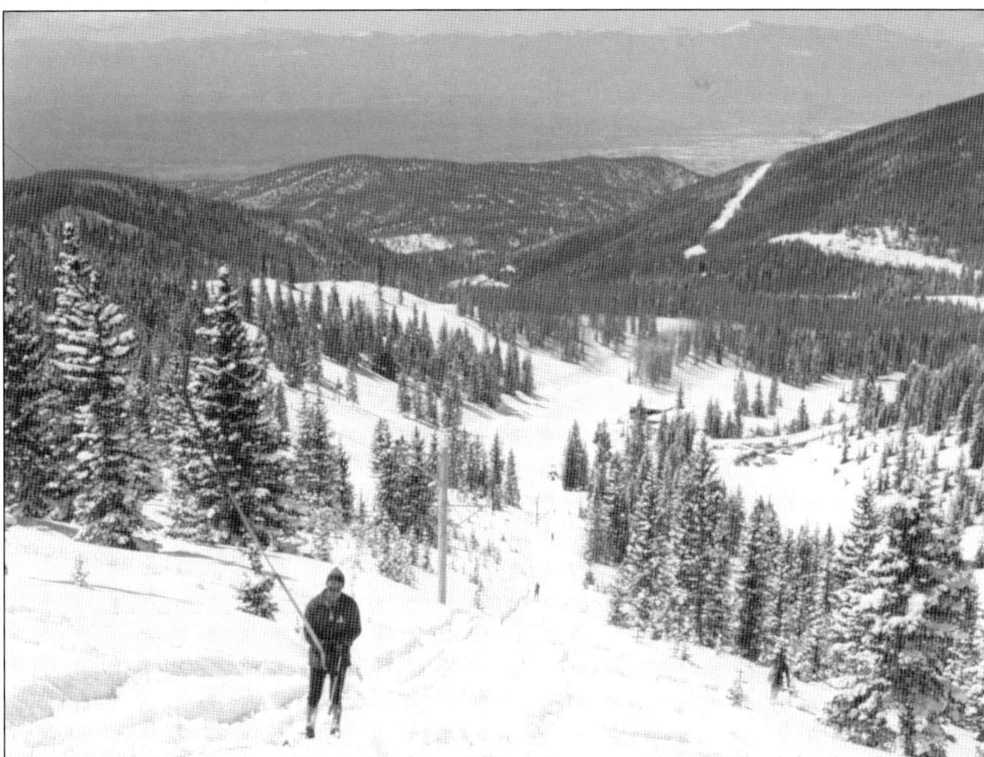

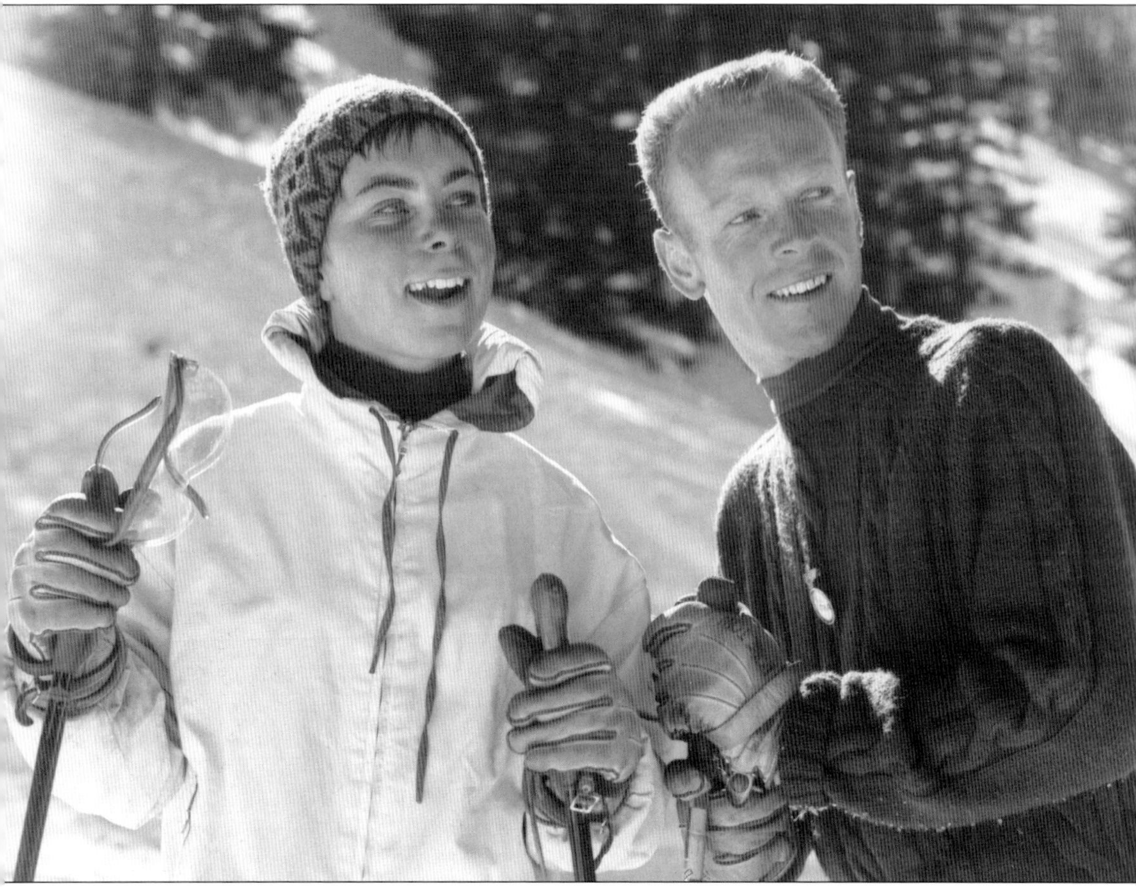

Reserl and Harvey Chalker are seen here at the Santa Fe Ski Basin in the early 1960s. He ran the basin's ski shop starting in the 1957–1958 season and served as general manger from 1960 until 1966, when the pair opened Alpine Sports in Santa Fe. They sold the shop in 2015, but it remains Santa Fe's premier ski shop today. Reserl grew up skiing in Bavaria, Germany, and Harvey skied on Mount Hood, Oregon. They met in 1956 in Garmisch, Germany, when Harvey was in the US Army. Despite the fact she spoke little English, Harvey was drawn both to her personality and to the fact she was such a fine skier. "We had the same interest, and the rest is history," he once noted. They married in 1959, and both are members of the New Mexico Ski Hall of Fame. (Courtesy PFC.)

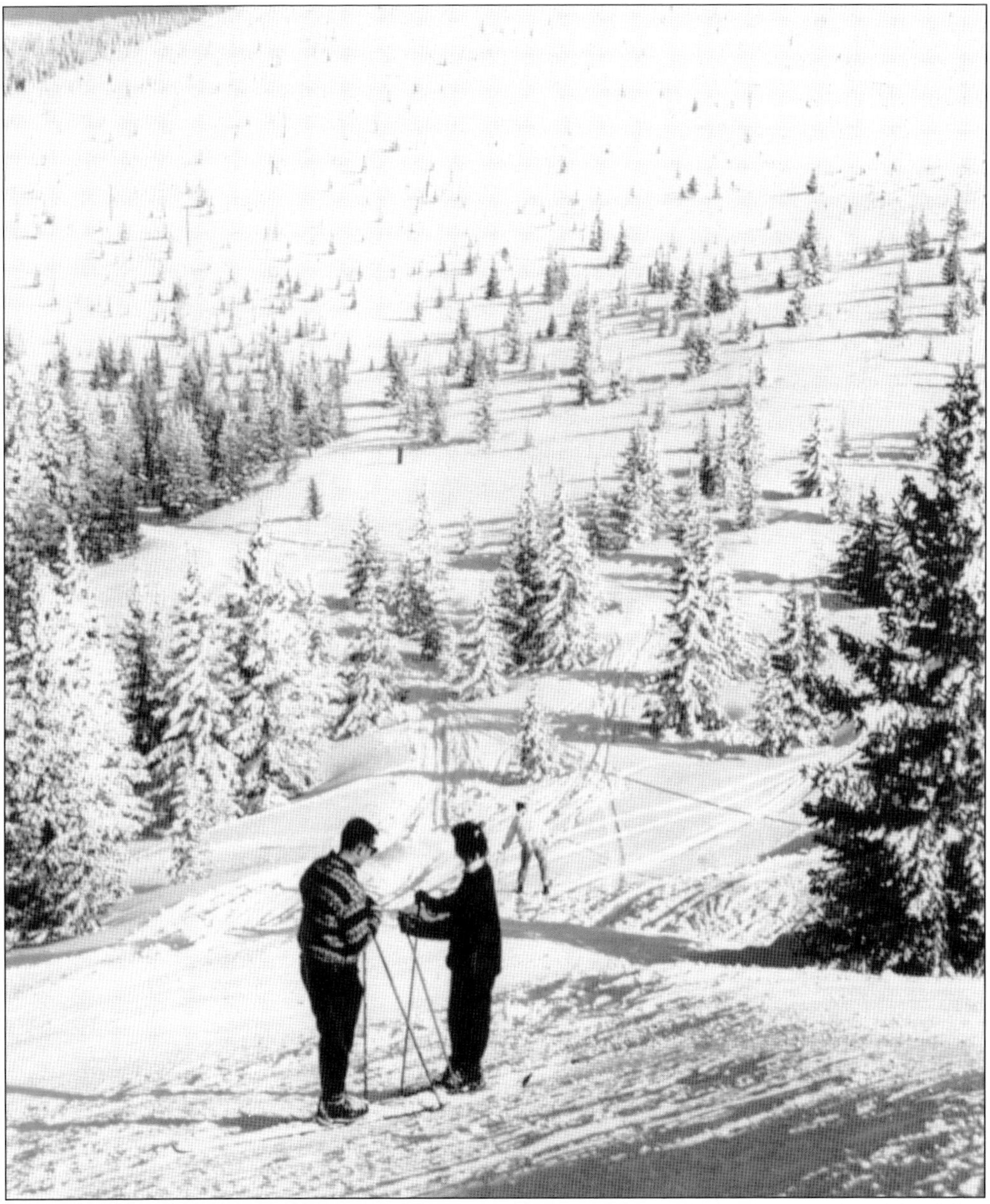

Two skiers pause for a view of the tremendous open terrain at Santa Fe Ski Basin in the 1960s. This was the same general area as the photograph taken in 1937 of what Graeme McGowan called the "Sacate Blanco." It was already beginning to fill in with young pines in this photograph; today, the area is thickly forested. As most skiers then avoided powder like the plague, it would often go untouched. As skiing the unnamed, untouched open spaces of the upper mountain gained appeal, the sheared-off stumps remained a hazard for decades, almost impaling a few skiers. The only way to reach the higher slopes was via the notorious "big poma." Few people in the 1960s ventured there. (Courtesy PFC.)

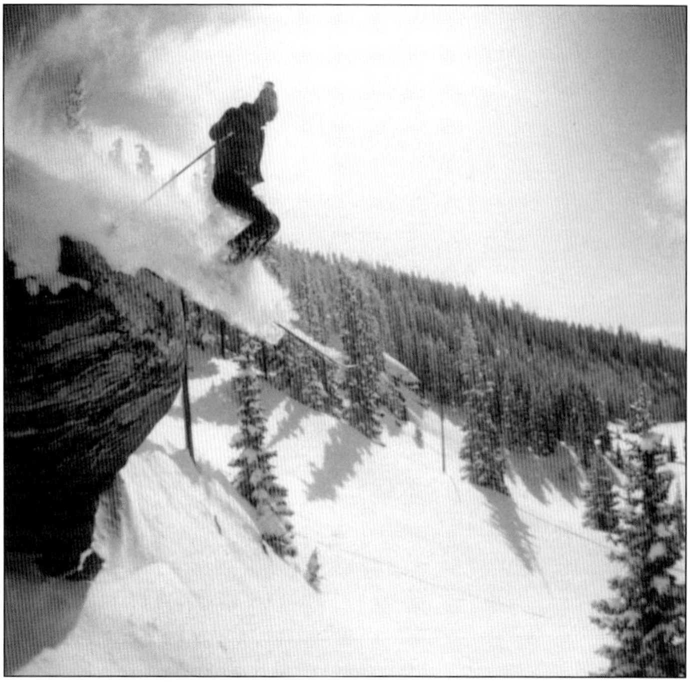

This classic image captures someone shooting off a small cliff at Santa Fe Ski Basin in the 1960s or 1970s. In addition to lift improvements, for several years the Pitchers also opened the Sierra Lodge for overnight accommodations with a handful of rooms, including a Bierstube with beer and wine offerings. But its isolation, as well as the fact that Santa Fe itself has many fine hotels, did in the lodging aspect. In 1973, a lift ticket cost $7, ski school ran $7.50, and deluxe rentals with release bindings were $6.60. (Courtesy SkiSF.)

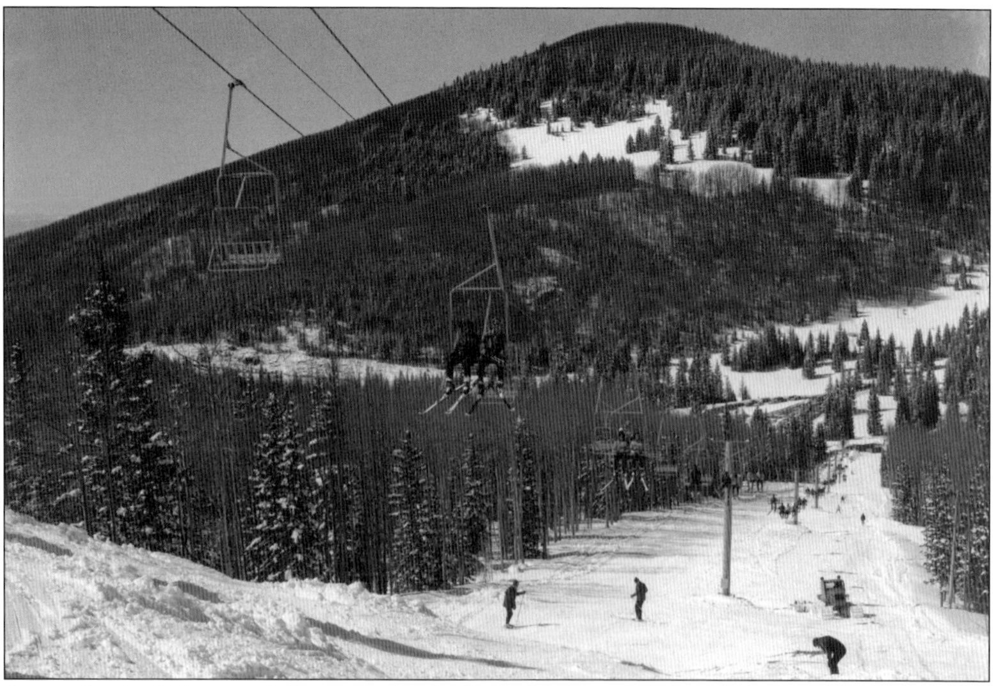

Pictured is the 900-vertical-foot Aspen Peak Chair at Santa Fe Ski Basin sometime in the 1960s or 1970s. It was named for the summit rising behind the lift's base. It was erected for the 1964–1965 season by the Pitchers, and its opening shifted primary skier services and all parking farther down the basin from the original lodge and lifts. It was replaced in 1988 by the current Super Chief quad-chair. Note the snowcat moving up an open slope. With today's liability issues, this is not common anywhere. (Courtesy PFC.)

Davey Pitcher grew up at Santa Fe Ski Basin and filled many roles there over the decades his family controlled it. Here, he is seen in the 1980s standing next to a snowcat grooming machine that he was thoroughly at home in. When the family sold the ski area to the Abruzzo family in 1984, Davey headed just north to Wolf Creek Ski Area in southern Colorado, his dad's childhood stomping grounds, which the family bought. He eventually became its manager, a position he still relishes today. (Courtesy PFC.)

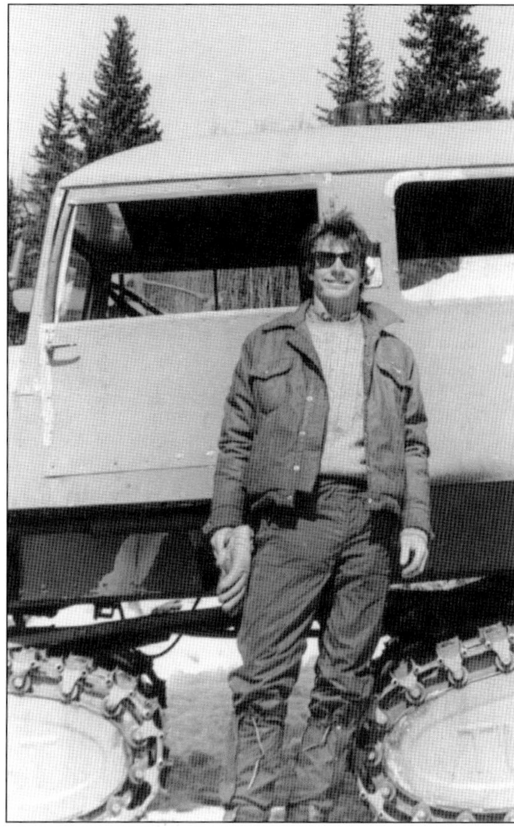

No job was too small, or too big, for Pete Totemoff to tackle. Here, he is driving a bulldozer in the parking lot of Santa Fe Ski Basin around 1963, before the ski area was extended downhill and the new base area was created. He followed Pitch Pitcher from Sierra Blanca back to Santa Fe and was making himself indispensable, as usual. Eventually, two triple chairlifts were strung up from this parking lot, the first by the Pitchers in 1983, and the second, the Millennium, by the Abruzzos in 1985. The latter is 5,730 feet long, rises 1,530 feet, and cost some $3 million. (Courtesy PFC.)

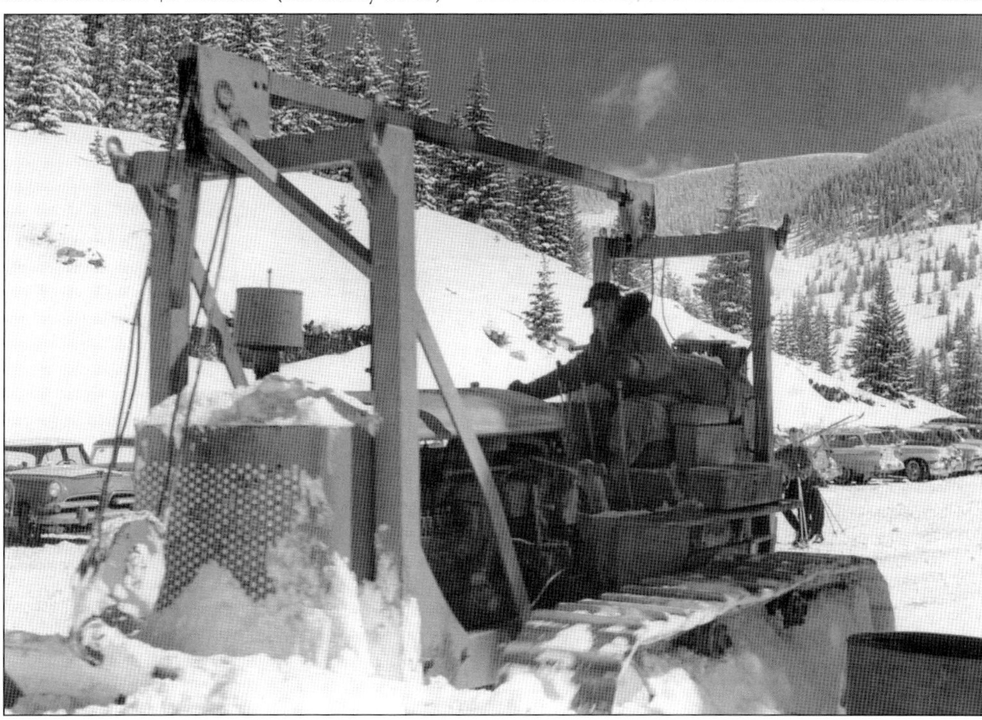

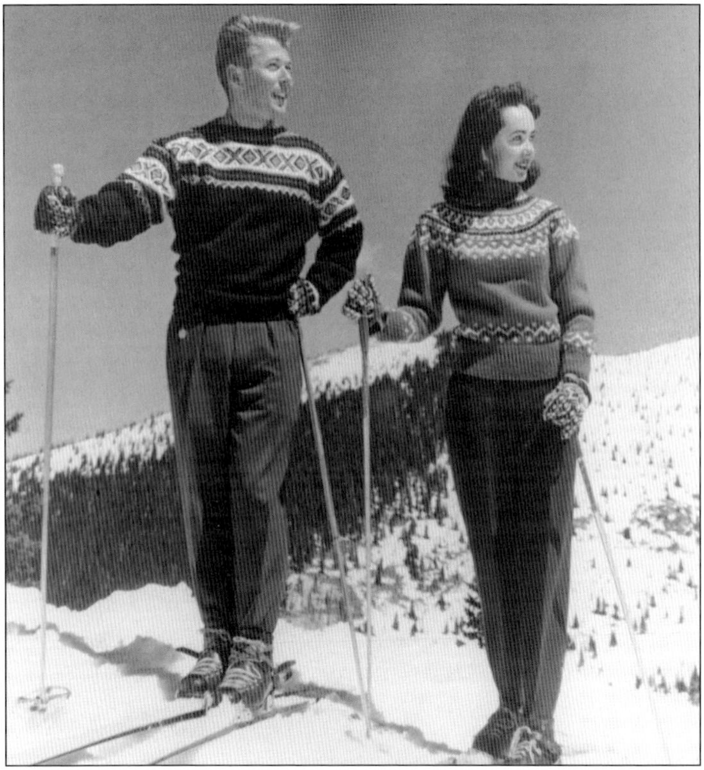

This young couple posed for the state tourism bureau at Santa Fe Ski Basin in the 1960s to promote skiing and develop it as an economic force, which it quickly became and continues to be. Behind them are the open slopes on what is now Raven's Ridge, created by a wildfire at the turn of the 20th century. It has largely been overgrown today, though skiers occasionally hike out and descend this slope, picking their way through glades and narrow alleys. (Courtesy PFC.)

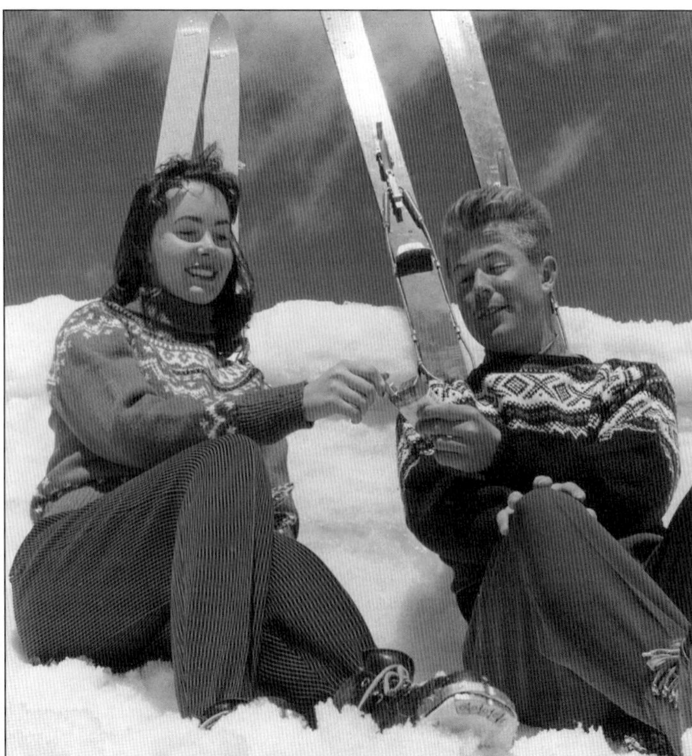

Another photograph of the same couple taken by the state's tourism bureau presents skiing and smoking as hip activities. It seems that the couple has made turns in the snow and sun and are now ready to relax with a cigarette. Could Dean Martin be close at hand? (Courtesy PFC.)

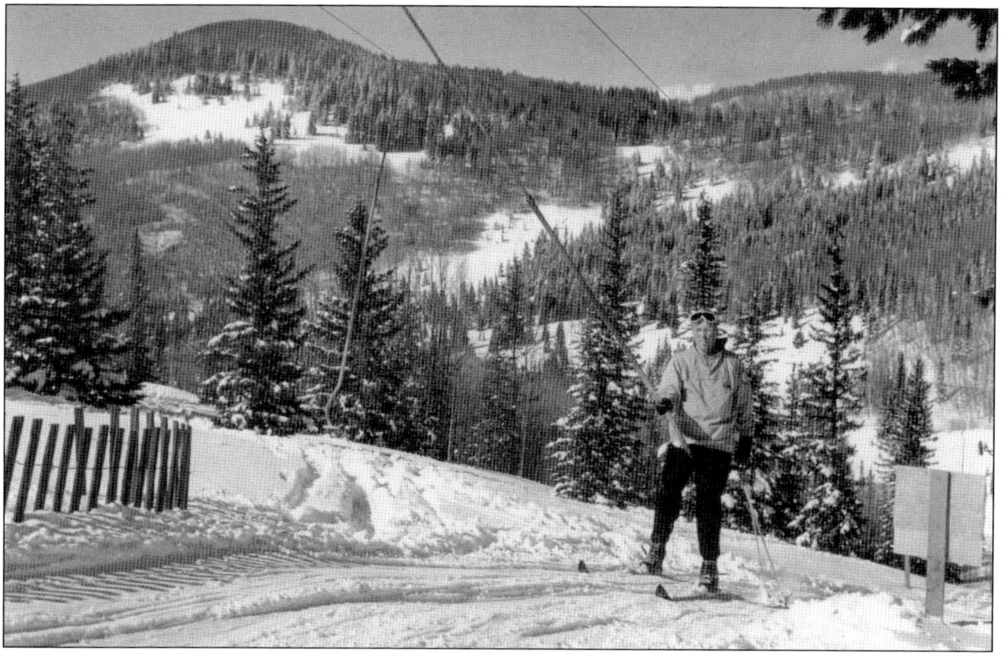

Another lift installed by the Pitchers at Santa Fe Ski Basin was the Alpine Bowl Poma. It went up into a subsection of Aspen Basin and is home today to such excellent runs as Alpine, Camp Robber, the tree run Central Park, Lobo, and Marmot. The same terrain can be reached now by both the Tesuque Peak Chair and the Millennium, and the surface lift is gone. (Courtesy PFC.)

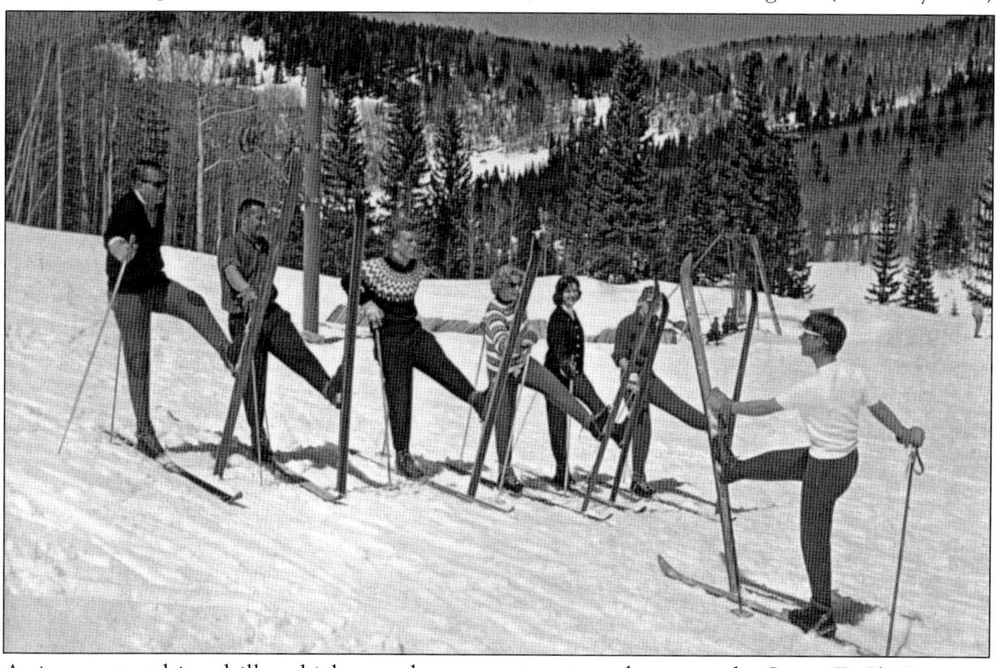

A tips-up stretching drill, or kick-turn demonstration, is underway at the Santa Fe Ski Basin in this photograph from the inside back cover of the November 1960 issue of *New Mexico* magazine. It was taken by the notable Harvey Caplin of Corrales, New Mexico, whose historical treasure trove includes some 50,000 photographs. (Courtesy NMSM.)

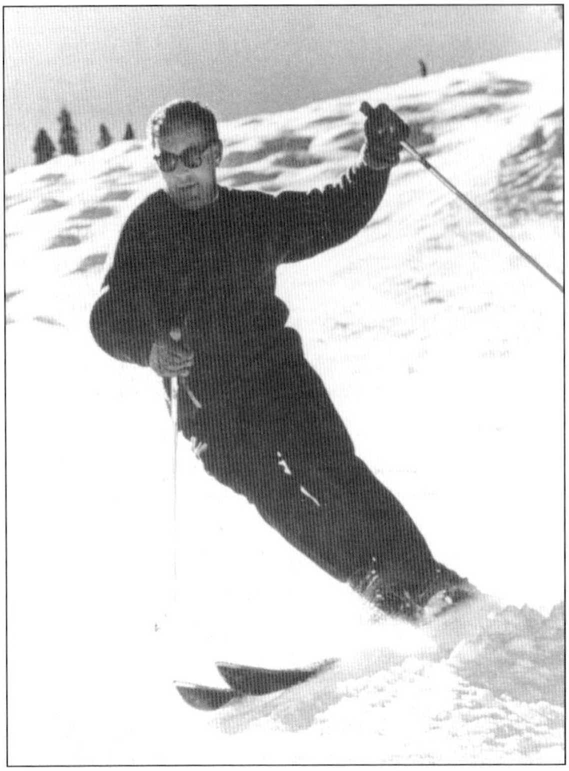

Santa Fe Ski Basin's head ski instructor Mike Leahy demonstrates the latest in form and style on the slopes in the 1960s. Instruction programs have been central to the ski area since its early days under Ernie Blake. Today, it has programs designed for toddlers to seniors, plus intensive workshops, multiple disciplines, and private group options under ski school director Bill Gould. (Courtesy PFC.)

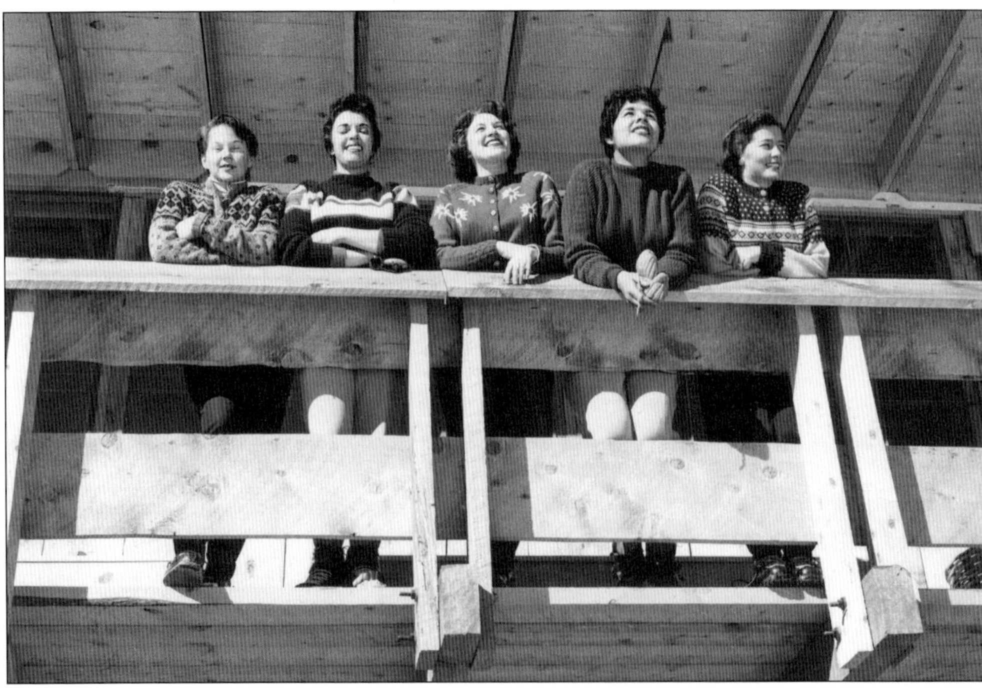

Santa Fe's motto is "the City Different," and its clientele of the 1950s and 1960s followed suit. Here, a group of Santa Feans gather on the upper balcony of the Sierra Lodge at Santa Fe Ski Basin. A good-looking wool sweater was de rigueur in those days. (Courtesy PCF.)

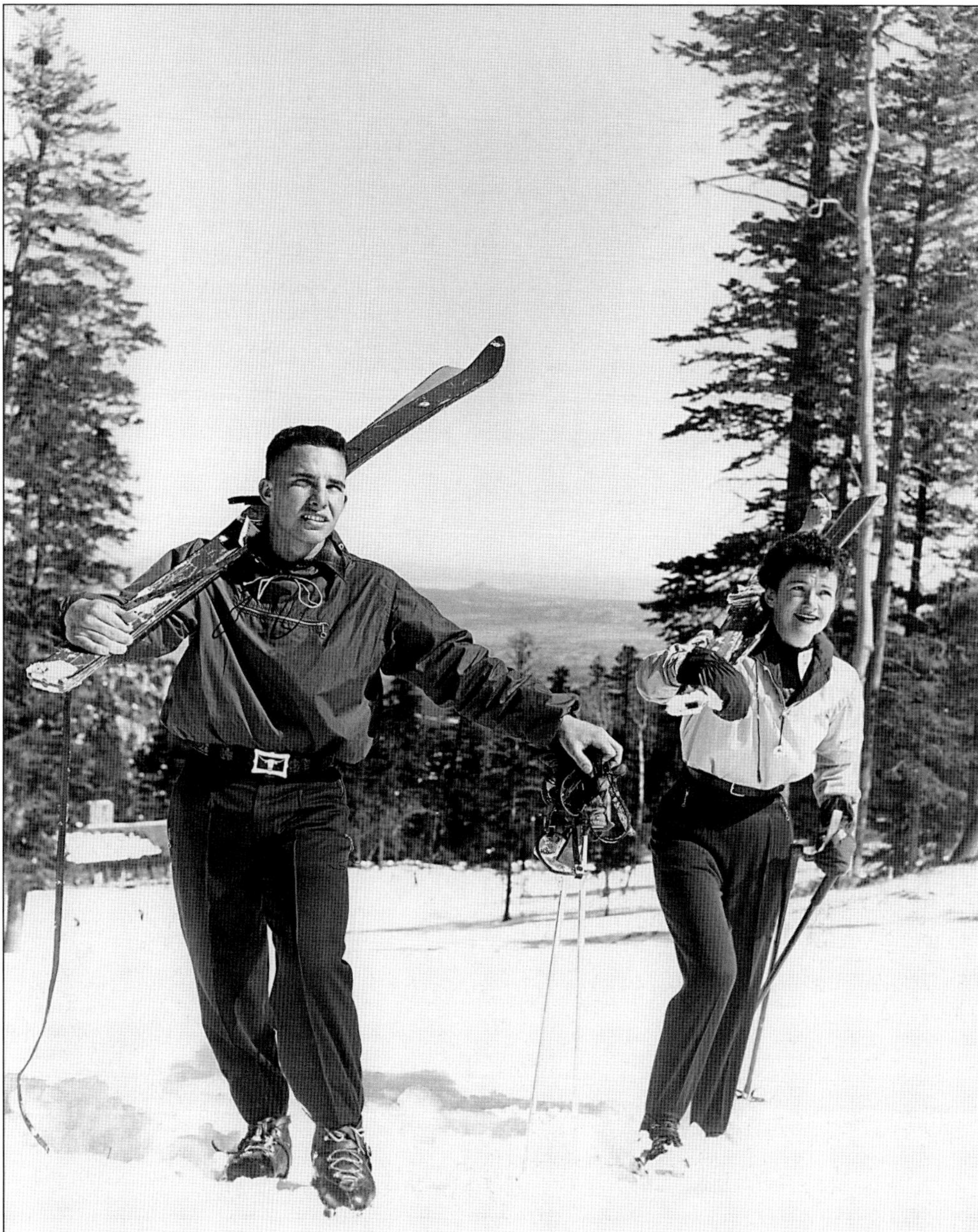

Sid Cutter (left) and Jeanne Eastep model the latest ski fashions, including a cool belt buckle, at La Madera in 1952. The City of Albuquerque took over operating La Madera in 1949, but after several poor snow years, it turned it back over to the La Madera Company, headed by Robert Nordhaus. A good snow year in 1952 made the operation viable, and future plans for new lifts were made. Sid Cutter went on to become a leader in the Albuquerque aviation community. In 1958, Ben Abruzzo purchased half ownership in La Madera, and in 1959, the road to Sandia Crest was paved by the US Forest Service, greatly improving the ski area's viability. (Courtesy SP.)

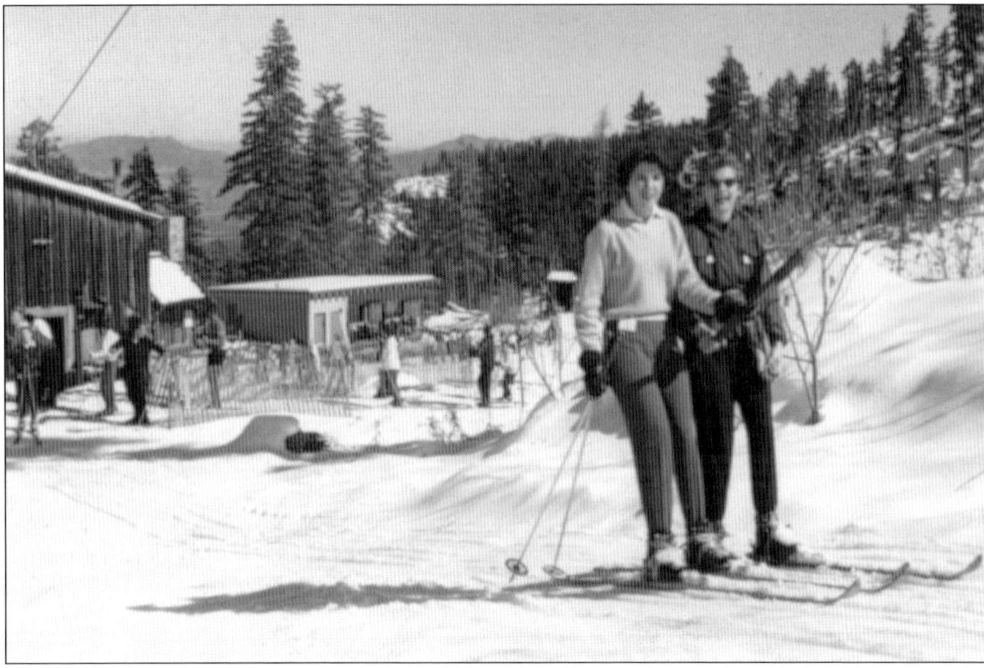

Two smiling women ride the Constam T-bar at La Madera in 1960. The 4,200-foot lift was installed in 1946 and was retired after a Stadeli double chairlift opened in 1963. They show unusual optimism about the rough ride ahead of them, which included deep troughs, extremely steep pitches, bare spots, ice, and flanks lined by thorny brambles. The building on the left is the lower terminal of the T-bar. Partly hidden behind it is the original log lodge built in 1938, and the building at center is the recently constructed café and snack bar. (Courtesy SP.)

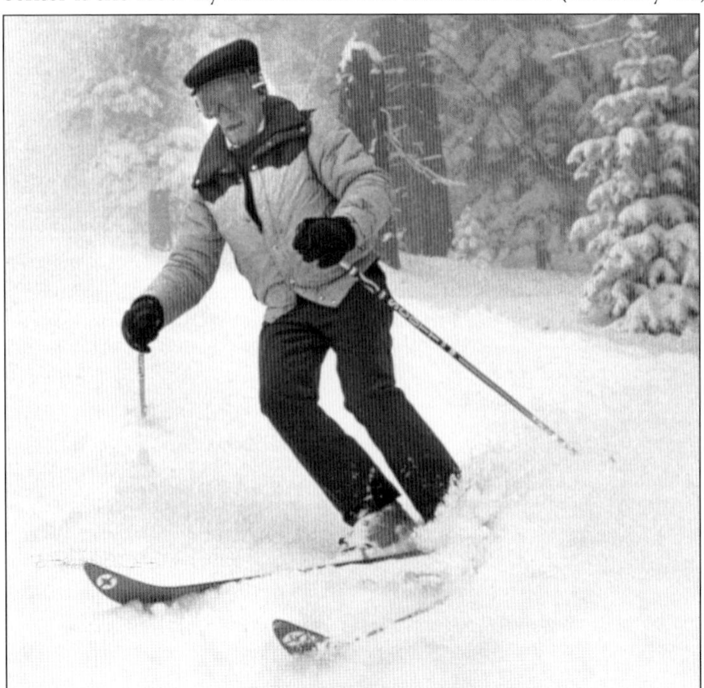

Robert Nordhaus, essentially the founder of La Madera and today's Sandia Peak, ended his active involvement in its operations in 1983 when he handed the ball off to Ben Abruzzo. But he continued to ski well into his 90th year, as seen in this image taken at Sandia Peak. A lawyer by training, he was renowned for his representation of American Indian tribes. The native son of New Mexico passed away at age 97 in 2007. (Courtesy SP.)

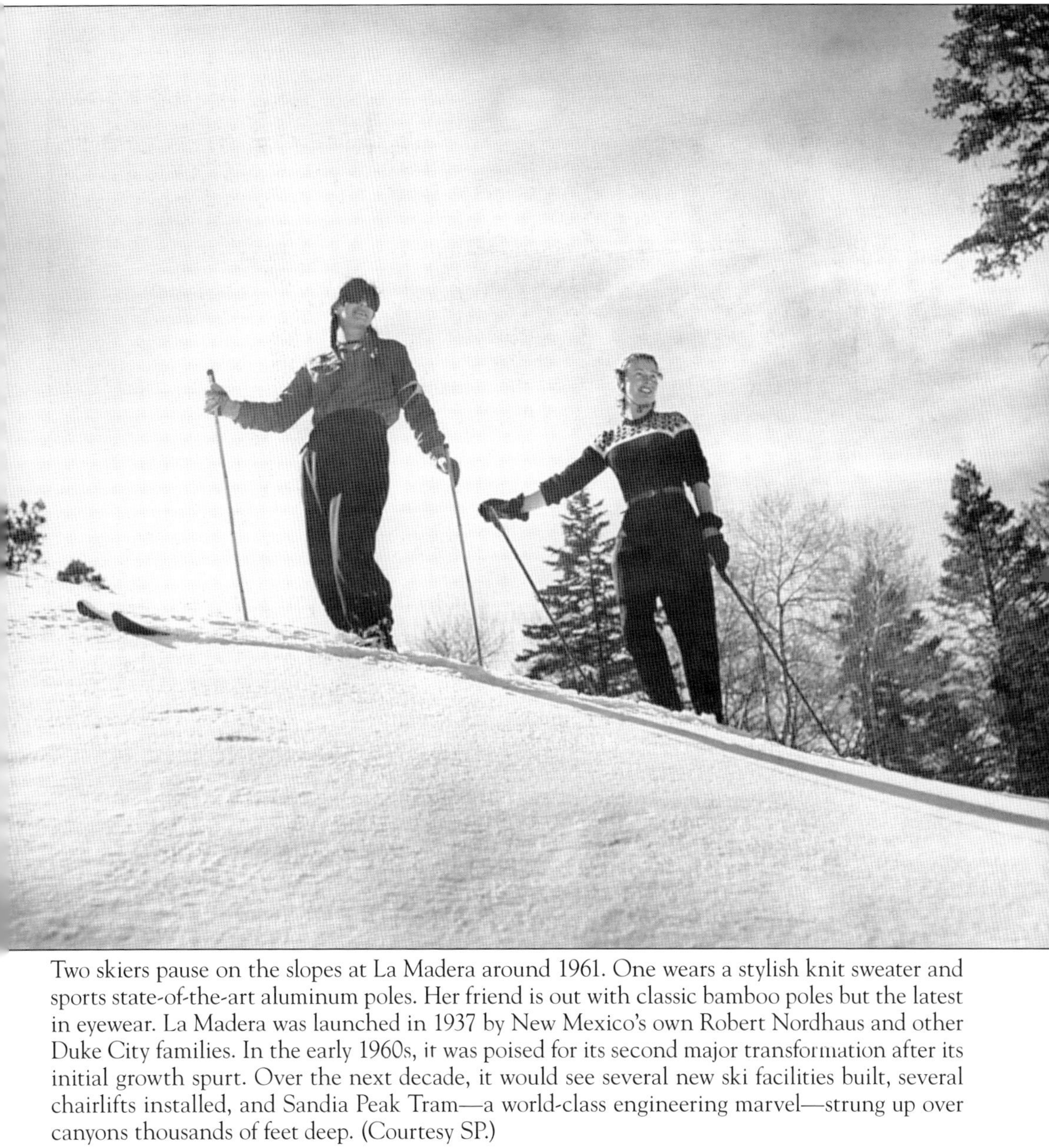

Two skiers pause on the slopes at La Madera around 1961. One wears a stylish knit sweater and sports state-of-the-art aluminum poles. Her friend is out with classic bamboo poles but the latest in eyewear. La Madera was launched in 1937 by New Mexico's own Robert Nordhaus and other Duke City families. In the early 1960s, it was poised for its second major transformation after its initial growth spurt. Over the next decade, it would see several new ski facilities built, several chairlifts installed, and Sandia Peak Tram—a world-class engineering marvel—strung up over canyons thousands of feet deep. (Courtesy SP.)

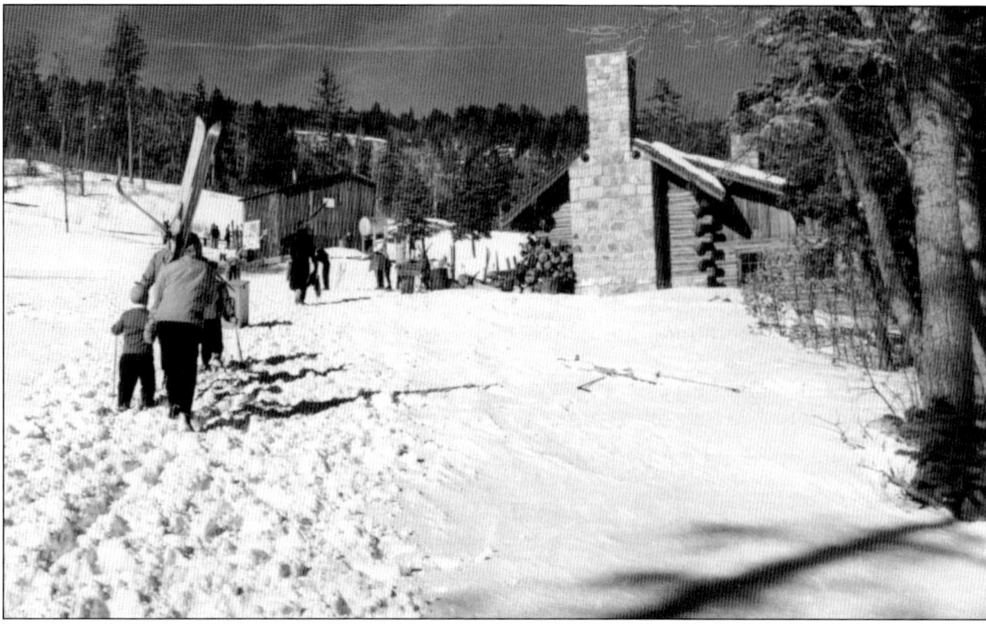

A ski family hikes up from the parking lot at La Madera in 1960 to the base area lifts and facilities. The building in the center is the bottom terminal of the Constam T-bar lift, and on the right is the day lodge, built by the CCC in 1938. In 1960, the ski lifts at La Madera consisted of a short rope tow on the beginner hill; the T-bar, which reached about two thirds of the way up the mountain; and a short platter pull lift above the top of the T-bar. (Courtesy SP.)

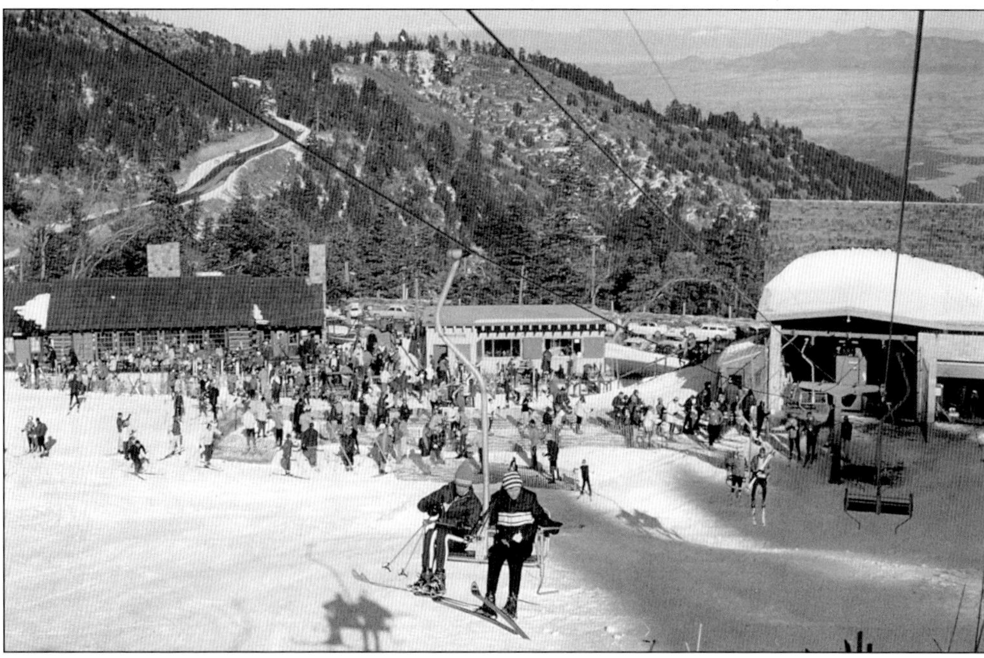

With big plans in the making, La Madera was rechristened Sandia Peak in the early 1960s. This photograph shows the new Stadeli double chair, which opened in 1963 and was the first lift to reach the top of the area along the rim of the Sandias and also accessed the new Summit House Restaurant. The old log lodge is on the left, and the new café and snack bar building is on the right. (Courtesy SP.)

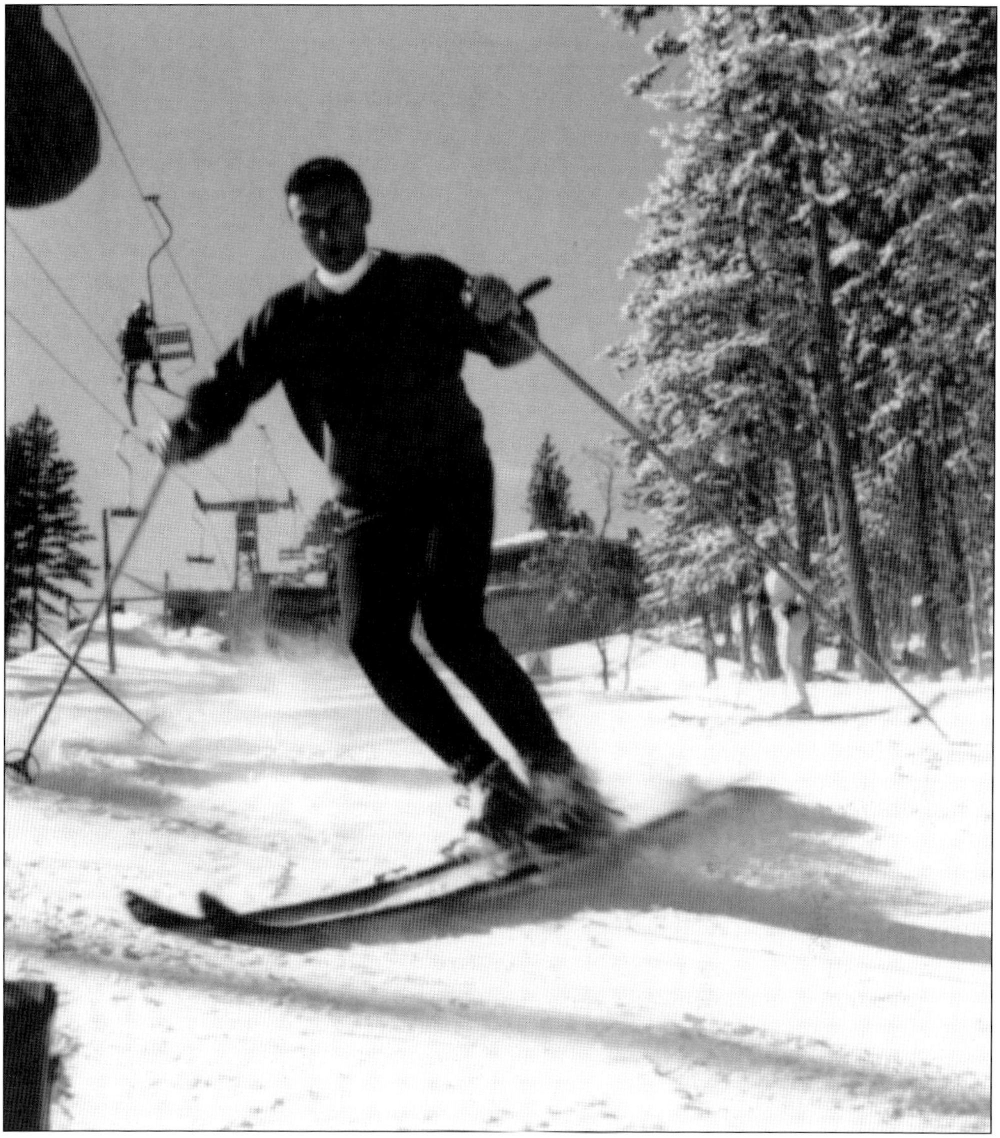

Skier Fred Dalem shows off his stuff on Exhibition at Sandia Peak in 1966 near the top of the newish double chair and Summit House. He is creating a nice flex in his skis at the bottom of this turn and is about to initiate his upward move to release his edges and begin his next turn. His ability was appropriate, as he directed Sandia's ski school from 1962 until 1970, when he perished in a car accident. The 1970 season ushered in another big change here, the opening of its second chairlift, the 4,000-foot Chair No. 2. Fred's Run at the top of Chair No. 2 commemorates Dalem. The award-winning Summit House in the background was designed by Max Flatow. (Courtesy SP.)

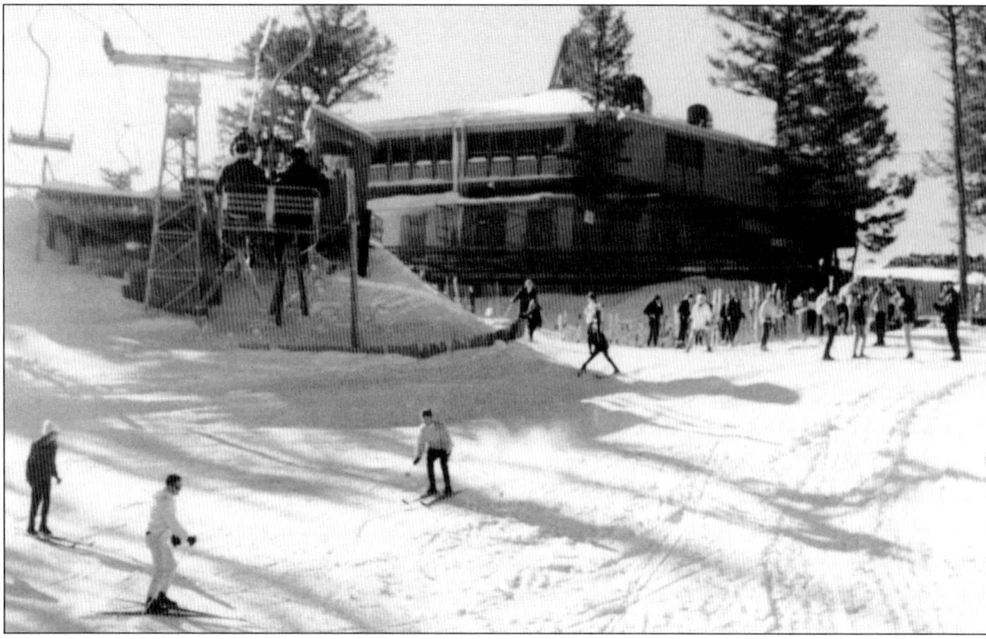

Sandia Peak's top is seen here, including skiers on Exhibition, the terminus of the 7,500-foot double chair, the octagonal Summit House restaurant and bar, and the top of the Sandia Peak Tram. The chair towers still stand, as does the tram—with new cables and cars—but the Summit House was replaced in 2020 with the restaurant and bar Ten 3, named for its elevation. All Summit House provisions had to be brought up on the chairlift its first winters, and many other challenges were overcome to provide food and drink at this elevation. (Photograph by Dick Kent, courtesy SP.)

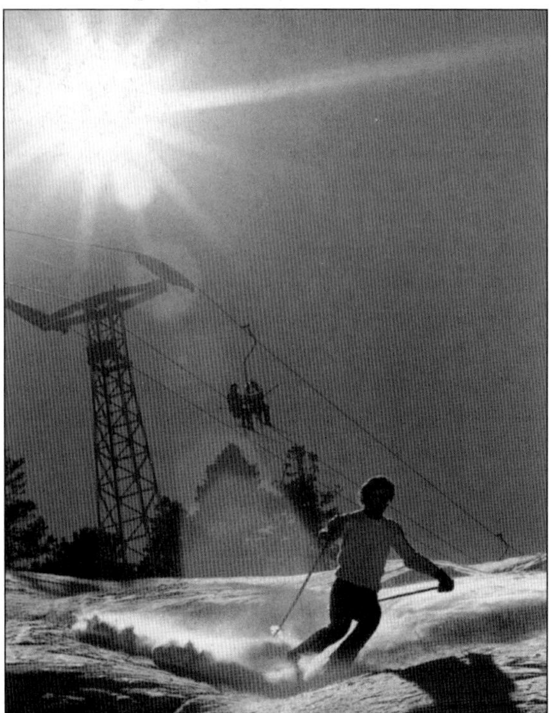

Another cool action image was captured by Ken Gallard of a skier in some big moguls at Sandia Peak in the 1970s. With declining snowfalls in later years, grooming took on additional importance. In 1978 or 1979, Sandia acquired a then novel blade for a snowcat that allowed for more precise grooming. Benny Abruzzo recalls in Pamela Salmon's book, "The ability to push the snow with the blade cats became the real art and science of keeping the ski area open." (Courtesy SP.)

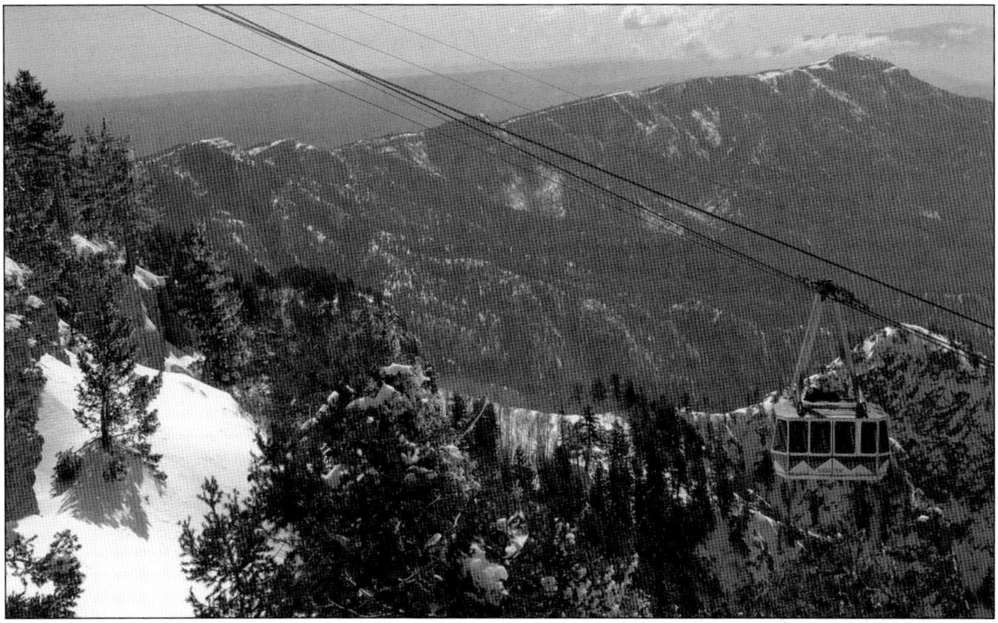

The greatest single evolutionary step in Sandia Peak's long history was the opening of Sandia Peak Tram in 1966. The tram cuts access from Albuquerque, via car, from about an hour to a 15-minute ascent from the city's edge amidst yucca and cactus to snow-laden fir trees. It is seen here approaching its summit terminal. From there, it is a minute walk to the ski slopes at the top of the ski area. The tram took more than two years to build and cost roughly $2 million. (Courtesy SP.)

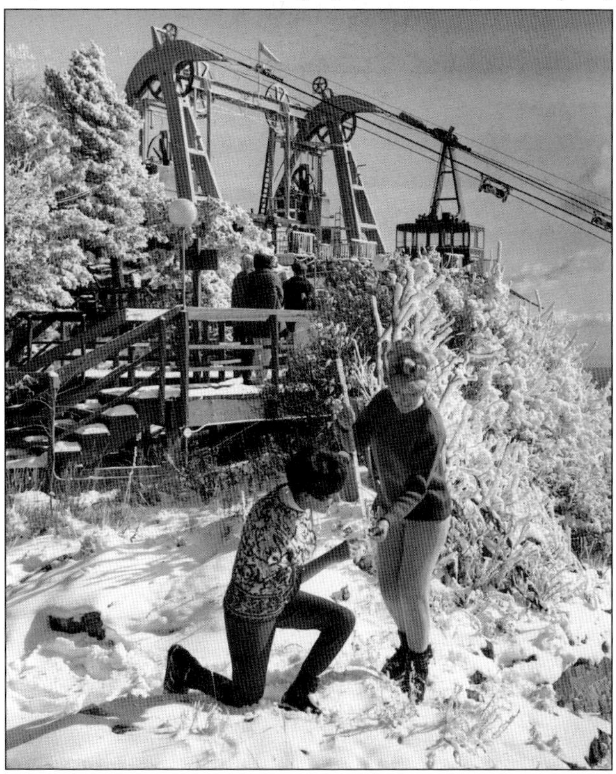

Anita Long (left) and Pat Abruzzo are measuring snow depth at Sandia Peak. Behind them is the top terminal of Sandia Peak Tram, a world-class engineering marvel that rises some 4,000 feet from Albuquerque, giving the city perhaps the nation's fastest urban-area-to-skiing experience. It was inspired by a ski tour of the Alps in 1956 by Robert and Virginia Nordhaus and Ernie and Rhoda Blake. Swiss engineers helped erect it with local construction company Martin and Luther, but New Mexicans like George Boyden and Jay Blackwood had to figure out how to safely run it. (Courtesy SP.)

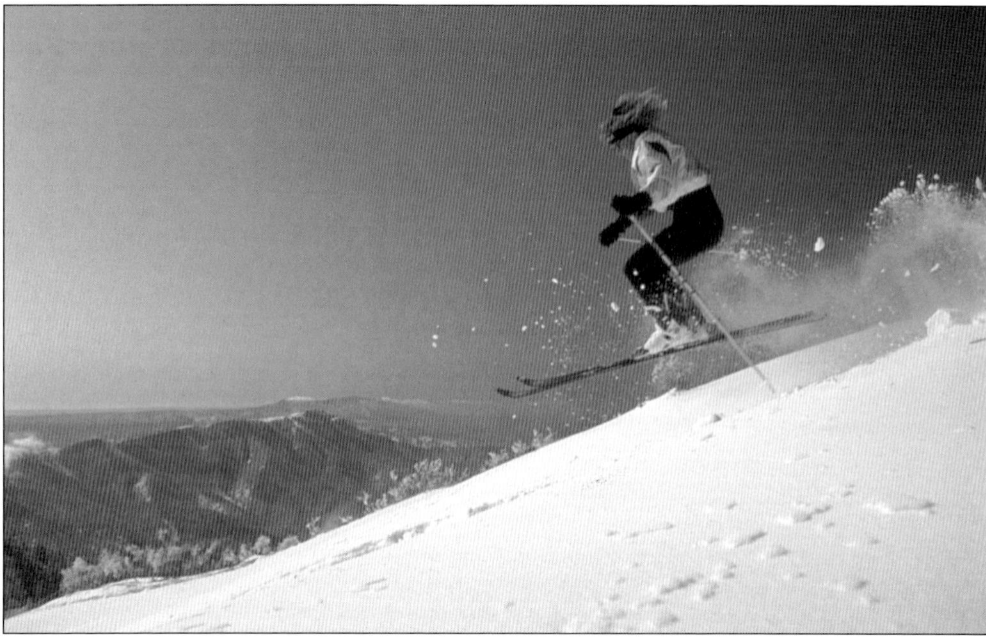

This hotdog skier at Sandia Peak around 1975 epitomizes the evolution in skiing that had occurred since the early 1960s. She is skiing aggressively, airing it out a bit, and wearing waterproof and stretchable fabrics tucked into her high plastic boots. Topping it all off is the headband. Behind her stretch the Sandias, running south toward the distant Manzano Mountains. (Courtesy SP.)

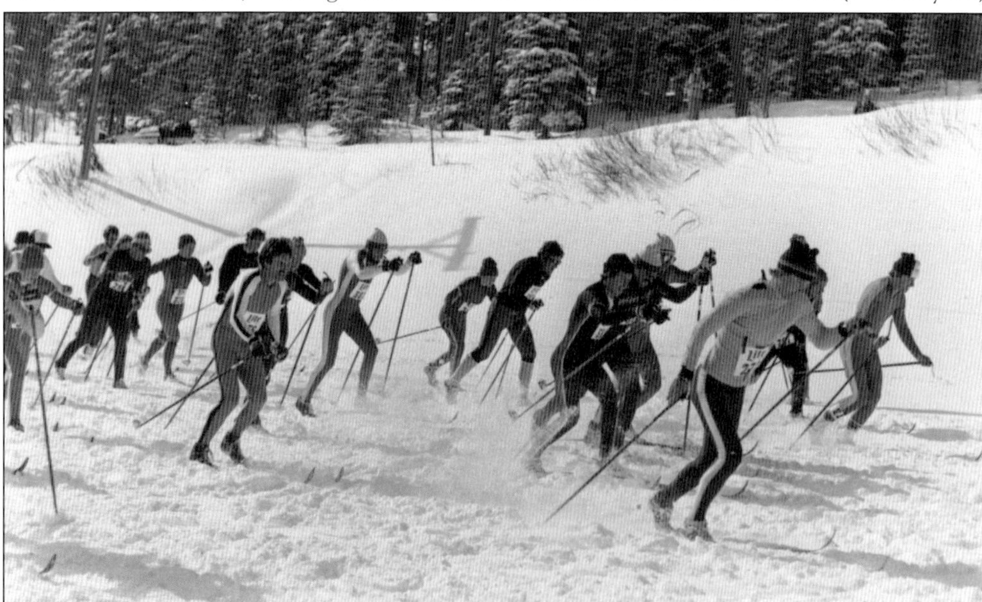

The Sandias have always attracted cross-country skiers, who mainly utilize the trail network at the summit of the range. But the ski area began to host organized races in the 1990s, as seen in this image, and served as home to the University of New Mexico's Nordic team. In the 1960s and 1970s, several cross-country clubs were founded in the state, and extensive guidebooks were published, including by Sam Beard, Kay Matthews, Jim Burns, and Cheryl Lemanski. (Courtesy SP.)

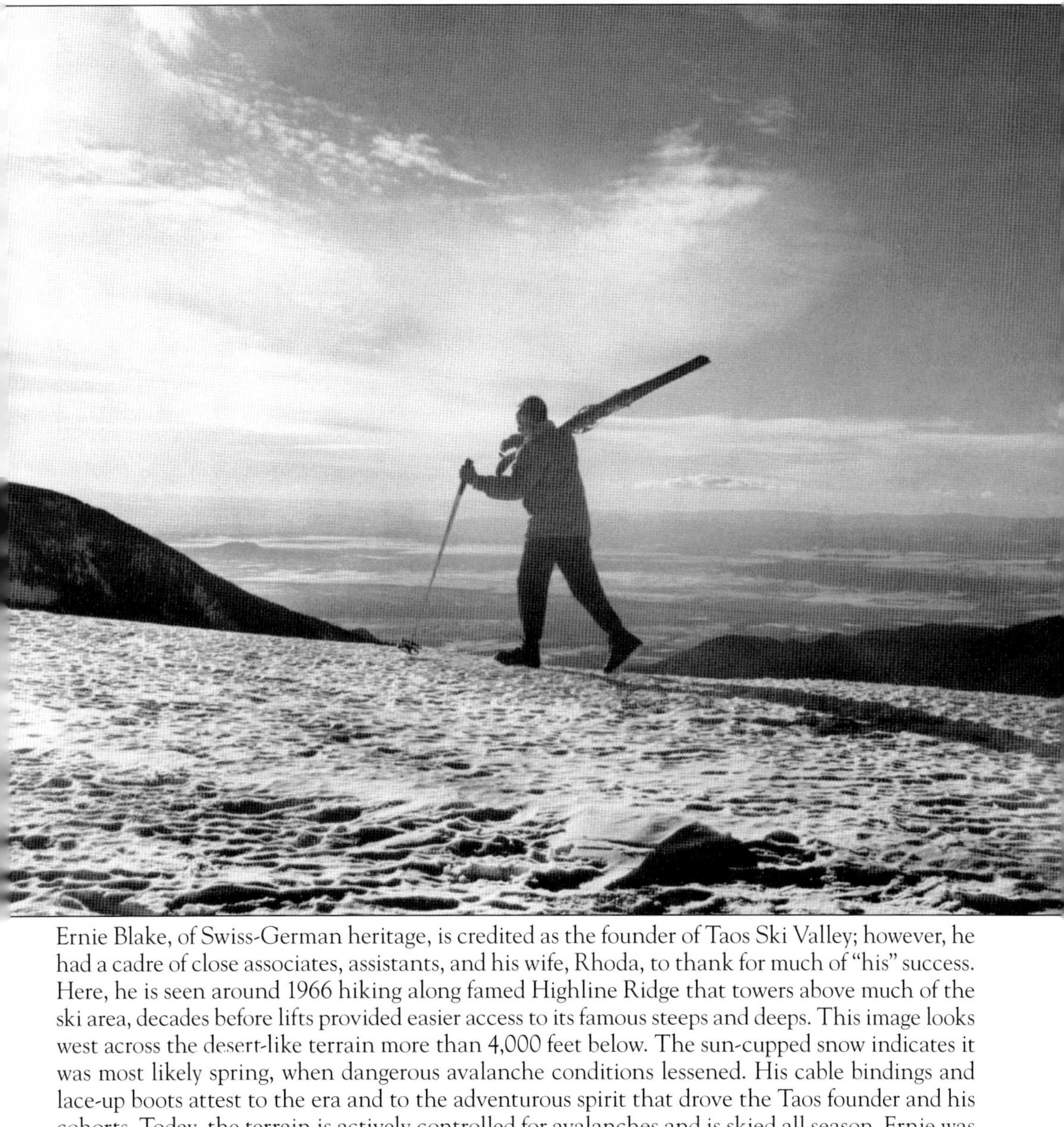

Ernie Blake, of Swiss-German heritage, is credited as the founder of Taos Ski Valley; however, he had a cadre of close associates, assistants, and his wife, Rhoda, to thank for much of "his" success. Here, he is seen around 1966 hiking along famed Highline Ridge that towers above much of the ski area, decades before lifts provided easier access to its famous steeps and deeps. This image looks west across the desert-like terrain more than 4,000 feet below. The sun-cupped snow indicates it was most likely spring, when dangerous avalanche conditions lessened. His cable bindings and lace-up boots attest to the era and to the adventurous spirit that drove the Taos founder and his cohorts. Today, the terrain is actively controlled for avalanches and is skied all season. Ernie was known as a skilled, strong, extremely competitive skier who challenged all comers in speed and daring-do. The photograph was taken by Wolfgang "Willy" Lert, an editor for *Ski* magazine and US sales representative for Bogner ski apparel. (Courtesy TSV.)

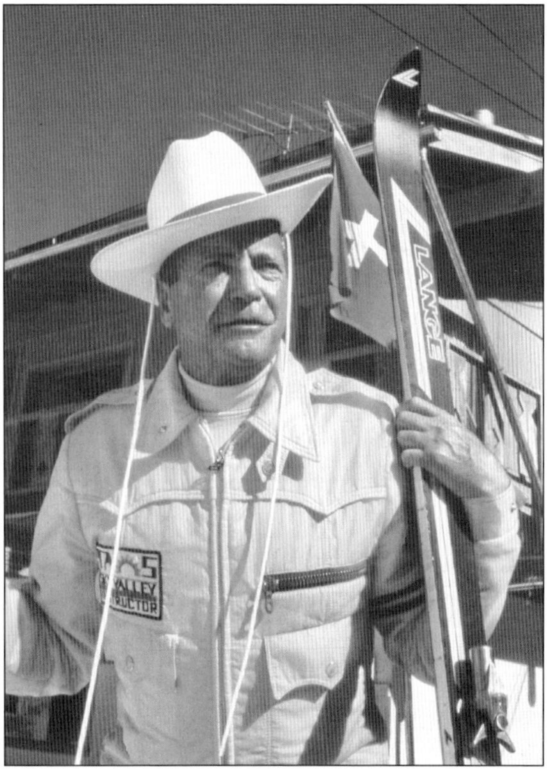

Ernie Blake of Taos Ski Valley wore many hats, literally. He had a notable way of connecting to diverse people and knew the value of a hat in solidifying relationships. Here, sometime in the 1970s, he dons a cowboy hat—the headgear of many northern New Mexicans and TSV's many visitors from Texas. (Courtesy BFC.)

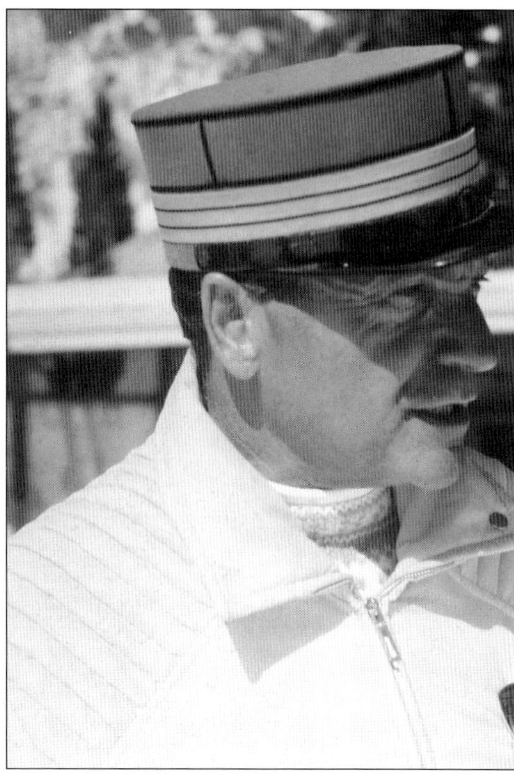

Here, Ernie Blake sports an official hat of a Swiss Army colonel. "It was a gift, I think, from Walter Widmer, and was genuine," notes son Mickey Blake, "I saw Swiss men visiting here stiffen at the sight of it." Ernie was known for his dictatorial style, fiery temperament, and strong opinions, but he was essentially a people person. He fired and then rehired many employees over the years. He died in 1989 at age 75. (Courtesy BFC.)

Ernie Blake and Rhoda Blake are seen here atop Highline Ridge at Taos, most likely sometime in the 1980s. Rhoda, as recounted earlier, was essential to the ski area's success, filling many roles, from ski tuner and instructor to lift operator, staff cook, mother, and mechanic. She also had a great eye for trail design, walking and skiing the mountain to lay out its early intermediate runs. She outlived Ernie by decades, dying in 2016. (Courtesy BFC.)

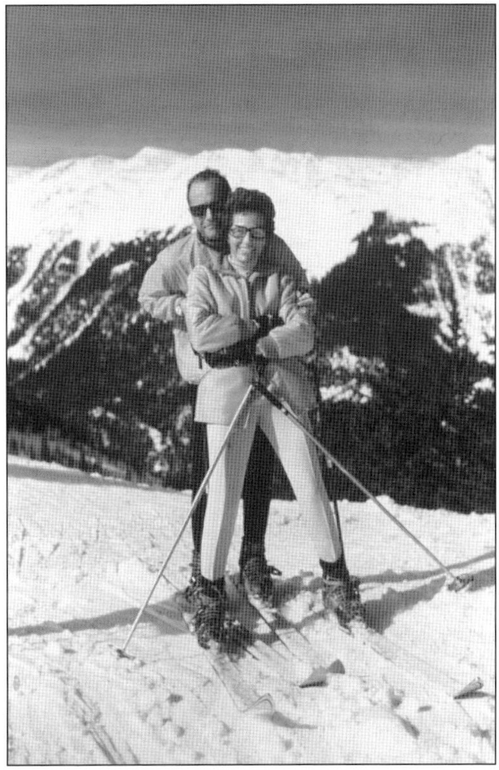

Pictured in the late 1960s or early 1970s is a mixed bag of TSV staff. From left to right are Georgia Hutton, Chilton Anderson, Clark Funk, Al Rosen, Rhoda Blake, and Ernie Blake. Some are sporting concho belts, a popular form of adornment created by Navajo silversmiths. Hutton was an essential assistant to Ernie Blake, Anderson was initially a lift operator whose height was helpful in restringing lift cables when they jumped off their tracks, Funk became a force in the ski school, and Rosen was a local mover and shaker. (Courtesy BFC.)

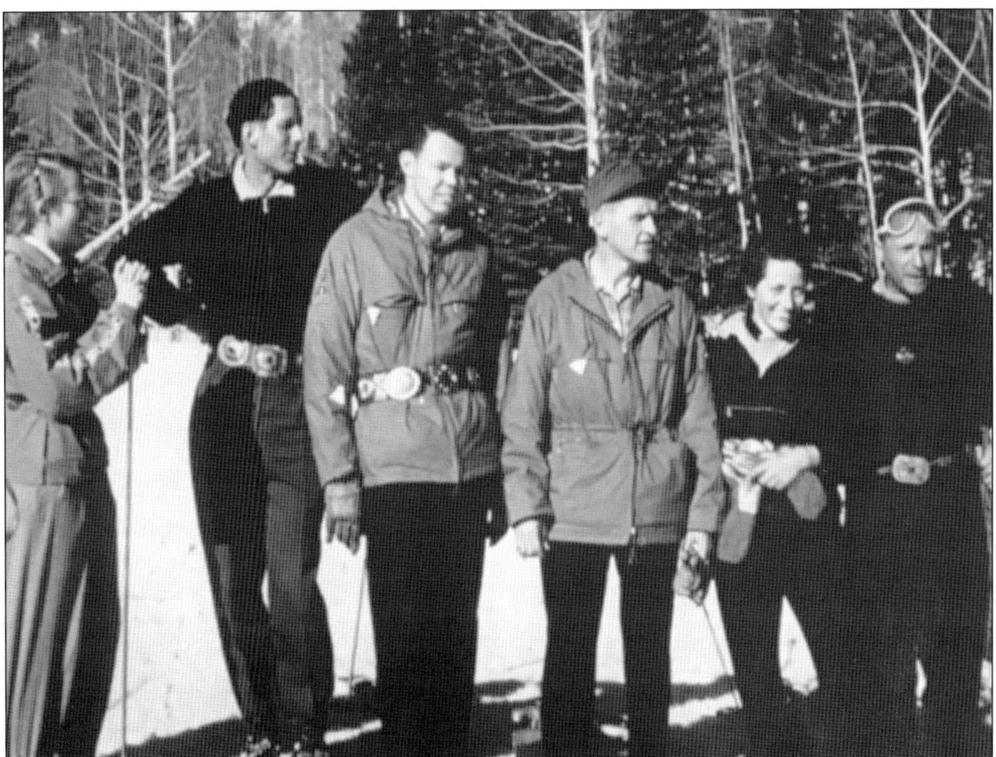

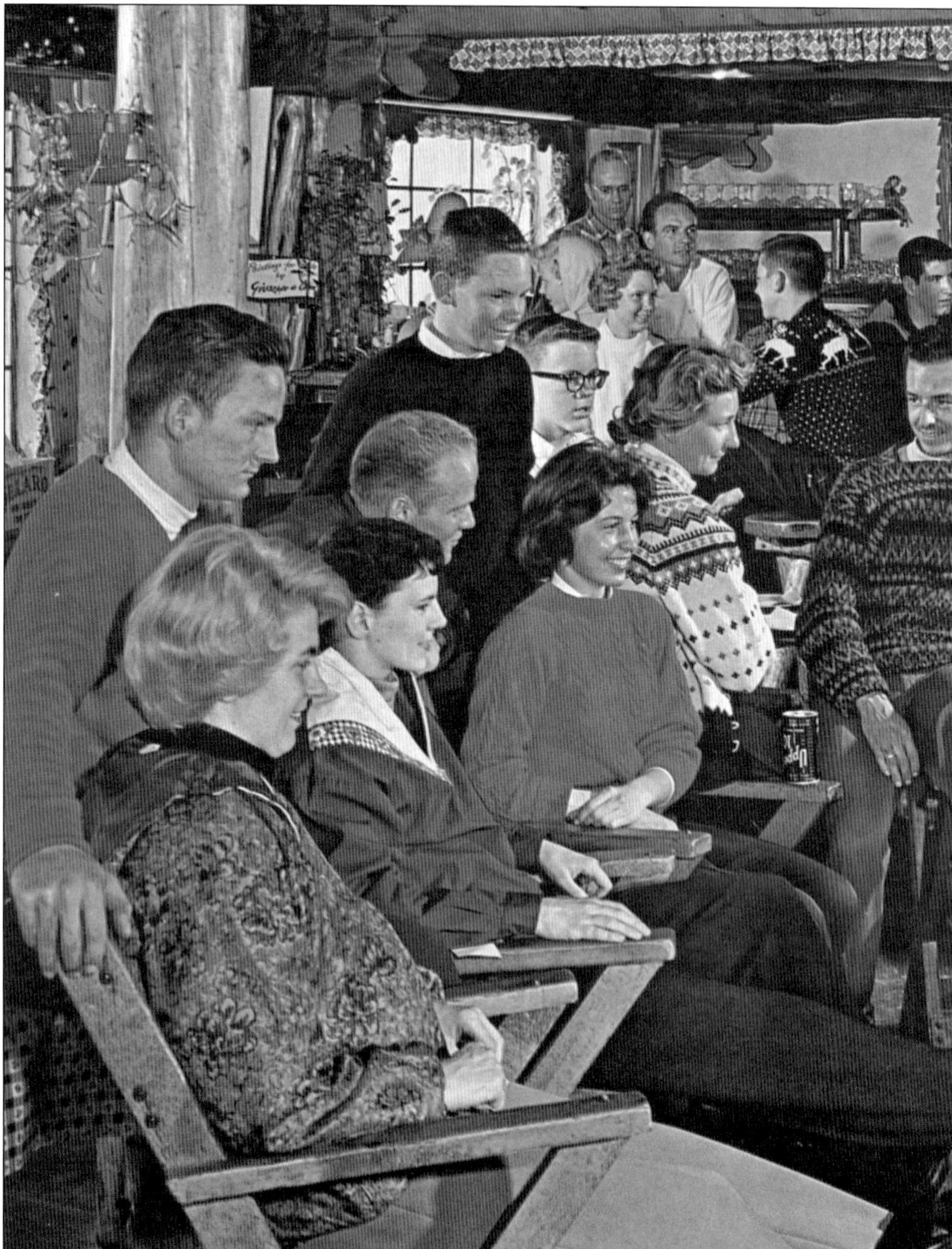

This image for *New Mexico* magazine in the 1960s portrays the interior of the beloved Hotel St. Bernard. The crowd is focused on the fireplace, seen in the adjacent photograph. It served as the eternal flame of the valley, as did the hotel's founder, Jean Mayer, seen here fourth from the left. He passed away in 2020 but skied almost up to his final days. The hotel was the first to be built from the ground up at TSV and opened in 1960. It had deeply loyal employees, many returning decade after decade to work for Jean, who was as charming as he was a fantastic skier and excellent cook. Guests often returned here annually for generations, and many a marriage began around its long communal dining tables. (Courtesy TSV.)

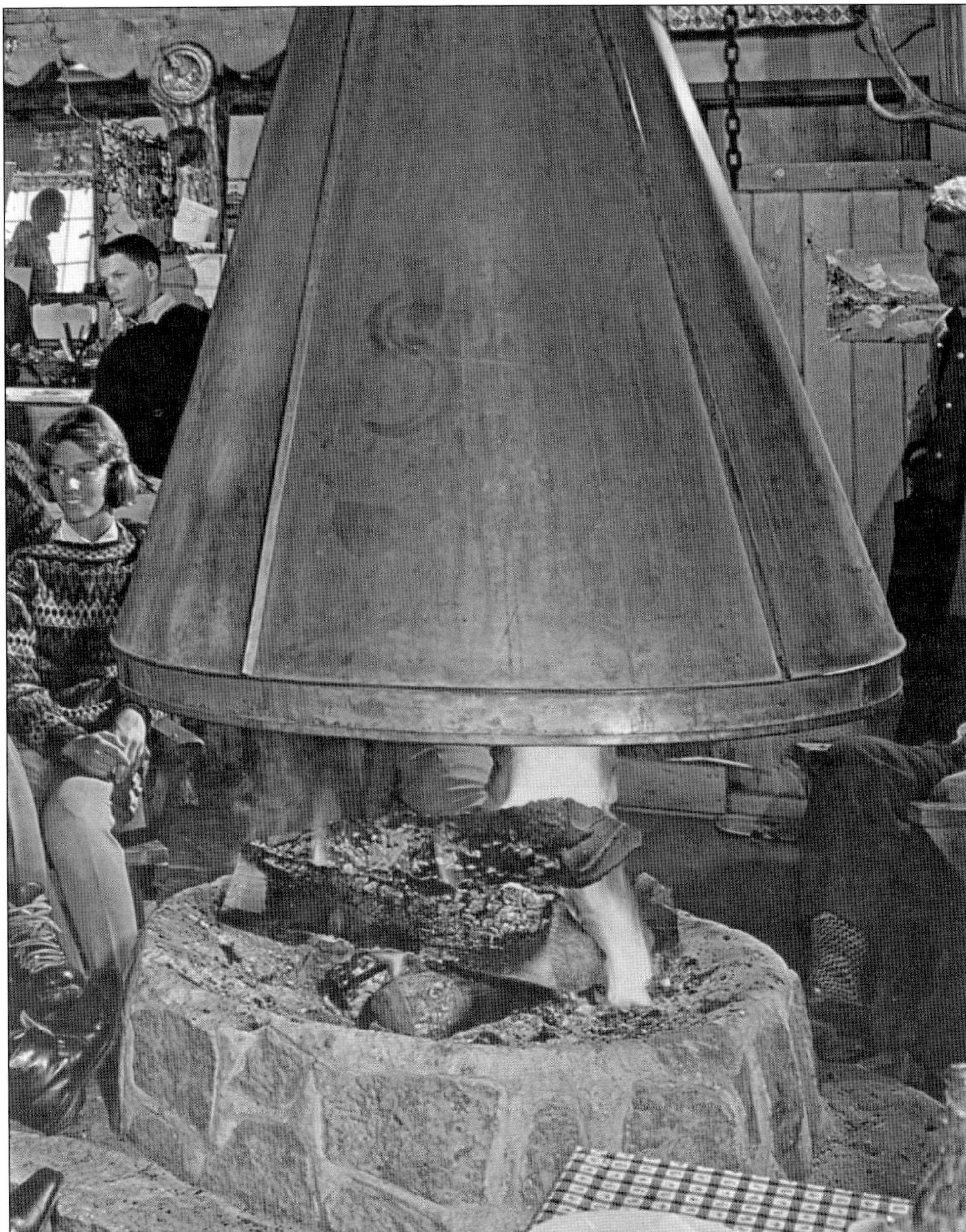

The copper-sheathed circular fireplace at the Hotel St. Bernard was the center of attention since the lodge's founding in 1960. Many a soaked, frozen child over the years perched on its stone bench thawing out, while adults scorched their woolen socks around it. The hotel's tiny but sufficient bar is back in the left corner. This large, open room also served as the dining room, where guests gathered for every delightful meal during the typical six-day stay. The lodge provided accommodations, dining, and twice-a-day lessons in the resort's acclaimed ski school in its popular Ski Week package deals. It looks exactly the same today, though with founder Jean Mayer's death in 2020, its ownership has transferred to Taos Ski Valley Inc., and it is currently closed. It is hoped this fireplace will warm patrons again in the years to come. (Courtesy TSV.)

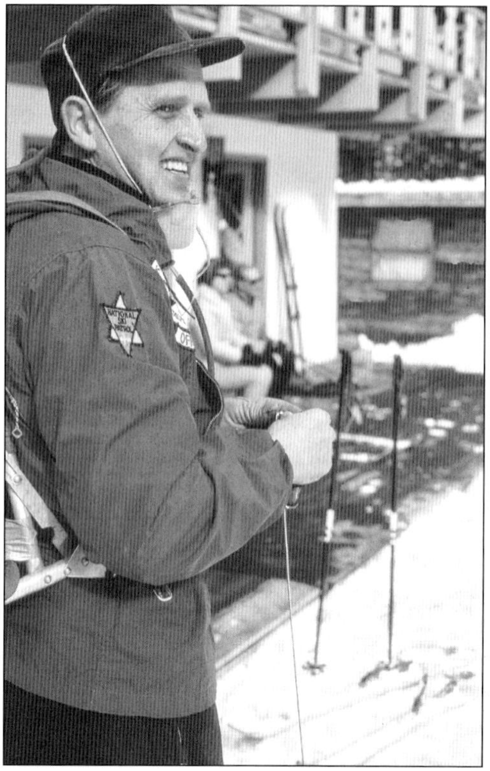

Dr. Al Rosen, seen here at Taos Ski Valley in the 1960s, was a diehard skier. A local mover and shaker, he was the first man in Taos who Ernie Blake approached with the idea of launching TSV, and he helped get the ski area road improved and electricity installed. He had bad lungs and skied with heavy oxygen tanks strapped to his back. Al's Run is named for him. (Courtesy TSV.)

Here, Pete Totemoff shows that he still has what it takes, executing a nice turn in wind-compacted powder at Taos Ski Valley sometime in the 1970s or 1980s. Though Totemoff ended his working career at Ski Santa Fe, where the mid-mountain restaurant and bar bear his name, he was always welcome at TSV and continued to ski here until his death. (Courtesy TSV.)

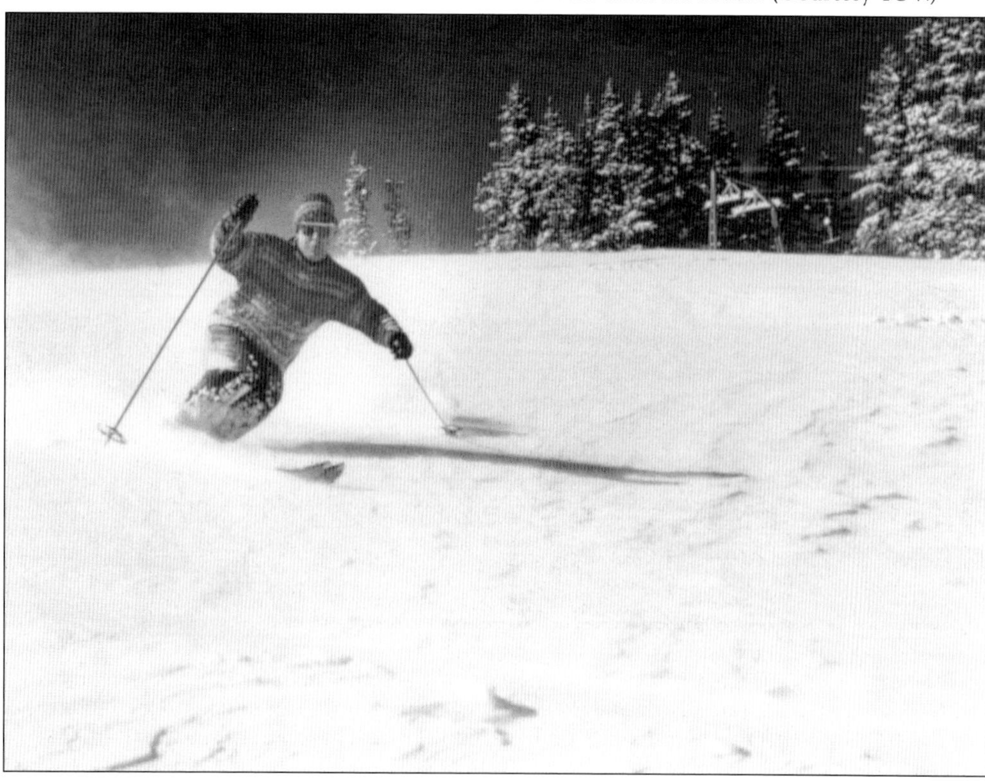

Jean and his brother Dadou Mayer have a few friendly words with guests in 1962 at their lodge in Taos Ski Valley, the Hotel St. Bernard. One season, Jean broke an ankle, and after a few weeks, he sawed off the cast, stating that a tight ski boot was as good as wearing a cast, and skied on it! (Photograph by Wolfgang "Willy" Lert, courtesy BFC.)

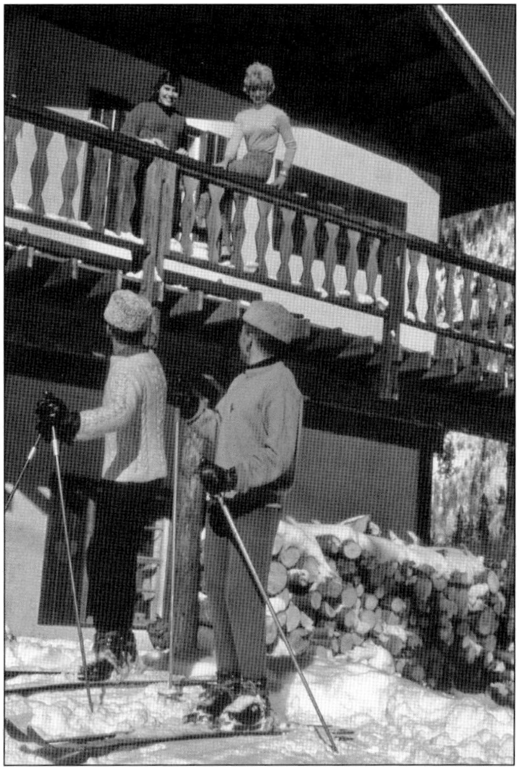

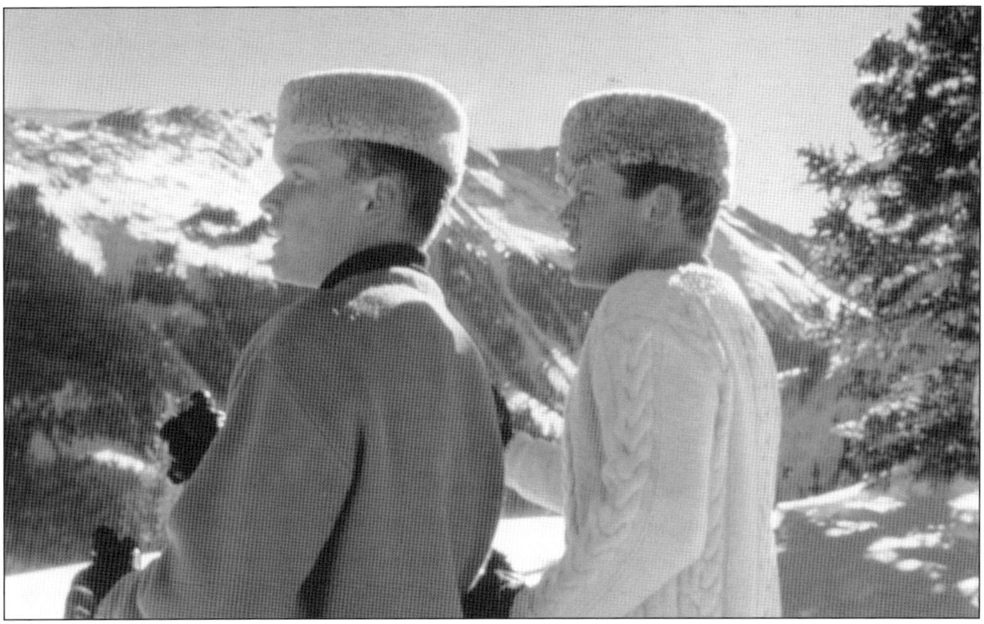

Brothers Dadou (left) and Jean Mayer stand atop Highline Ridge at Taos Ski Valley in this 1962 photograph taken by Bogner USA's representative Willy Lert. Their mother, Nicole "Maman," and father, Charles "Papa," also immigrated to New Mexico after their sons and played vital parts in helping to establish and run Red River Ski Area. (Photograph by Wolfgang "Willy" Lert, courtesy BFC.)

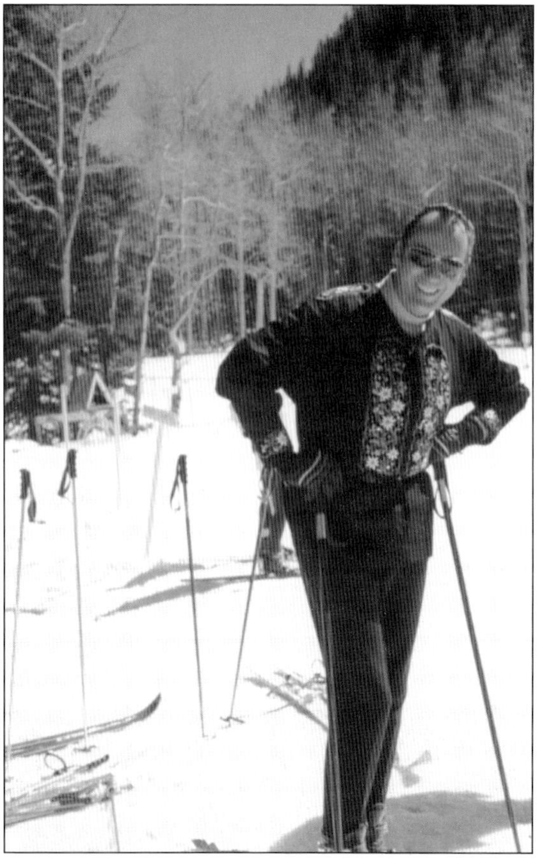

Yet another of the many Europeans Ernie Blake recruited to Taos was the handsome, courteous, graceful Swiss-raised Walter Widmer. Among his many roles, he directed the ticket office for many years. Ernie Blake filled his ski school with Austrian instructors, TSV's kitchens with French chefs, and various lodges with oodles of Germans, creating a unique hybrid American–European vibe that still characterizes the ski area today. (Courtesy BFC.)

This scene of Taos Ski Valley on a typical morning in the 1970s reveals the former Thunderbird Lodge in the back and T-bird Chalet to the left. The lodge began as a low-cost dorm-style accommodation, but under the Brownell family, it blossomed into a fine establishment. Both structures were later removed, and in their place, a new condominium complex is being built by the ski area management. (Courtesy TSV.)

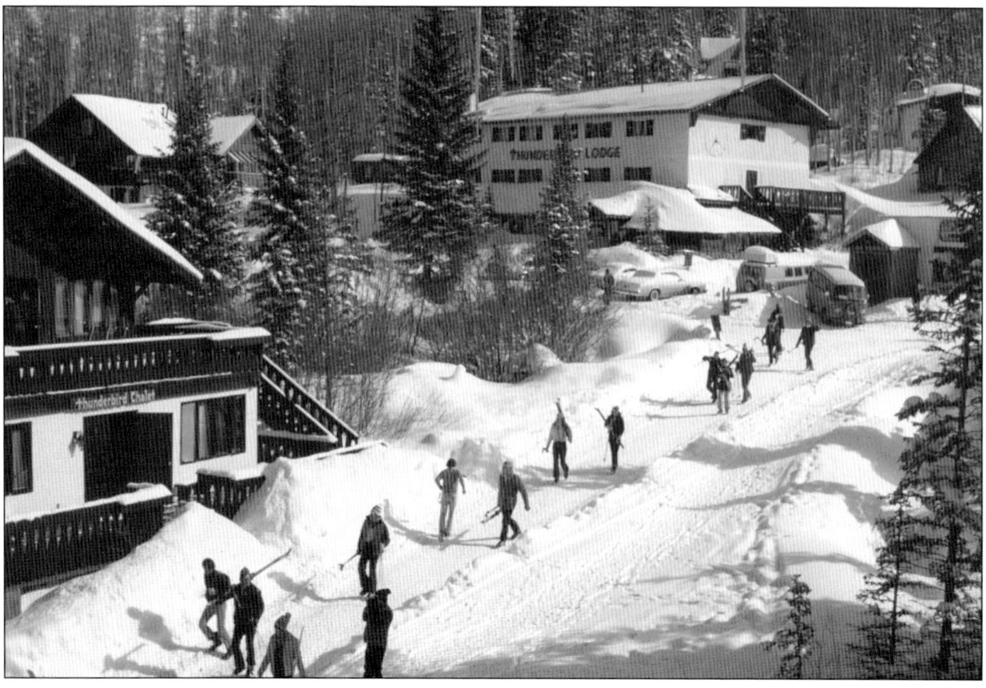

Five

A Maturing Industry 1980s and 1990s

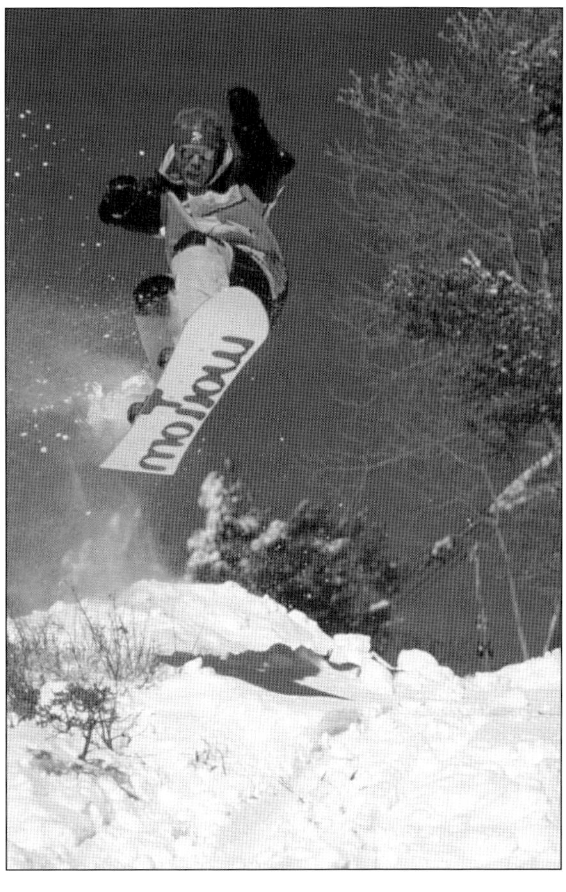

Richard Abruzzo, the youngest son of Ben and Pat Abruzzo, was an early convert to snowboarding and was often seen catching air on the slopes of his family-owned Sandia Peak and Ski Santa Fe. He was a world-class balloon pilot, but died in a tragic balloon crash off the coast of Italy in 2010. (Courtesy SP.)

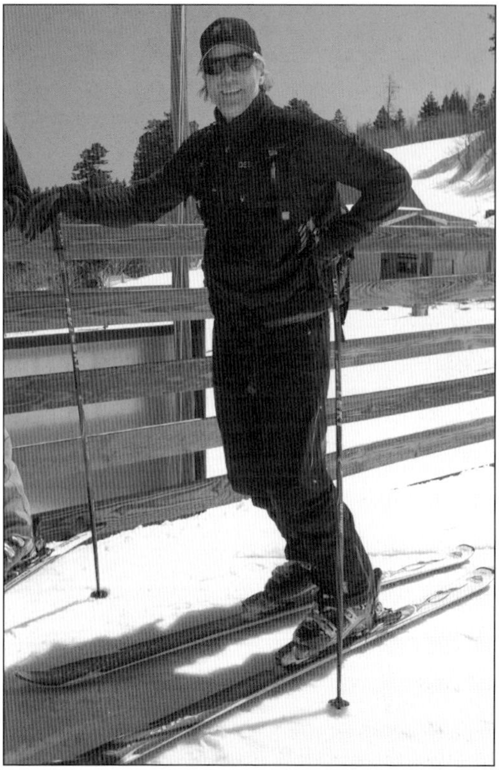

Benny Abruzzo, pictured here at Sandia Peak, was thrust into his father's shoes way sooner than expected. Ben Abruzzo Sr. had assumed full control of Sandia Peak in 1983, and in 1984, the family also acquired Santa Fe Ski Basin, changing its name to Ski Santa Fe. But in early 1985, Ben was killed in a small plane accident, and Benny was called upon to manage both ski areas. His son Ben Jr. directs operations today, but his father continues to provide on-the-ground guidance. (Courtesy SP.)

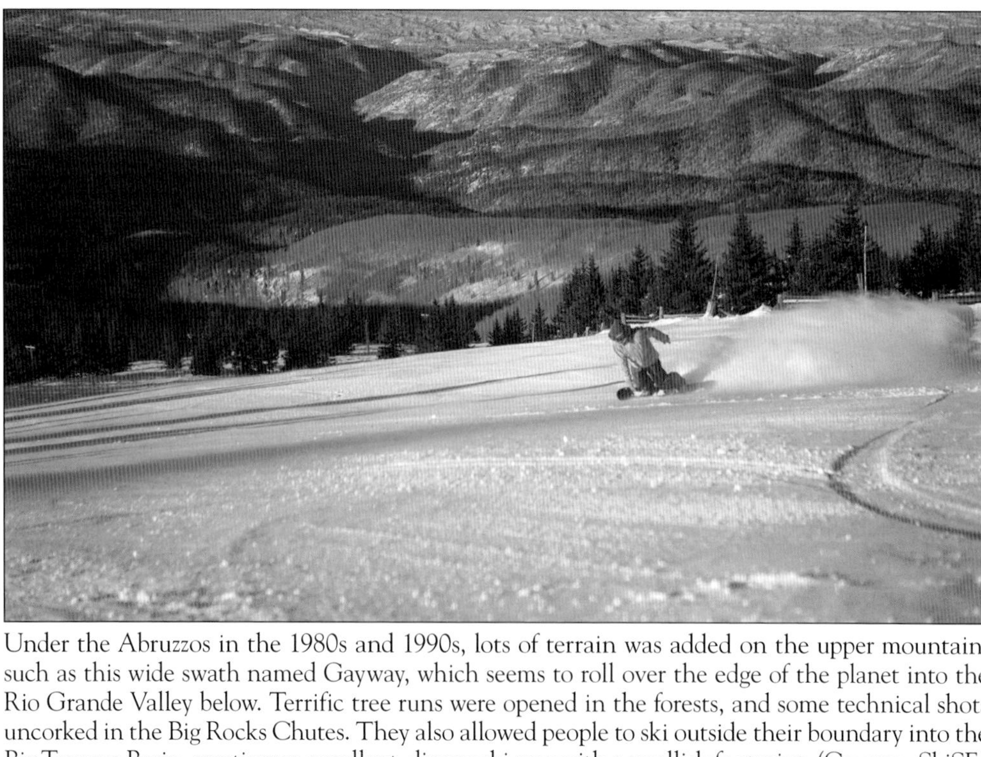

Under the Abruzzos in the 1980s and 1990s, lots of terrain was added on the upper mountain, such as this wide swath named Gayway, which seems to roll over the edge of the planet into the Rio Grande Valley below. Terrific tree runs were opened in the forests, and some technical shots uncorked in the Big Rocks Chutes. They also allowed people to ski outside their boundary into the Big Tesuque Basin, creating an excellent, diverse ski area with a smallish footprint. (Courtesy SkiSF.)

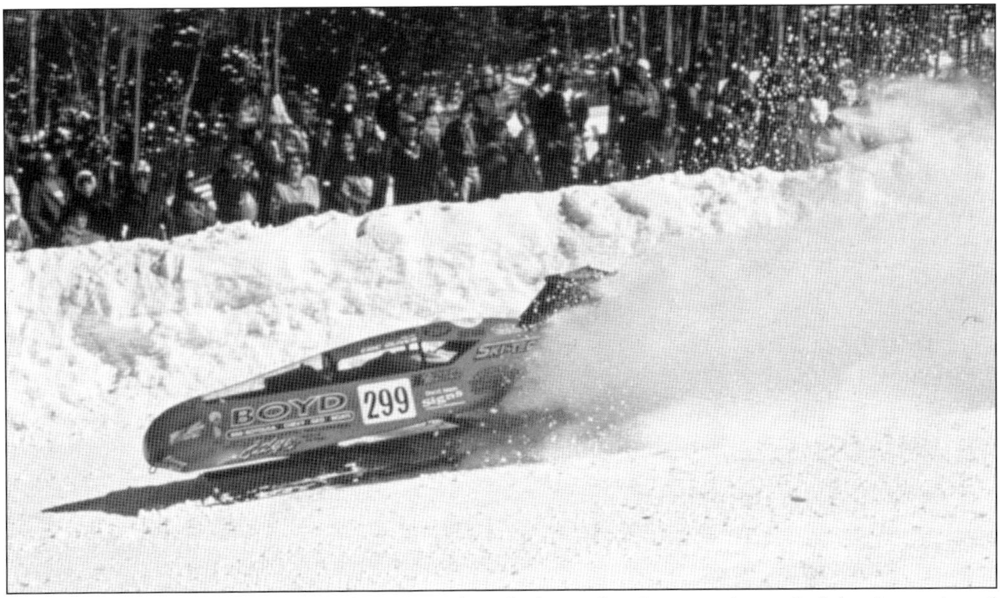

What began with lift operators riding snow shovels down the slopes at the end of the day at Angel Fire eventually turned into the annual World Champion Shovel Races. This included the modified division models seen here, which only required a shovel to be in contact with the snow. These beasts often hit speeds over 60 miles per hour, and were involved in some serious crashes. The unofficial motto was "Faster and faster, until the thrill of speed overcomes the fear of death." The event was killed following the 2019 competition. (Photograph by Bill Blankenburg, courtesy AFR.)

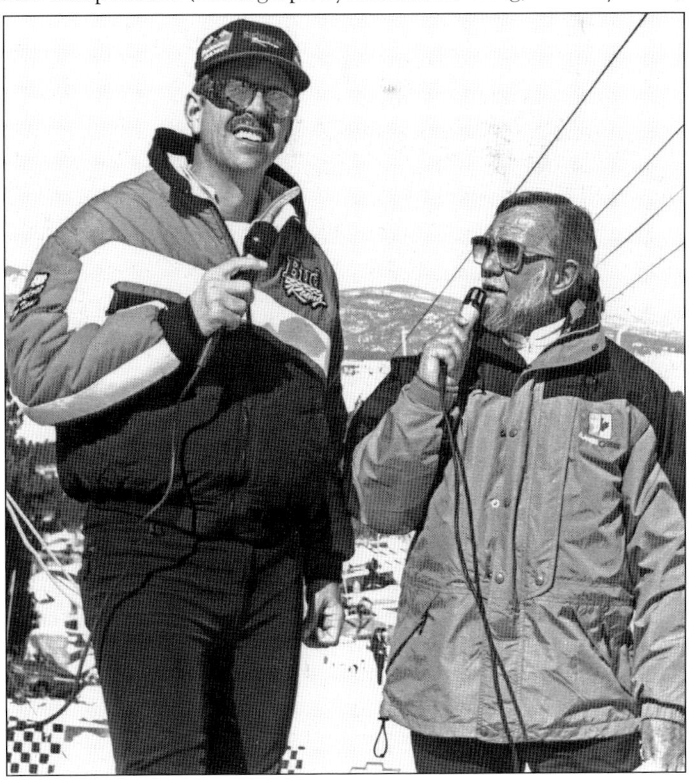

Angel Fire carved out a unique niche in winter sports with its annual World Champion Shovel Races, which were broadcast a few times by ESPN and ABC's *Wide World of Sports*. Seen here covering the competition are Curt Hanlen (left) and Bill Burgess. Starting in 1979, it grew into a multiday event with hundreds of participants coming from near and far. The elite shovelers clocked in at 60 miles per hour and higher. (Courtesy AFR.)

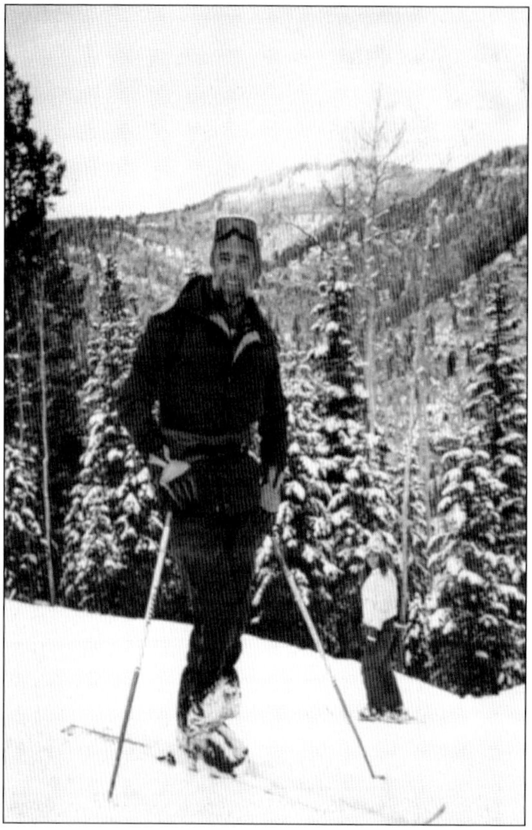

Sipapu continued to grow, slowly, over the 1980s and the 1990s. Here, founder Lloyd Bolander is seen around 1980, when he would have been 53. He eventually relinquished control to his adult son Bruce, who managed the area for several decades and continues to have a hand in its operation. At age 86, Lloyd died in December 2002. Sipapu is still an unpretentious, small, relaxed retreat, with an emphasis on its terrain park, and hosts lots of junior snowboarding and ski competitions. (Courtesy Bolander family.)

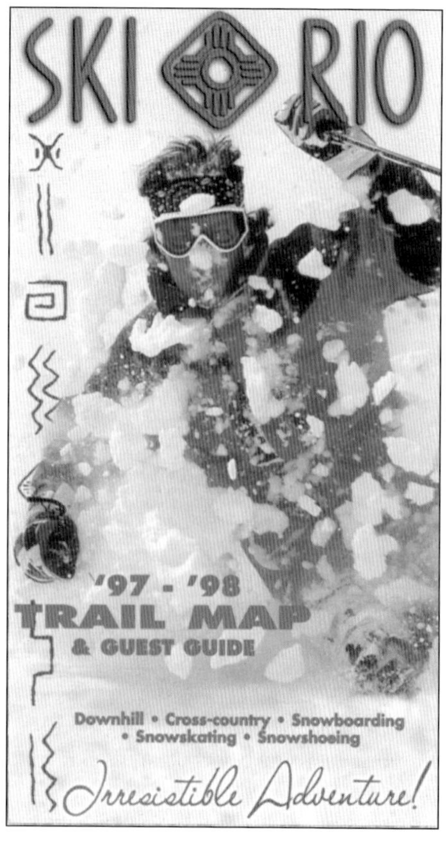

Some things have vanished. This is the brochure for Ski Rio, located north of Taos in the Sangre de Cristos very close to the Colorado border. It operated from 1982 to 1990 and from 1995 to 2000 and was a substantial endeavor, with two triple chairs and a double and a significant 2,150-foot vertical drop. There were three small hotels, a nice base lodge with a massive stone fireplace, and numerous condos. It is but one of the state's "ghost" ski areas; others include Agua Piedra, Sawyer's Hill, Hyde Park, Powder Puff, Sugarite, and Val Verde. (Courtesy NMSM.)

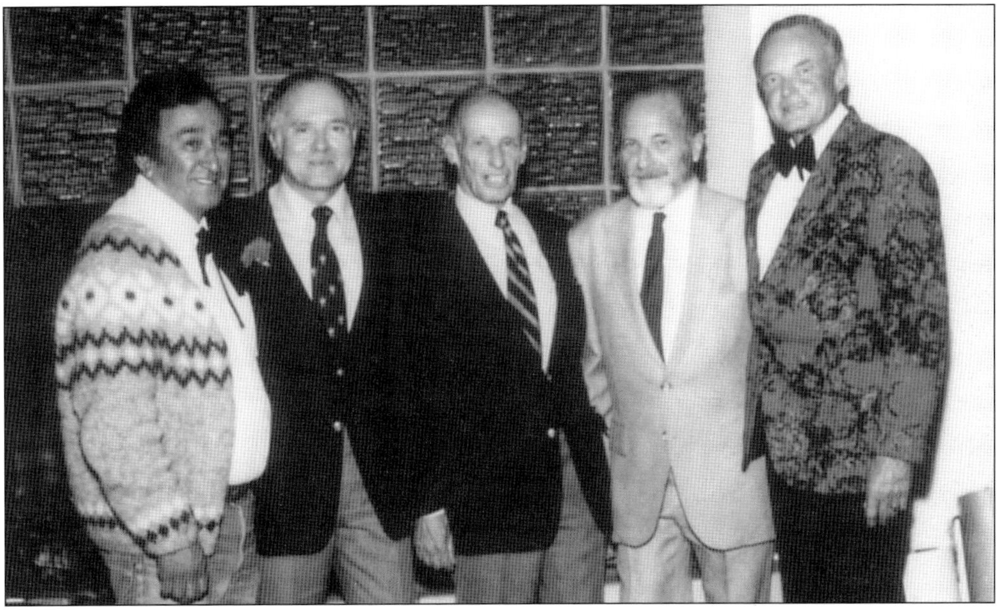

A who's who in New Mexico skiing lore is seen here at some unknown event, probably in the early 1980s. From left to right are Pete Totemoff, Ben Abruzzo, Robert Nordhaus, Ernie Blake, and Buzz Bainbridge. All are members of the New Mexico Ski Hall of Fame, and all worked directly with one another to build its ski community. Ben Abruzzo was also a world-class hot air and gas balloonist. In 1978, with Larry Newman and Maxie Anderson, he made the first trans-Atlantic balloon crossing in the *Double Eagle*, and in 1981, he was on the team to first transit the Pacific. (Courtesy NMSM.)

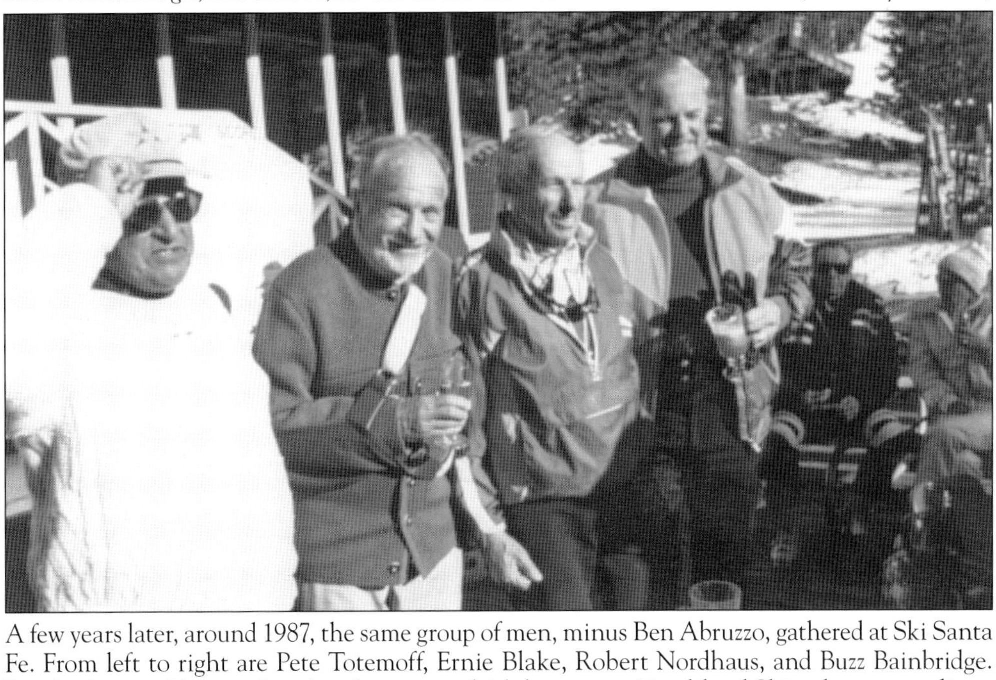

A few years later, around 1987, the same group of men, minus Ben Abruzzo, gathered at Ski Santa Fe. From left to right are Pete Totemoff, Ernie Blake, Robert Nordhaus, and Buzz Bainbridge. Bainbridge would go on from his ski career, which began as a Northland Skis salesman, to direct the state tourism bureau. Blake has his arm in a sling, the result of an accident during an old timers' ski race at Taos. (Courtesy SkiSF.)

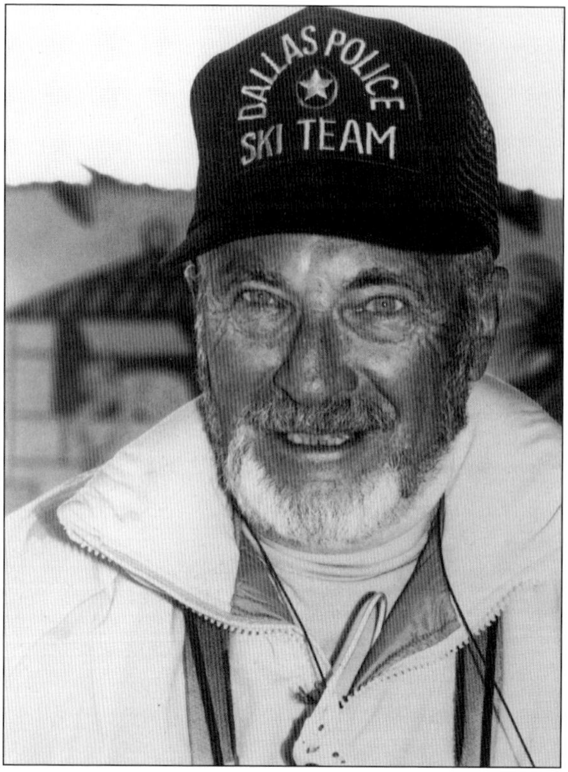

Ernie Blake wears yet another cap at Taos Ski Valley in the early 1980s, given to him, says son Mickey Blake, by visiting members of the Dallas police force. "My parents would invite all kinds of people up to their modest, little apartment right at the foot of the chair. Everything they ever made went right back into the operation." (Courtesy TSV.)

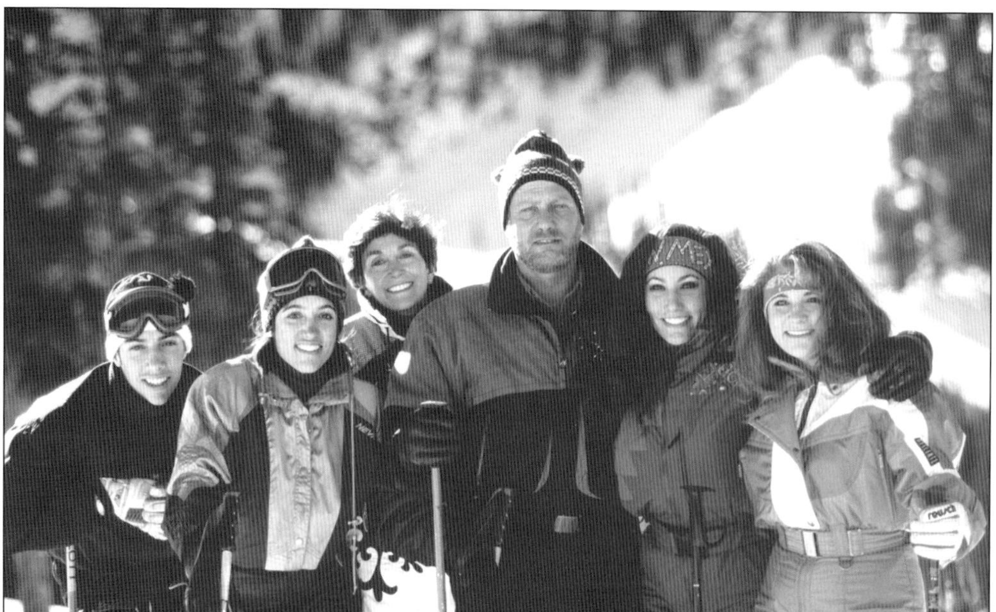

With Ernie Blake's death, eldest son Mickey was passed the Taos Ski Valley torch. He managed it for decades, with the aid of men like Gordon Briner, Chris Stagg, and many others. His son Alejandro and daughter Adrianna also spent years overseeing its operation in the 21st century. Seen here is his immediate family, which includes, from left to right, son Alejandro; daughter Adrianna; wife, Ann; and daughters Alyda and Alexsis. (Courtesy BFC.)

Jean Mayer, seen here around 1985—judging by his new Course Dore Dynastars—directed the Taos Ski School for decades. He was a true student of skiing's always-moving cutting edge, studying racing videos to keep up with the latest developments in skiing technique and equipment. To be placed in his weeklong ski school program was both a huge thrill and a challenge. He gave hundreds of people their start in skiing careers and left many cherished friends behind. (Courtesy TSV.)

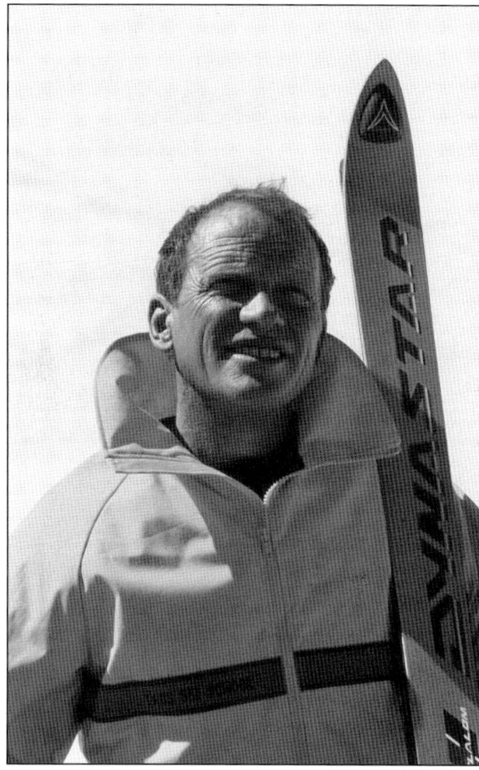

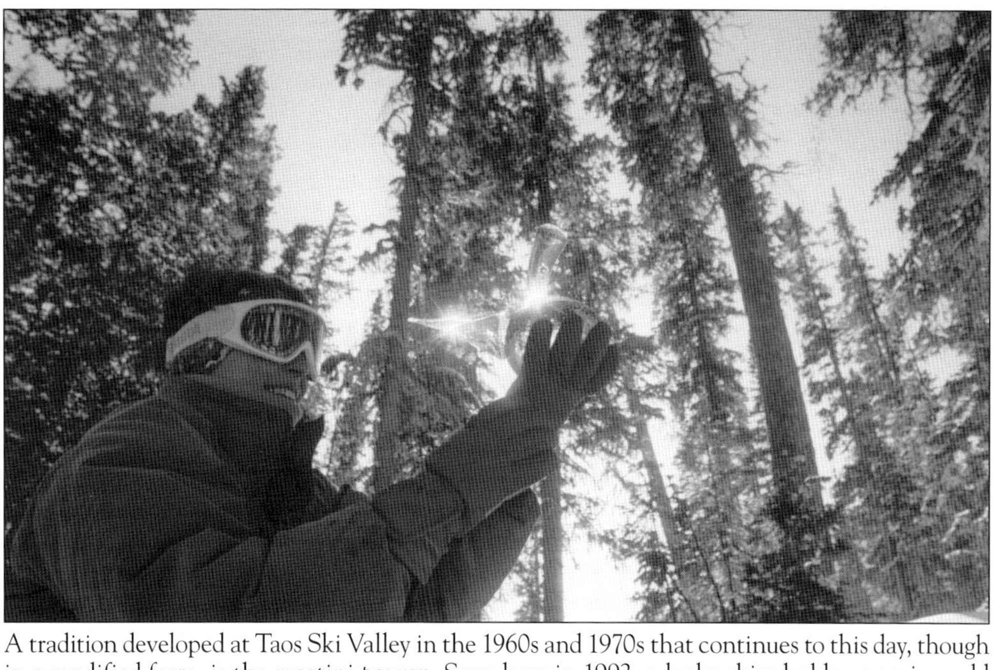

A tradition developed at Taos Ski Valley in the 1960s and 1970s that continues to this day, though in a modified form, is the martini *pouron*. Seen here in 1992, a lucky skier holds up an ice-cold glass pouron filled with a martini mix that has been hidden at the base of a tree festooned with a discrete ribbon. Stashed in remote woods, if one came across a ribboned tree, assiduous digging at its foot would turn up the liquid courage. (Photograph by Kitty Leaken.)

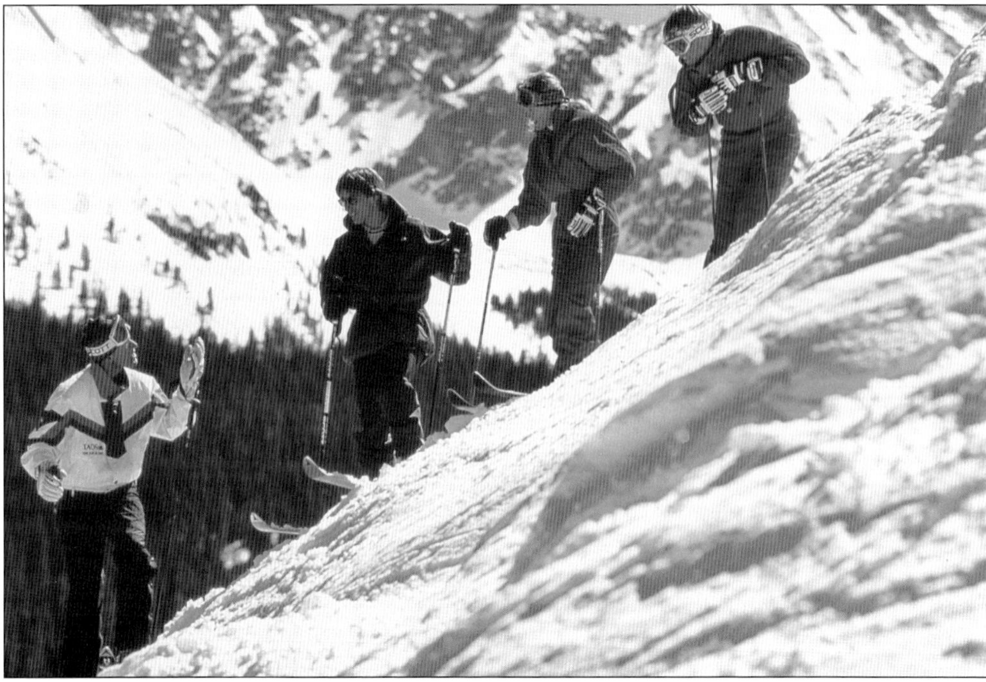

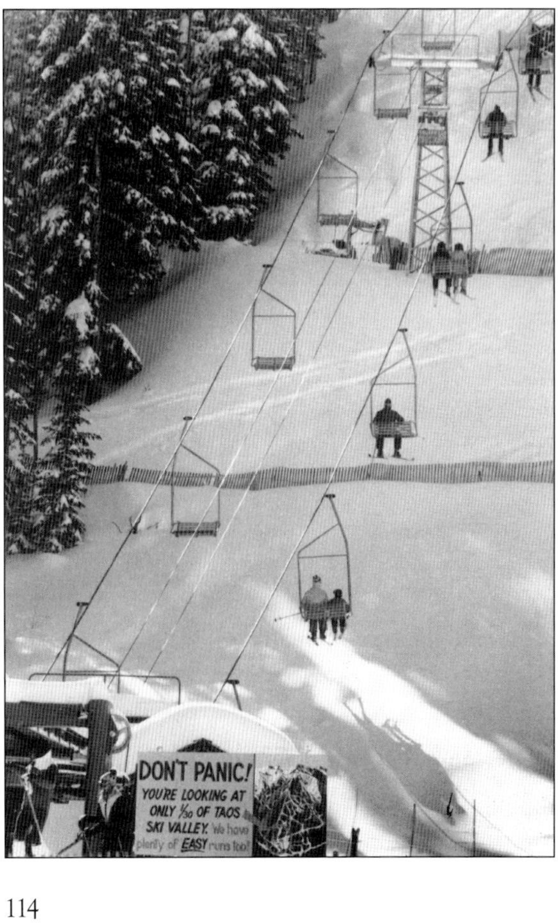

Taos Ski Valley's ski school was often picked as the best in the United States by major ski publications. This photograph, taken in the 1980s or 1990s by Taos's best-known and prolific photographer of the ages, Ken Gallard, shows the typically small class for experts on a rather steeply inclined slope. Unlike many ski schools that focus on beginning and intermediate skiers, the sentiment at Taos is that anyone can, and should, get better. They pioneered the idea of classes focused on skiing its steepest, most moguled, and deepest terrain—among the continent's most challenging. (Photograph by Ken Gallard, courtesy TSV.)

Ernie Blake had this sign posted at the foot of Al's Run at Taos Ski Valley to try to dissuade skiers from taking one look up it and the adjoining Snakedance, and turning around to leave, as was known to happen. This photograph was probably taken in the early 1980s on another powder morning. (Courtesy TSV.)

By the 1990s, people were regularly skiing off the high ridges above tree line that encircle Taos Ski Valley. The most sought-after, and hard-won, prize was Kachina Peak, seen here in the 1990s in the center foreground. It required an hour hike along Highline Ridge, much of it above 12,000 feet, to the summit at 12,481 feet. At its foot sprawl the runs of Kachina Basin, which gather together at the base of Chair No. 4 at the Phoenix Lodge. Ernie Blake long contemplated a lift up Highline Ridge or to Kachina Peak itself but did not live to see that happen. (Photograph by Chris Dahl-Bredine, courtesy TSV.)

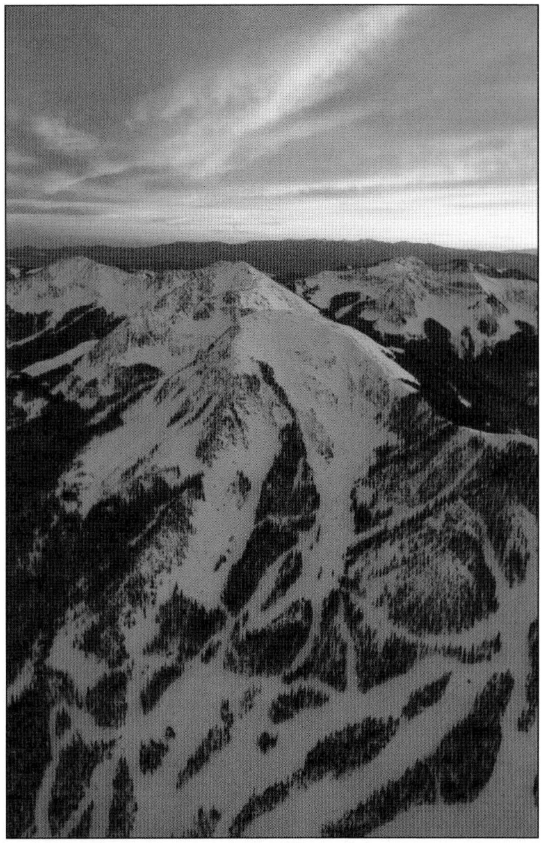

With the increase in interest in skiing the above tree line chutes and bowls at Taos Ski Valley in the 1970s and 1980s, the area undertook an ambitious program to control avalanches. Here, the ski patrol mans an avalauncher in the 1990s, which shot explosive projectiles into the upper reaches of Highline Ridge's couloirs and cornices to intentionally set off slides, reducing the danger from uncontrolled avalanches. (Photograph by Daniel Gibson.)

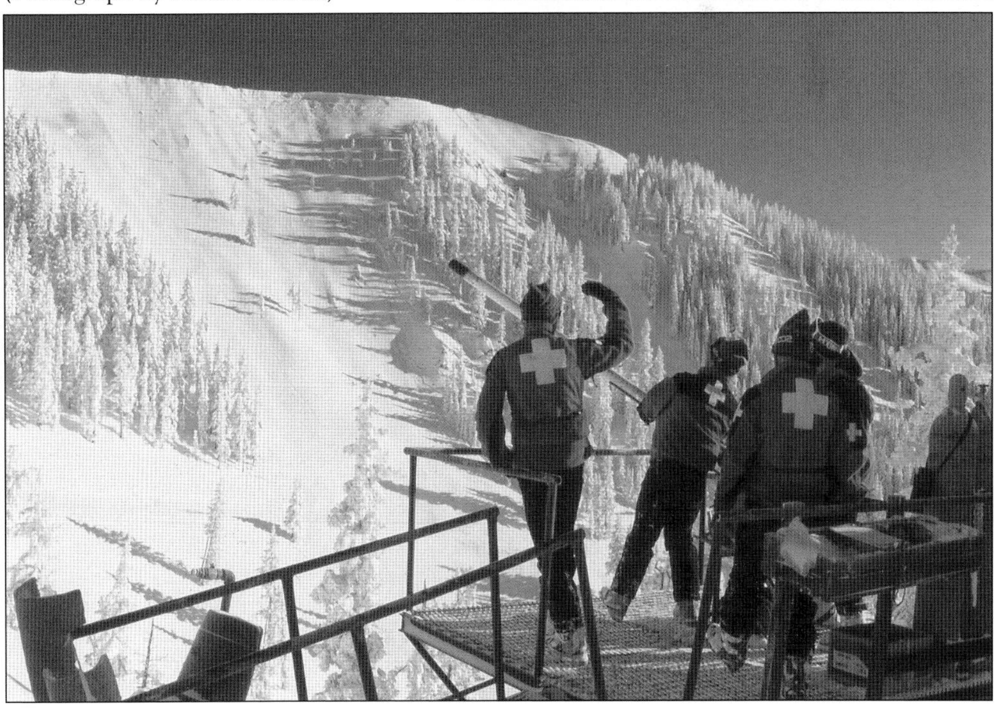

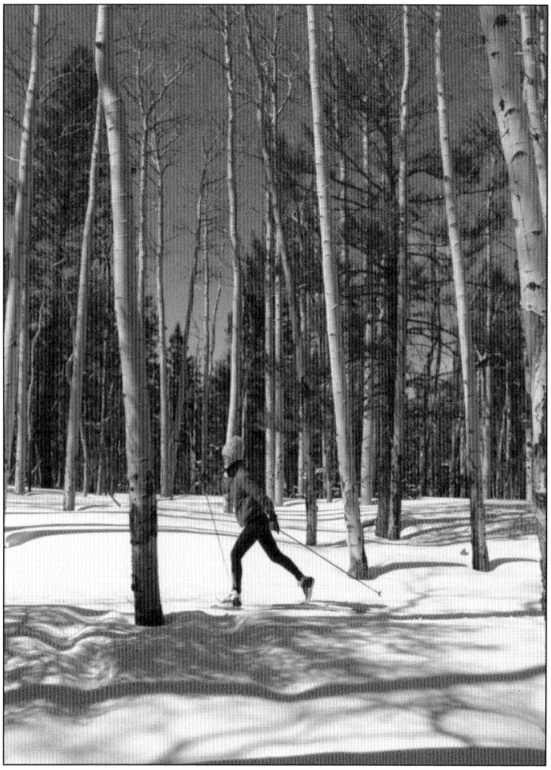

The 1980s and 1990s also saw an increased interest in cross-country and backcountry skiing across New Mexico, from the Sacramentos south to Mount Taylor in the west and the Jemez, Sangre de Cristos, and Brazos mountains of the north. Here, in 2007, Marlise Unger strides nicely through the aspens at the state's first, and still only, dedicated cross-country area, Enchanted Forest. Opened in 1985 by Judy and John Miller, their daughter Ellen Miller-Goins oversees its 32 kilometers of groomed trails today. Both senior Millers are members of the New Mexico Ski Hall of Fame. (Courtesy Enchanted Forest.)

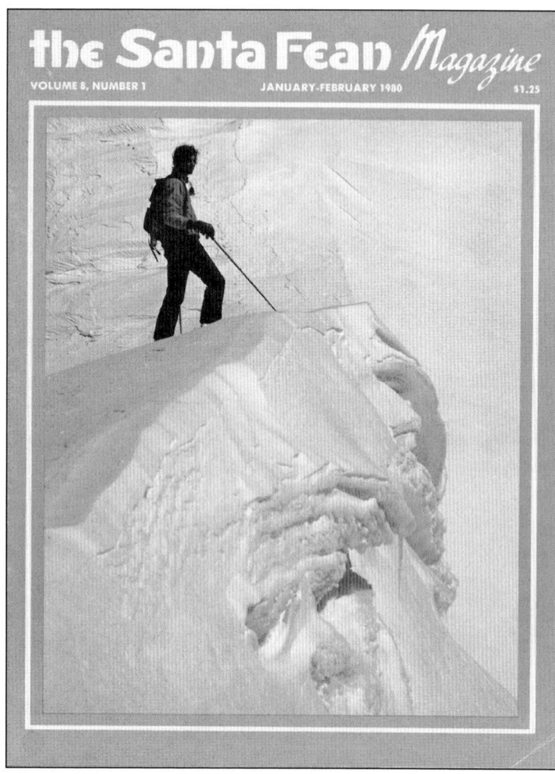

From the 1980s onward, skiers began venturing once again outside of the developed ski areas, seeking solitude, greater challenge, or to save a buck. This image on the cover of the January–February 1980 *Santa Fean* magazine, taken by Lee McAllister, captures a solo skier standing atop a huge cornice on Lake Peak, the highest point immediately above Santa Fe. (Courtesy NMSM.)

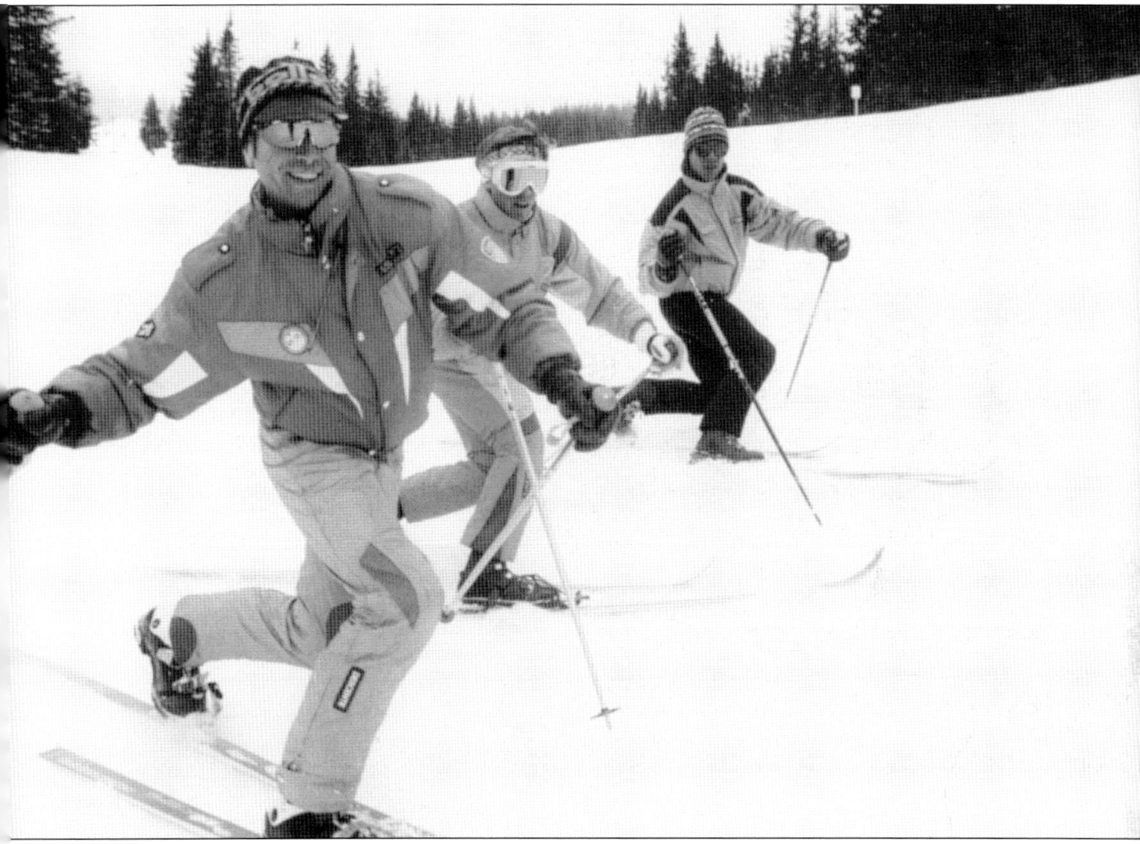

"Free the heel, free the mind" is the credo of the telemarker skier. But once upon a time in Santa Fe and Taos, it was the rage, and few did it better than Tony Forrest, seen here in the forefront. Forrest is a nationally known figure in the field and visited New Mexico annually since 1987 to hold workshops, as with this one at Ski Santa Fe in the 1990s. The area hosted a telemark festival for 30 years running, but it was interrupted by the pandemic in 2020. Forrest was a leader in crafting telemark skiing as it is known today, with heftier, plastic boots on bigger skis with metal edges. He skied on the first Professional Ski Instructors Association telemark demo team and went on to coach it, helped write the curriculum, and was one of the first three examiners for telemark teaching certification. (Photograph by Kitty Leaken.)

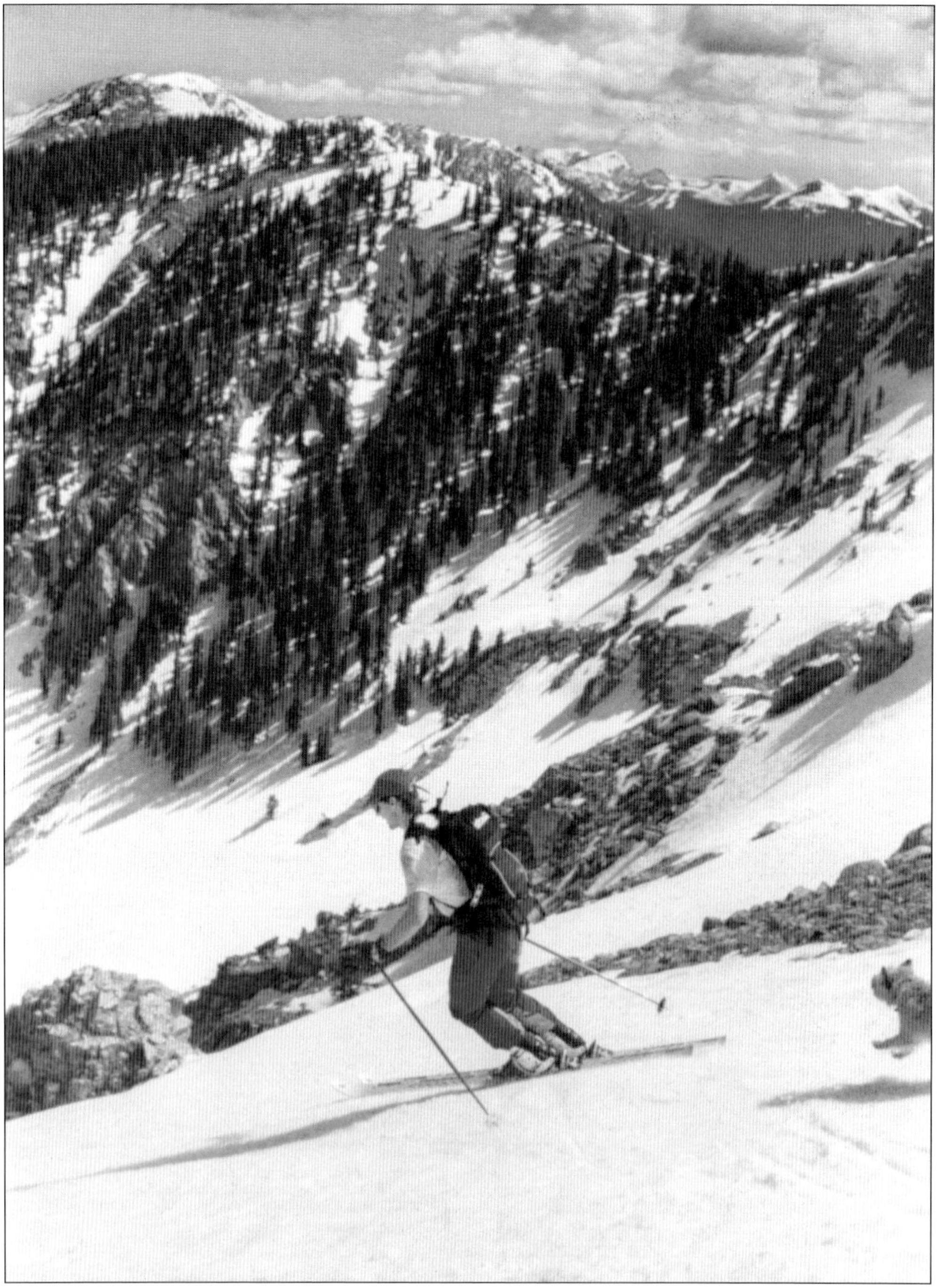

Early backcountry enthusiasts tackled some of the steepest terrain above Santa Fe, such as in this c. 1992 image of Biddle Duke on a snowfield on Lake Peak, which echoes the images found at the front of this book. Skiing is an eternal endeavor, immersed in the laws and mysteries of the physical realm. Backcountry skiing is now growing by leaps and bounds in New Mexico, but there are still many remote lines that have yet to be tackled, including some on the Truchas Peaks seen in the background here. (Photograph by Kitty Leaken.)

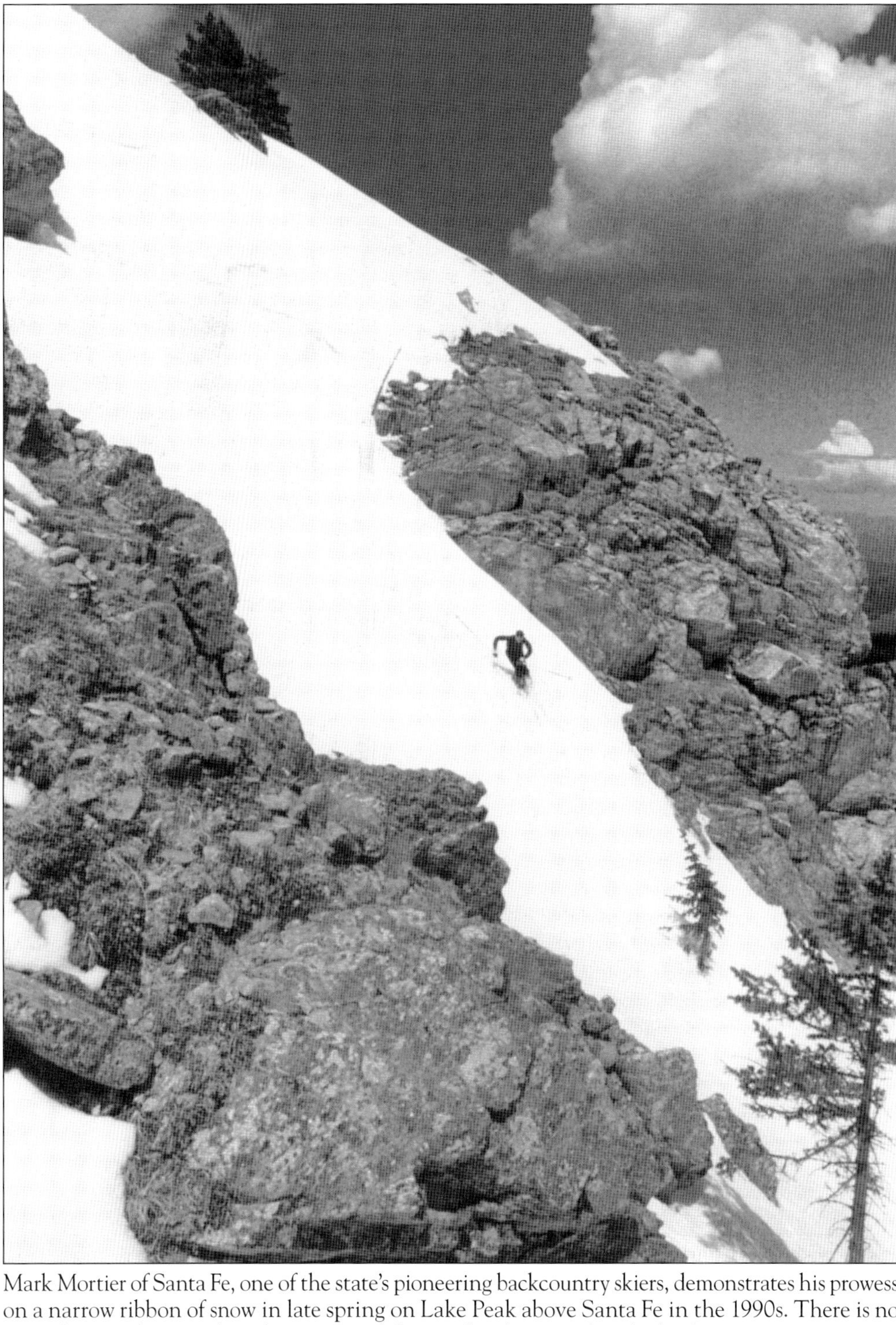

Mark Mortier of Santa Fe, one of the state's pioneering backcountry skiers, demonstrates his prowess on a narrow ribbon of snow in late spring on Lake Peak above Santa Fe in the 1990s. There is no room for error here, with unforgiving rock lining the chute. Today, the backcountry community's primary focus is the Lake Fork Valley above Taos Ski Valley, but Lake Peak's challenging slopes have lots of devotees as well. (Photograph by Kitty Leaken.)

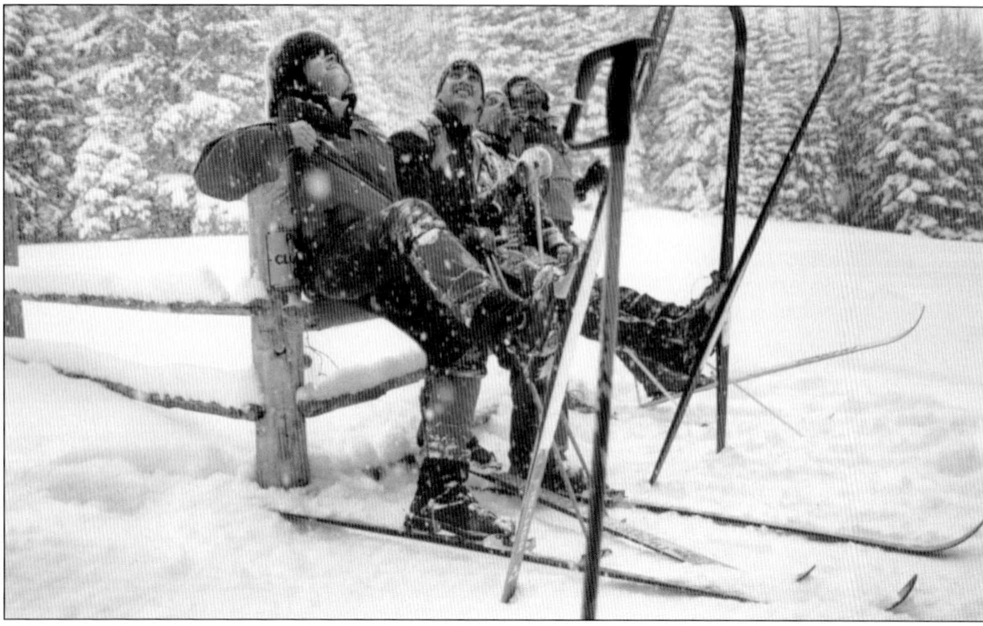

One longs for whatever these backcountry skiers are drawing upon in a snowstorm during a skinny skis convention on the Winsor Trail Saddle above Santa Fe in the early 1990s. The Winsor trail is the gateway to the Nambe Saddle, Santa Fe Baldy, and the Pecos Wilderness and was skinned up by the earliest of New Mexico's ski pioneers. From left to right are Kitty Leaken, Hugh Gagen, Tom Long, and Dave Parsons. (Photograph by Kitty Leaken.)

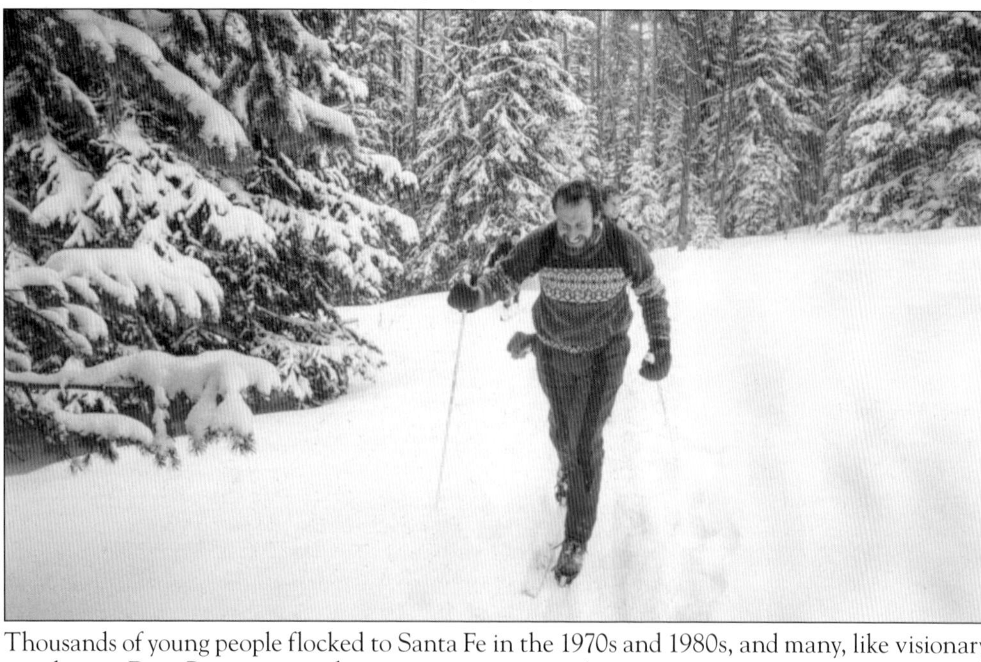

Thousands of young people flocked to Santa Fe in the 1970s and 1980s, and many, like visionary woodcarver Dave Parsons, were drawn to its mountains. A common winter outing was up toward the ski basin and out Aspen Vista on the radio towers maintenance road, which was closed to traffic in winter. The route switchbacks up Tesuque Peak toward the fabled Horse's Head of yesteryear and is still a favored quick ski today. (Photograph by Kitty Leaken.)

Six

The Contemporary Scene
21st Century

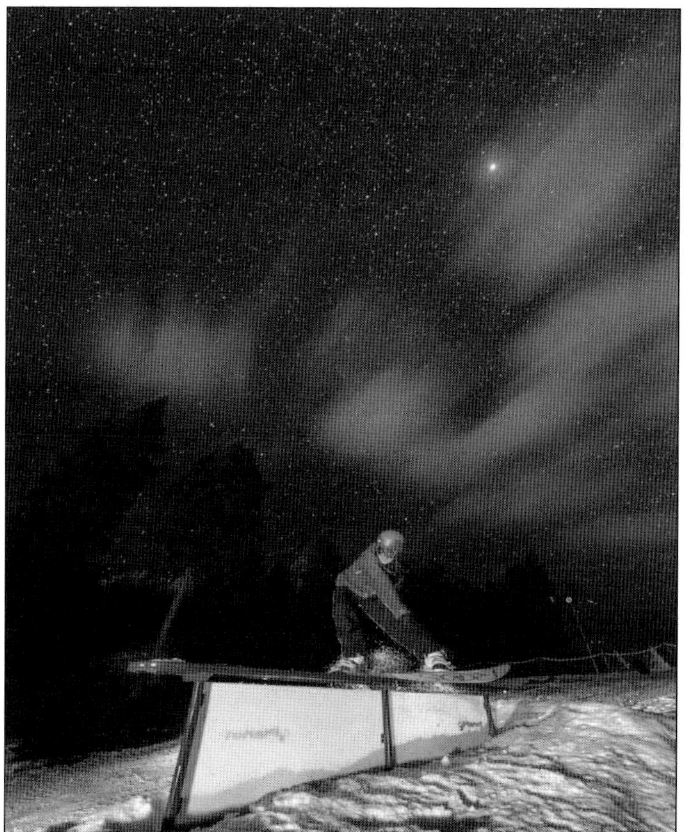

Angel Fire Resort has the only night skiing and snowboarding in the state today, including some terrain park features, as this shot of a night trickster around 2015 attests. It operates the state's largest terrain park, with progression feature lines to build skills safely, and hosts lots of park competitions. (Courtesy AFR.)

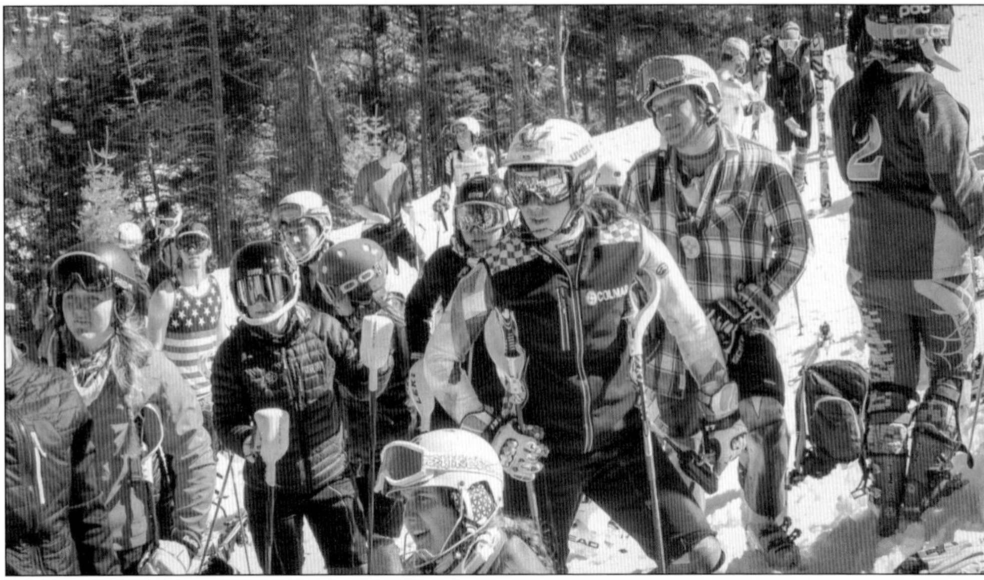

For decades, Red River hosted the annual home meet of the University of New Mexico's alpine ski team. Skiing is the only NCAA–sanctioned sport UNM ever won a national championship in, under coach George Brooks in 2004. Brooks went on to head the trade organization Ski New Mexico. However, the college racing program is now moribund. Here, a fine group of racers from around the Rocky Mountain region, including some who skied in the Olympics for their national teams, is seen preparing for a slalom in March 2016. (Photograph by Kitty Leaken.)

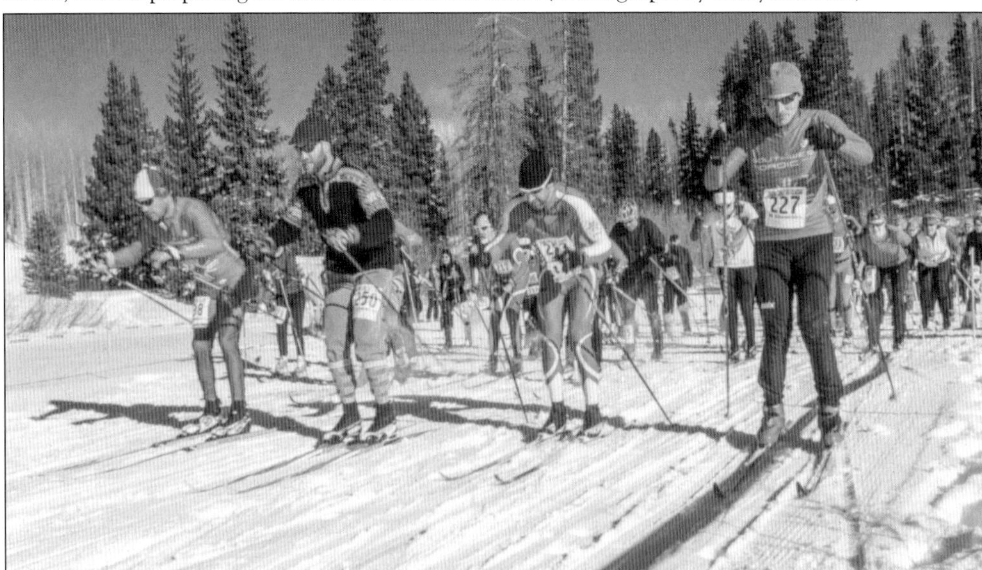

Cross-country skiing remains a significant aspect of the state's skiing scene today. The Chama Chile Ski Classic was first held in 1973 and has been held every winter since, except in 2020 and 2021 due to COVID-19. It is the major annual competitive cross-country gathering in the state and attracts racers from around the Southwest, Colorado, and farther afield. This is the start of the men's 12-kilometer race in 2016. Two of the region's best, and eventual winners that day, were Clay Mosely of Los Alamos, second from left in traditional garb, and Steve Ilg of Durango, Colorado, third from left. (Photograph by Kitty Leaken.)

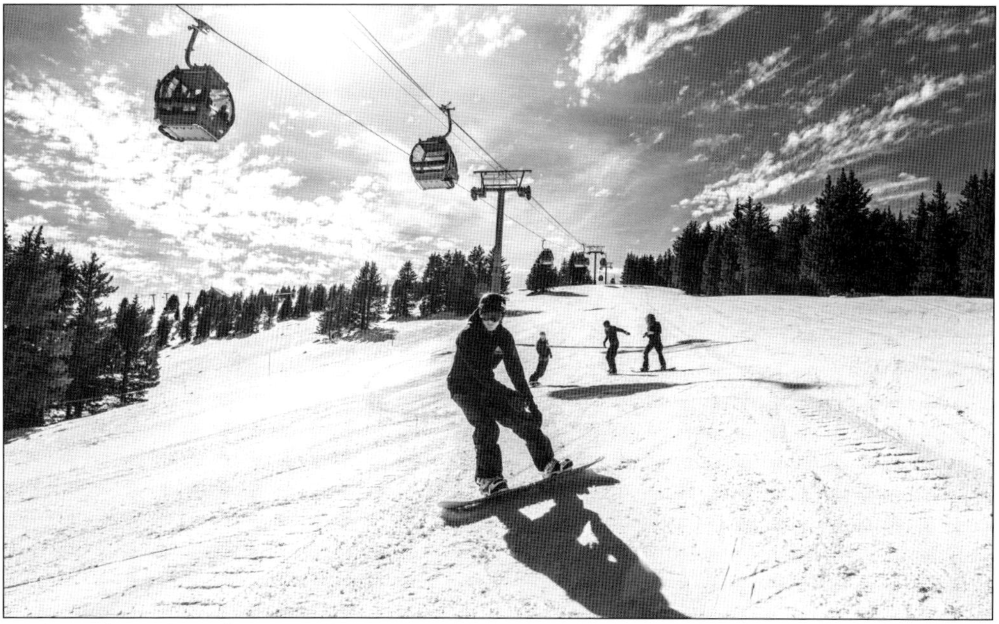

With Pitch Pitcher's departure from Sierra Blanca, the ski area was purchased by the Mescalero Apache, under tribal chairman Wendell Chino, becoming the first tribe in the nation to own a ski operation—another New Mexico first. In 1984, its name was changed to Ski Apache. Pitcher built the state's first gondola in 1962; in 2013–2014, it was finally replaced by this beauty. The circle remains unbroken. (Courtesy Ski Apache.)

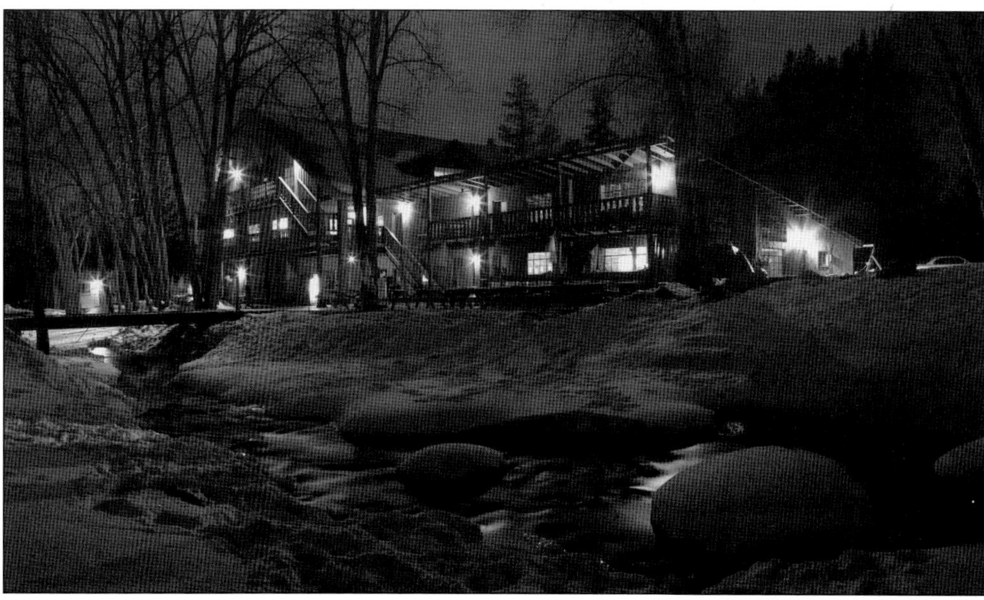

Overlooking the Rio Pueblo, the main lodge at Sipapu, built by the Bolanders over many decades, was expanded and renovated in the new century and looks like this today. Ernie Blake wrote of the family in the 1953 *American Ski Annual*, "Clan Bolander is the team to watch in all New Mexico meets. They have been beaten on occasion, but it is always an upset and cause for great rejoicing." Lloyd Bolander died in 2014 in his late 80s. His son Bruce remains involved today. (Courtesy Sipapu Ski & Summer Resort.)

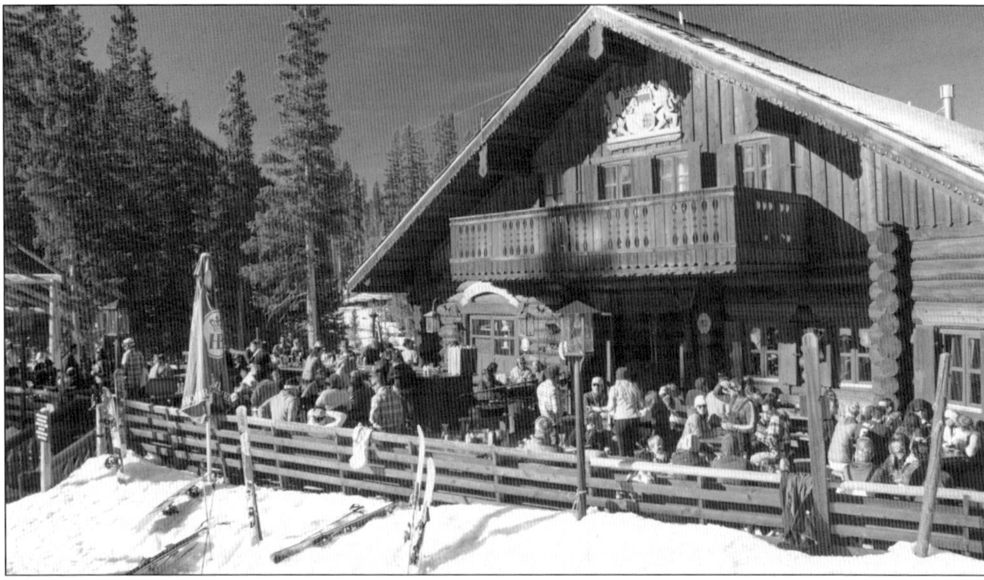

Energy at Taos Ski Valley has migrated a bit to the Kachina Basin in the past 20 years. It used to be that the Hotel St. Bernard bar was the place to be après-ski, but now, the deck of the Bavarian Lodge and Restaurant is often so. Opened in 1994 by Thomas and Jamie Schulze, it reflects Ernie Blake's roots—from lederhosen-clad bar maids serving big frosty mugs of German brews to the delicious *saurerbraten*, *kasespatzle*, and schnitzel. The interior takes one right into the Alps, with ceiling murals painted by Swiss artist Reto Messmer, and thick down comforters on the beds. (Courtesy TSV.)

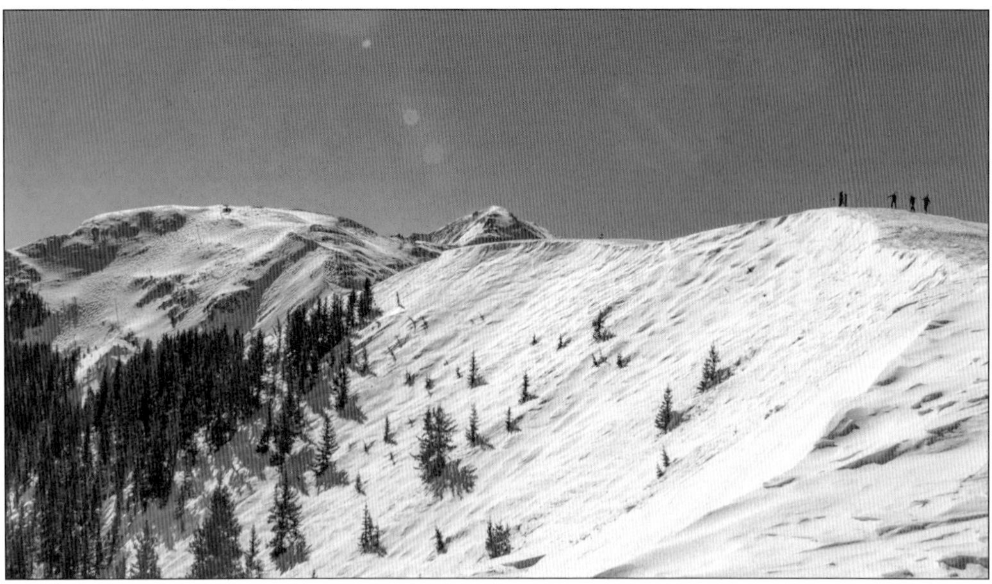

Ray Deveaux, a native Taoseno and head of ski patrol at Taos Ski Valley for many years, once spoke of Highline Ridge and Kachina Peak, seen in this photograph around 2017: "Sometimes on really cold mornings, as the sun is breaking over Wheeler Peak, snow lingering in the air after a storm catches the light and there's this flash and a massive cross and diamond shape appears in the air over Kachina Basin. Guys here aren't religious but the intense beauty has silenced us for five minutes while we watch these things unfold." (Courtesy TSV.)

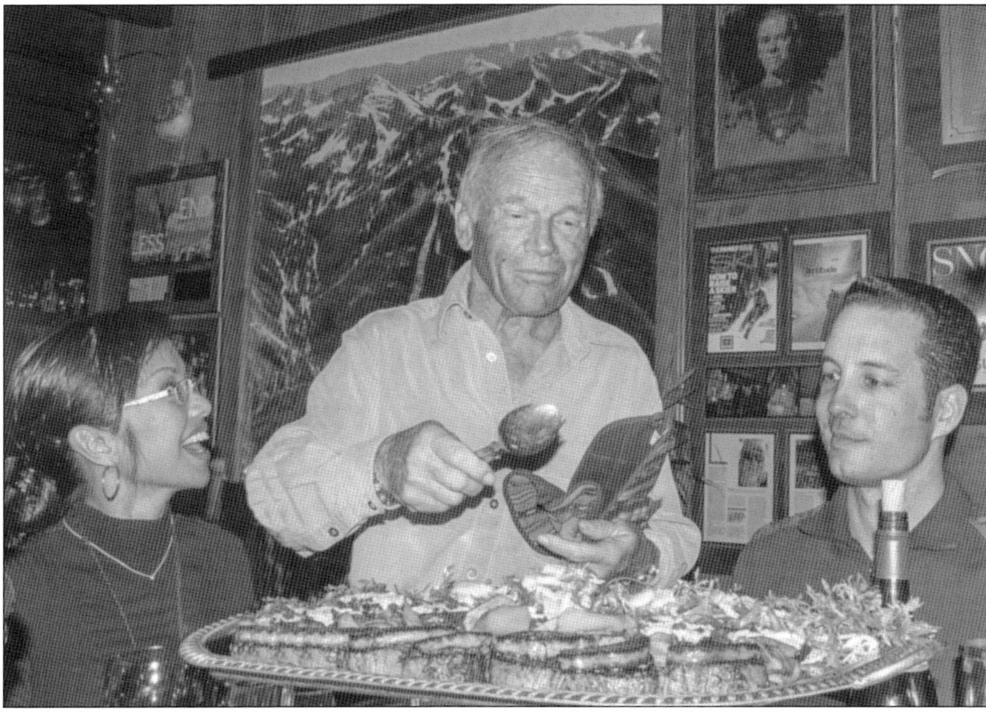

Jean Mayer serves up another delectable dish at his Hotel St. Bernard in Taos Ski Valley in 2014 to his rapt guests. He hosted dinner here almost every night during the ski season from 1960 to 2020. Guests had priority, eating every delightful meal here, so to score an open seat for dinner as a drop-in was a coup. (Photograph by Kitty Leaken.)

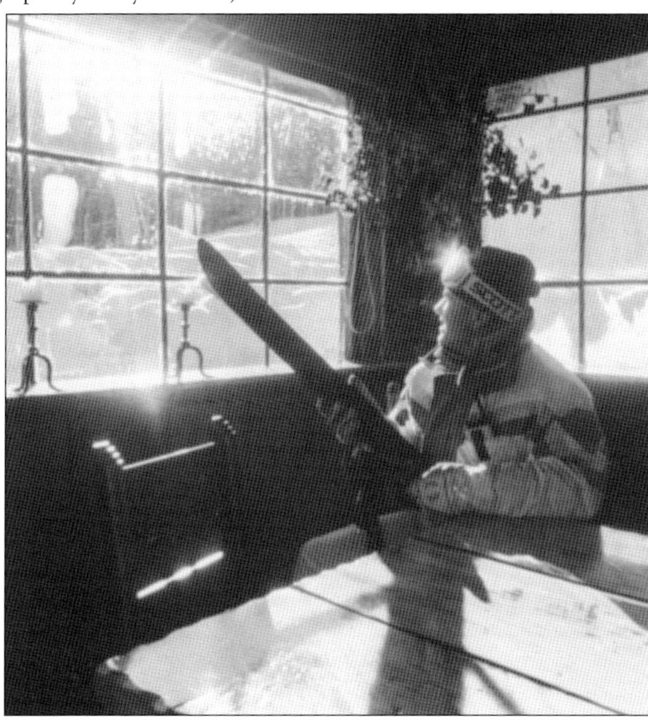

Here is a last shot of Jean Mayer, who, with family members like his brother Dadou and some of his grown children, turned the Hotel St. Bernard at Taos Ski Valley into a world-renowned accommodation. He sits here in the coveted sunny dining room corner window table looking out into the realm he loved so deeply. He left this earthly plane in 2020 with eight children and seven grandchildren, but his spirit hovers over Taos today like a snowflake refusing to come down to earth. (Photograph by Kitty Leaken.)

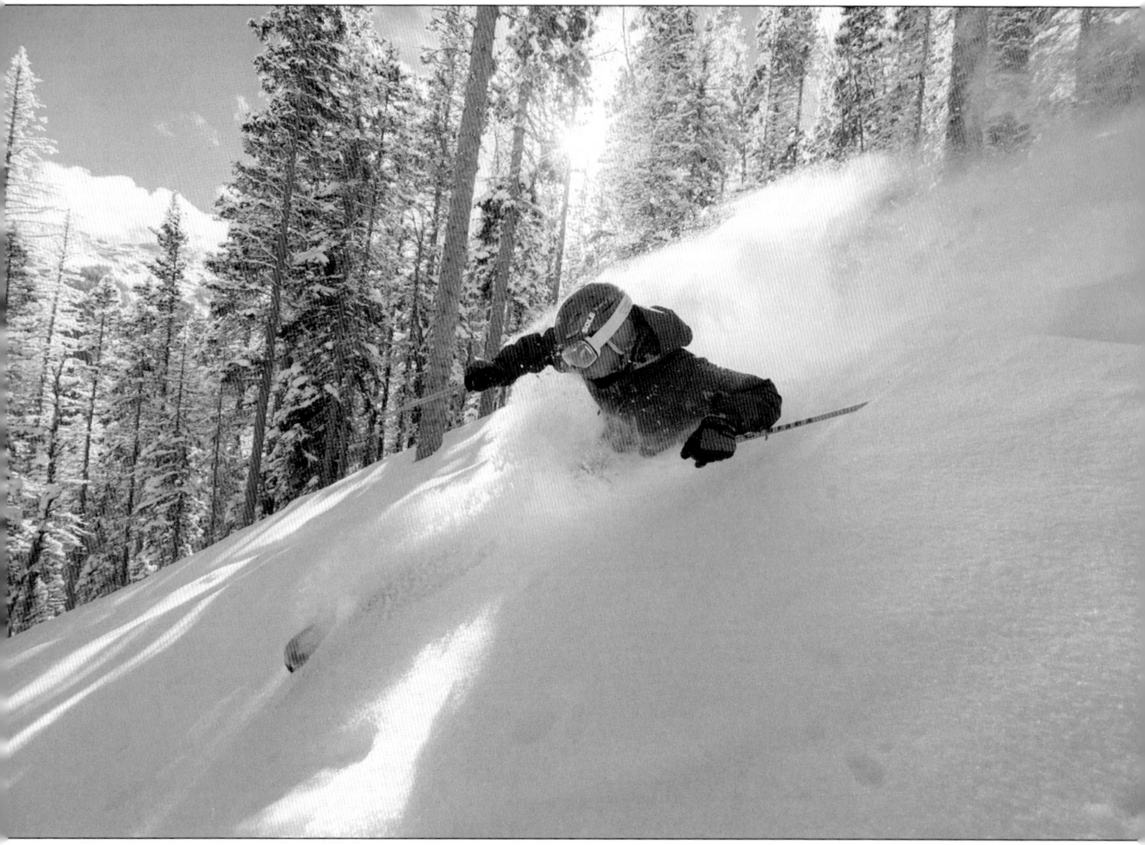

It is still deep and steep at Taos Ski Valley, as this c. 2017 shot reveals. Decades ahead of most American ski areas, Taos okayed, and even encouraged, people to hike to the double-black diamond terrain off Highline and West Basin Ridges. Under new ownership since late 2013 by Louis Bacon, conservation philanthropist and founder of Moore Capital management, it continues to place emphasis on the quality of the experience and the power of mountains to transform people positively. (Courtesy TSV.)

Index